D1256744

OUR RIGHTFUL PLACE

Our Rightful Place

*A History of Women at the
University of Kentucky,
1880–1945*

TERRY L. BIRDWHISTELL AND
DEIRDRE A. SCAGGS

UNIVERSITY PRESS OF KENTUCKY

Copyright © 2020 by The University Press of Kentucky

Scholarly publisher for the Commonwealth,
serving Bellarmine University, Berea College, Centre
College of Kentucky, Eastern Kentucky University,
The Filson Historical Society, Georgetown College,
Kentucky Historical Society, Kentucky State University,
Morehead State University, Murray State University,
Northern Kentucky University, Transylvania University,
University of Kentucky, University of Louisville,
and Western Kentucky University.
All rights reserved.

Editorial and Sales Offices: The University Press of Kentucky
663 South Limestone Street, Lexington, Kentucky 40508-4008
www.kentuckypress.com

Library of Congress Cataloging-in-Publication Data

Names: Birdwhistell, Terry L., author. | Scaggs, Deirdre A., author.
Title: Our rightful place : a history of women at the University of Kentucky,
    1880–1945 / Terry L. Birdwhistell and Deirdre A. Scaggs.
Other titles: Topics in Kentucky history.
Description: Lexington, Kentucky : The University Press of Kentucky, [2020] |
    Series: Topics in Kentucky history | Includes bibliographical references and index.
Identifiers: LCCN 2020013487 | ISBN 9780813179377 (hardcover) |
    ISBN 9780813179391 (pdf) | ISBN 9780813179407 (epub)
Subjects: LCSH: University of Kentucky—History. | Agricultural and Mechanical
    College of Kentucky—History. | Women—Education (Higher)—Kentucky—
    History.
Classification: LCC LD2773 .B57 2020 | DDC 378.769—dc23
LC record available at https://lccn.loc.gov/2020013487

This book is printed on acid-free paper meeting
the requirements of the American National Standard
for Permanence in Paper for Printed Library Materials.

Manufactured in the United States of America.

Member of the Association
of University Presses

For Zoe, Jessie, John, Janice, and Dean

Contents

Preface   ix

Introduction   1

1. First Women and the Will to Succeed   9

2. Frances Jewell McVey and the Refinement of Student Culture   57

3. Sarah Blanding and the Modern College Woman   101

4. Economic Depression and an Uncertain Future   130

5. World War II and the Illusion of Equality   164

Epilogue   191

Acknowledgments   195

Notes   197

Bibliography   227

Index   237

Preface

This study, a history of women at the University of Kentucky (UK) through World War II, begins to pull back the curtain on the lives and experiences of UK women over seven decades. By the 1950s, that struggle would include African American women. Still, the push for a more diverse and inclusive University of Kentucky does and must continue. Many more stories remain to be told, preserved, and shared.

UK's Martin Luther King Center, established in 1987, sponsors programs that focus on "the importance of cultural awareness and cross-cultural understanding." The Disability Resource Center works with students with disabilities in gaining equal access and opportunities. The stories of the struggle for LGBTQ rights at UK have only begun to be more fully told and preserved. Today, UK has an Office for Institutional Diversity that seeks to empower "all to be their best selves and strives to create a sustainable climate where all can benefit from the highest quality education, care, and work environment." Looking forward, these diverse voices can be joined together to present the mosaic that UK has become and serve as examples of why it is important to seek equality, always.

Introduction

During the first quarter of the twenty-first century women have comprised a little over half of all students attending the University of Kentucky (UK), including undergraduates, students in professional programs, and graduate students. Women held 40 percent of the faculty positions, but only under a quarter of the women were full professors. All twelve of UK's presidents have been men, and only two women have served briefly as the highest academic officer in the university. In 1939 Georgia Monroe Blazer became the first woman to serve on the UK Board of Trustees, and in 2007 Mira Snider Ball, class of 1965, became the first woman to chair the UK Board. Without doubt, the women who first attended UK as students and those who taught on the faculty during those early years would be astonished, and most likely pleased, to see what women have accomplished. But some would question whether women have reached true equity. A UK report issued in 1990 concluded that much work remained to be done. Ten years later a follow-up report, "Blueprint for Gender Equity at America's Next Great University," noted some gains by women but still concluded that not enough was being done. In 2001 a Commission on Women was created at UK to take "as long as needed" to address women's issues on campus. A year later the chair of the commission, law professor Carolyn Bratt, resigned, noting, "We've been able to get things done around the edges and some of them have real impact, but there's a fundamental issue of women being at the table where the real decisions are being made, and there doesn't seem to be a real commitment to making that happen." Bratt was especially concerned about the very low number of women administrators at the

1

highest levels. These have been consistent themes in women's experiences at UK from the beginning.[1]

Since 1880, when they first entered the University of Kentucky, women have sought, demanded, and struggled to find equality within the university. It has been a journey of multiple generations of women during a time of significant changes in American society in regard to women's lives. The period between 1880 and 1945 witnessed women's suffrage, two world wars, and an economic depression. It was during this time, prior to the modern women's movement of the 1960s and later, when women worked to take their rightful place in the university's life.

Over the decades, the history of women at the University of Kentucky has remained mostly buried in the university's published accounts, except for making note of "firsts" by women and cases of exception rather than the rule. Slowly but surely, that history is now being rediscovered by the university community and celebrated. But the story of women at UK is not about women triumphant, and it remains untidy. After pushing for admission into a male-centric campus environment, women attempted to create women's spaces, women's organizations, and a woman's culture often patterned on those of men. At times it seemed that the women were replicating a woman's college within the larger university rather than integrating. However, coeducation meant that women competed with men academically while still navigating the evolving social norms of relationships between the sexes. Nonetheless, coeducation created opportunities, challenges, and problems for women students and faculty.

Rather than simply tracing the evolution of the women's experience on the UK campus, our aim in this book is to uncover how women's roles and place at the university were constructed for and by UK women. Moreover, taking a more women-centric view of the campus shows more clearly the impact that women had over time on the culture and environment as well as on the development of a specific institution. It also allows us to compare, and perhaps contrast, the experiences of women at UK with those of women at other public universities across the United States.

Women in public coeducational universities between 1880 and 1945 faced challenges as well as choices. They ultimately made decisions regarding their education and their professional careers in the context of traditional social and cultural roles and under the constant pressure of a patriarchy. Some women chose the path that Geraldine Joncich Clifford has described as the "Lone Voyager," resisting the traditional limits to their sex. Others resisted very little and followed the courses that they found available. Still others chose to attempt to assimilate their traditional roles as women into the new educational and vocational opportunities.[2]

Before the mid-1800s private colleges and academies offered the only avenue for white women in the United States to seek college-level educations. The University of Iowa allowed women students upon its founding in 1855, followed by Wisconsin admitting women into its Normal Department in 1863. Other public universities admitting women by 1870 included Kansas, Indiana, Minnesota, Missouri, Michigan, Cornell, Penn State, and California. In her study of coeducation in the western United States, Andrea G. Radke-Moss suggests that "the openness of newly founded institutions in the post–Civil War west more easily implemented coeducation," as opposed to more established eastern colleges, which had "held out against the admission of women." Of 582 private and public colleges in 1870, only 29 percent were coeducational. Two decades later, the number of colleges had grown to 1,082, but only 42 percent admitted both women and men.[3]

The Civil War created significant disruption in education at all levels in the South. Coeducation in private colleges and public universities across the South came later than other regions of the United States, as white southerners chose to educate their daughters, if at all beyond finishing schools, close to home in women's colleges. Even though public universities in Mississippi admitted women in 1882, the state of Mississippi created the Mississippi State College for Women in 1885, making it the first public women's college in the United States. North Carolina created what became the Woman's College of the University of North Carolina in 1892; the college first admitted men in 1964 when it became the University of North Carolina at Greensboro. The Florida State College for Women did not admit men until 1947 upon becoming Florida State University.[4]

The following list names southern state universities in order of the date they admitted women:

University of Kentucky, 1880
University of Mississippi, 1882

Mississippi State University, 1882
Auburn University, 1892
University of Tennessee, 1892
University of Alabama, 1893
University of South Carolina, 1895
University of North Carolina, 1896
Louisiana State University, 1906
University of Maryland, 1917
University of Georgia 1918
Virginia Tech, 1921
University of Florida, 1924
Florida State University, 1947
Clemson University, 1954

Amy Thompson McCandless, who does not include Kentucky in her study of women's higher education in the South, suggests that the expansion of higher education for women in the region "between 1890 and 1920 created unprecedented personal and professional opportunities for white women in the region, but the recipients of that educational largess were in turn expected to conform to the chivalric images of womanhood promulgated by their benefactors." Moreover, "Women were to be educated for their families, not for themselves. They were to become better mothers, better housekeepers, and better public-school teachers." Yet, as McCandless points out, "some Southern women employed these very same cultural prescriptions to justify their social activism."[5]

Kentucky's Berea College, founded by abolitionist John Fee, began college-level work around 1869, becoming one of the South's first coeducational colleges. Berea also provided educational opportunities to both African American and white students until 1904, when a state law prohibited the practice. Shannon H. Wilson notes that Berea College's founders "were clear in their commitment to provide education for women. Their reasoning that Christianity elevated everyone did not lead immediately to equality in education." Initially, Berea's "Ladies Course" provided a three-year classical education that "prepared women to be wives, mothers, teachers, and interesting companions for their spouses." While not a public college, Berea College offered a work-study program that made it possible for students with very limited financial means to attend. Other private colleges in Kentucky would become coeducational later. Georgetown College first admitted women in 1884, Transylvania University in 1889, and Kentucky Wesleyan College in 1892. Women students attended Eastern Kentucky University and Western Kentucky University when they were founded in 1906 as coeducational state normal schools. The University of Louisville did not admit women until 1907.[6]

The Morrill Act of 1862 expanded postwar educational opportunities for men in Kentucky and many other states at newly created land-grant colleges. Kentucky's Agricultural and Mechanical (A&M) College (now the University of Kentucky), founded in 1865 under terms of the Morrill Act, began as a college within the quasi-public Kentucky University.[7]

In 1878, following a controversial rift within the governing body of Kentucky University over denominational control of the university, the Kentucky legislature separated the A&M College, making it an independent public institution that would evolve into the University of Kentucky. Concerns over the college's survival were real and widespread, as it faced daunting challenges about both finances and enrollment. The separation left the struggling college with little funding and no permanent campus. During the academic year 1877–1878 total enrollment fell to only 78 students from a high of 295 only eight years earlier. But Lieutenant Governor John C. Underwood, chair of a commission to evaluate the college, predicted a bright future, suggesting that the school would "provide for the proper education and cultivation of their sons." Under the forceful leadership of founding President James K. Patterson, the school slowly began to achieve some semblance of stability.[8]

In the split with Kentucky University, UK had lost its campus and had to begin immediately to search for a permanent home. Frankfort, the state capital, and Cynthiana, a small town thirty miles north of Lexington, hoped to attract the college. But it was Bowling Green that made the most competitive bid to move the school from Lexington to western Kentucky. Ultimately, state and college officials accepted Lexington's offer of a fifty-two-acre former fairground near Maxwell Springs on the city's south side as well as $30,000 in city bonds to retain the college. Fayette County added an additional $20,000 in county bonds as incentive to remain in Lexington. The fairground, established in 1850 by the Kentucky Agricultural and Mechanical Society for

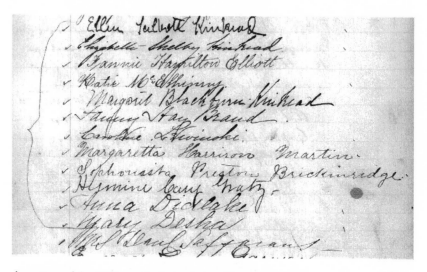

A portion of the 1880 matriculation ledger. These women pioneers who walked into President Patterson's office to sign the ledger one by one probably experienced great excitement, anticipation, and even trepidation. (UK matriculation ledgers.)

animal fairs and horseracing, had become a city park by the time the college took ownership. But buildings on the new campus would need to be constructed, forcing the A&M College to rent its former campus from Kentucky University at the Woodlands for a time.[9]

During its 1880 session the Kentucky General Assembly passed legislation creating a Normal Department within the A&M College to train teachers needed for the state's growing number of white elementary and high schools. Because a growing percentage of teachers entering the field were women, the new legislation allowed each Kentucky county to send a student, regardless of sex, to the A&M College as a county appointee. These appointments provided a tuition waiver for both the men and women appointees as well as free board for the men. Women appointees apparently received no boarding allowance.[10]

When fourteen-year-old Sophonisba Breckinridge and forty-two other young women walked into President Patterson's office to sign the student register in the fall of 1880, they initiated a new era in Kentucky public higher education. They began an unprecedented journey toward an uncertain future. Over the next seven decades, these women, and the generations of women that followed, not only created a place for women at the University of Kentucky but also created a social and cultural environment that both mirrored the existing male traditions and created and defined their own experiences and expectations.

Andrea G. Radke-Moss reminds us that "the defense and promotion of coeducation became an integral part of the land-grant ideology and culture." Moreover, even after gaining access, rules regulating women's academic pursuits, social activities and spaces, and interactions with male students had to be negotiated and defined. Women might attend classes with the men, but they were segregated in a special space between classes. Radke-Moss adds that "in spite of the practices of gender separation, many women and men students sought to push these boundaries by expanding the educational space for women." Young women moving into this environment must have caused concern among parents and college administrators alike. Nevertheless, women continued to bear the burden of stricter rules than those of the male students.[11]

Coeducation was at times lonely, at times harsh, and at times the most freedom and fun the young women had ever known. Their individual experiences created a mosaic of shared women's experiences that sometimes differed as much as they were alike. These public coeducational colleges would change rapidly, accelerated by transformations in the student culture and the influence of the Progressive Era on education and society generally. Each generation of women students would face new opportunities and new challenges that had to be negotiated. Some scholars have argued that the earliest generation of women students in the coeducational universities may have been more serious than those who followed. Perhaps the efforts to create separate women's organizations and spaces within the universities actually hindered and delayed the struggle for full equality. What is certain, however, is that each institution exhibited similarities and distinctions in dealing with coeducation over time. To understand the totality of women's history in public education in the United States, it is imperative to consider each college's experiences as they were shaped by its particular social and cultural environment and the influence of its students and women faculty and staff over time.[12]

From the vantage point of the "Me Too" era in the United States, we should acknowledge that it is time to reevaluate the strict rules women encountered in coeducation. An important issue that has yet to be addressed fully by historians of women's higher education is sexual harassment and even sexual assault of women on college and university campuses. Once women entered UK, strict rules were placed on the students. Viewed through one lens, these rules seem oppressive and antiquated. Why did women students have to be under the watchful eye of a matron at all times when not in class? Why did universities such as UK concern themselves so much about contact between men and women on the campus?[13]

Perhaps it was actually a concern for the safety of women students, and not entirely about their morality. An examination of almost any public university campus in the late nineteenth century will turn up often inappropriate and unpredictable behavior of the male students. Many of them, when not in class, drank alcohol to excess, fought sometimes viciously among themselves, used guns inappropriately, intimidated male professors, and generally caused disruptions on the campus and in the larger community. Who would not have been apprehensive about young women in this environment?[14] In addition, while documented incidents are nearly absent from the public record, stories have survived over the decades of male faculty acting inappropriately with their female students. Perhaps the scarcity of reports about male students harassing their female counterparts at UK results from the rules that were in place for the women. More likely, of course, is that those records are scarce because at that time women would have been even more unlikely to report any type of sexual harassment or even sexual assault.

It is past time to examine the successes, the failures, and the impact women students at UK made during the latter decades of the nineteenth century and the first half of the twentieth century. The present volume is an attempt, at long last, to offer a more complete story. It is a story of women seeking access to academic equality, creating a separate women's culture and spaces within a male-centric environment, and attempting to create a truly coeducational learning environment and social culture.[15]

1

First Women and the Will to Succeed

White women in Kentucky first gained access to public higher education in 1880. Over the next thirty-five years women civic leaders, faculty, staff, and students strove to create an identifiable and distinct women's environment within the University of Kentucky (UK). A pioneer generation of Kentucky women created a space for themselves within a traditionally male campus. Lynn Gordon, in her study of women and higher education during the Progressive Era, argues that this was a significant period in the history of women's higher education. With a majority of college women being educated in public coeducational universities, this generation of women students began to redefine what higher education meant for women and their future. Their successes challenged the prevailing notions of career and marriage, even as it remained generally unresolved for what purpose women were attaining college degrees.[1]

The initial entrance of women into public universities like UK came often through the institution's "normal," or teacher training, department. Historian John Thelin has noted, "Any discussion of the advanced education of women in the nineteenth century ultimately overlaps with the subject of teacher education." In her pathbreaking history of women's education in the United States, Barbara Miller Solomon notes, "The first thirty women to attend the University of Wisconsin came for teacher training." Permitted to take other college courses during the Civil War when enrollment generally shrank precipitously, "they were not allowed to sit down until all male students were seated." After the war and the return of the men students, coeducation abruptly halted and did not return until six year later.[2]

Kentucky was no exception to the entrance of women students through the normal department. The state legislature's revision of UK's charter in 1880 called for the creation of a normal school within the newly independent college to increase student enrollment and income as prospective teachers sought certification. The legislature also stipulated that one student from each Kentucky county who had been a teacher, or sought to teach, could receive free tuition. The opening of the normal school to women provided the first access to public higher education to white women in Kentucky. Previously, women pursing college work or teacher training attended a wide range of private women's academies and colleges or teacher institutes spread across the commonwealth. The first public access to higher education for African Americans in Kentucky was the State Normal School for Colored Persons, which opened in Frankfort in October 1887 and eventually became Kentucky State University.[3]

The initial enrollment in the fall of 1880 of women at UK was "at first meager," but "grew to respectable portions" as forty-three women students entered. The following year the college anticipated sixty "young ladies" to matriculate "on equal terms with the males." Professors reported that the first class of women students "held their own fully with the young men, making quite as good recitations and examinations."[4]

In late fall 1881, a Lexington newspaper reported that the "system of co-education of the sexes works well at the State College. The girls have invaded almost every class, and are 'holding the fort manfully.'" Perhaps with purposeful hyperbole, the report concluded that upon arriving at State College, a new student "was astonished to see so many girls in attendance. He inquired if this was a female school, and if so why they allowed the boys to attend." But, as Helen Lefkowitz Horowitz has argued, the first women in these coeducational public universities were by definition "outsiders" and that it "took a certain courage to attend."[5]

Even after legislation made it possible for women to attend UK, the details regarding who was most responsible for making it a reality at the college remain vague. It is clear, however, that once the "experiment" was deemed a success, many came forward to claim credit. President

James K. Patterson later recounted that he had convinced a reluctant Board of Trustees that the new normal department should be open to both men and women. Patterson recalled that the chair of the Board, Judge William B. Kinkead, gave him "his cordial support" on the issue. Kinkead's son, George Kinkead, who would himself later serve on the board from 1900 to 1908, wrote that through his father's "initiative and personal force, and in the face of persistent and vigorous opposition, the coeducational system was introduced, which has proven a pronounced and admitted success."[6]

Patterson's biographer considered the admission of women to UK a moment of discord for the institution. He further argued that "the controversy over the admission of women to the university bore the bittersweet fruit with the least visible relation to any merits of the case." Patterson's role in the episode was described as "at first apparently that of an innocent bystander, which is perilous enough."[7]

Young Sophonisba Breckinridge, one of the original women students at UK, reflected years later in the local newspaper about her experiences. She noted that she had been given too much credit for being a pioneer in opening the doors of higher education to women. She added that her father, W. C. P. Breckinridge, and several other "gentlemen" deserved most of the credit for accomplishing the "miracle" of admitting women. She explained, "They managed to insert a clause" into the legislation regarding UK that allowed women to enter the Normal Department and "very cunningly" added that any student attending the college could take courses in any department. Breckinridge considered her father's strategy to be "pretty foxy."[8]

Patterson first admitted Sophonisba Breckinridge and two of Judge Kinkead's daughters, Ellen Talbott Kinkead and Elizabeth Shelby Kinkead, to the college but warned that "a trial of thirty days would be granted them." Breckinridge remembered that "no one expected to see them succeed, but they did, and soon after this the college was obliged to admit other women students from families where there were girls . . . [who] wanted to do the work." Even though she was in the top three students in her class, Breckinridge recalled that she "encountered professors who did not want girls in their classes, including one who she claimed tried to humiliate her by giving her a problem he thought she could not solve in front of the school trustees."[9]

Looking back on her UK experience, Breckinridge admitted that coeducation "rubs some of the bloom off the feminine character." But she quickly added that women who study alongside men "gain wider, more liberal views, honesty, directness and other things which more than compensate for the little amount of femininity she loses." After leaving UK and completing her undergraduate degree at the all-women Wellesley College, Breckinridge noted, "The great charm that Wellesley had for me was that it was made or established for me or the likes of me." Helen Lefkowitz Horowitz concluded in her study of women's colleges that Wellesley, "by having only women teach women and by housing students within the same large building," created "a totally female world," or a world that Breckinridge believed was designed for the likes of her.[10]

Never one to miss an opportunity for an argument, President Patterson responded to Breckinridge in the same newspaper just two days later regarding her claims for her father's role. Patterson countered that, even though he had earlier opposed allowing women at his college, there was "not the slightest reference to the admission of women" in the April 23, 1880, act of the Kentucky General Assembly and that W. C. P. Breckinridge "had nothing to do, either directly or indirectly, with the framing of the acts." Instead, he claimed that he and Judge William B. Kinkead alone "induced" a reluctant Board of Trustees "to admit females." Regardless of who received, or took, credit for coeducation at UK, the college did admit women for the first time in 1880 and gained another source of revenue from the higher enrollment. Patterson was no maverick, but he repeatedly showed that he would do almost anything to assure the continued existence of his college. With the creation of a normal department and the addition of 43 women students during 1880–1881, the total enrollment jumped dramatically, from 137 students in 1879–1880 to 234 the following year.[11]

Once enrolled at UK, women students found an environment controlled by men and dominated by male students wearing military-style cadet uniforms. When the Normal Department first opened, students attended classes in a one-windowed room in the Old Masonic Temple on Walnut Street in downtown Lexington before relocating to the Woodlands campus. But even after UK moved to its permanent campus in 1882, there was no women's dormitory. Conveniences taken for

The military-like environment at UK must have seemed very unwelcoming for women. Denied access to the all-male cadet corps, women students had a little fun by forming the "Broom Brigade," which mimicked the men's military drills. (UK general photographic prints.)

granted by later students, such as proper restrooms, dining facilities, and even a library, did not exist. Men held all faculty and administrative positions.[12]

Odd campus policies banned newspapers and any books other than textbooks from the men's dormitory rooms. But male students could carry guns, and it was not unusual to hear shots fired out of a dorm-room window. In February 1882 the cadets were awaiting new side arms that reportedly would "make the three infantry companies look splen-didly." Professors lived in trepidation of practical jokes and even retalia-tion from the male students. On occasion their fears became reality as violence erupted on the campus. In March 1883 a student "under [house] arrest for a violation of the regulations of the college" went into town and "came back intoxicated." Around noon the student "dis-charged pistols from his room in the dormitory with promiscuous threats." Colonel M. C. McFarland, commander of the cadet corps, was dispatched to disarm the student and dismiss him from the college. A rumor that the student had "loaded rifles and twenty rounds of ammu-nition" was dismissed as "purely a gratuitous myth." By the turn of the century President Patterson would question whether male students should even be housed on campus, as they caused so much disruption and destruction of property. But for the time being, the UK campus was far from genteel, and stereotypical male bravado ruled.[13]

Despite an unwelcoming, if not hostile, physical and social environment, women succeeded academically from their arrival at UK. But it would take time, and intense lobbying from the Kentucky Equal Rights Association and women reformers such as Laura Clay, to achieve the opening of a women's dormitory, the establishment of a Department of Domestic Science, the creation of the office of Dean of Women, and the founding of women's academic and social organizations. Yet women students fortunate enough to attend UK during those first decades probably did not dwell on their lack of opportunities on the campus. Many undoubtedly did not look to the university to provide social activities, as they led full social lives within the larger Lexington community.[14]

The lack of a women's dormitory did not affect women as much in the early years as it would later. All but one of the women students in the first class in 1880–1881 were from Lexington or Fayette County. Even though "Mrs. Daniel Saffarrans" (as she signed herself in the matriculation ledger), one of the women to attend that first year, listed her hometown as Yazoo City, Mississippi (her native state), she lived in Lexington with her husband, Daniel T. Saffarrans, and two small children. At age thirty-two, Ada Saffarrans may have been the first married woman with children to attend UK. She became a teacher at the Dudley School in Lexington just a few blocks from campus. She also had a third child in 1884, Ada Mead Saffarrans, who became a famous actress in the early 1900s. Daniel Saffarrans died in 1894.[15]

By 1890, however, UK women students came from communities and counties across the commonwealth. Out of necessity, these out-of-town students sought lodging in boardinghouses. In many cases, UK women students in the boardinghouses shared housing and meals with male students from UK and other private educational institutions in Lexington. As pointed out by Helen Lefkowitz Horowitz, ironically the first women attending coeducational universities experienced more freedom because while they were off campus, "fewer codes or rules separated the sexes." Only later would university administrators, especially the dean of women, exert their control over the women students' off-campus residences.[16]

The elevated site of the college's new fifty-two-acre campus, referred to at the time as College Park, commanded a good view of downtown Lexington only a few blocks to the north, as well as the rolling fields of rural Fayette County to the south. The newly completed Main Building contained a "commodious chapel, society rooms," and "lecture and recitation rooms sufficient for the accommodation of 600 students." The "large and well ventilated" dormitory next to the Main Building could house ninety students and included a "suitable dining room and kitchen" and "matron and servants rooms." A home for the president was built overlooking Maxwell Springs, where "an abundant supply of water" rendered "the construction of an artificial lake, with boating course a quarter mile in length . . . providing for a beautiful sheet of water to add to the attractions of the landscape."[17]

The dedication of the new campus in 1882 featured a parade from downtown Lexington to the new campus, with Governor Luke P. Blackburn and other dignitaries in carriages, a brass band from Cincinnati, the college faculty, and the cadet corps in uniforms. The parade ended at the Main Building, where numerous speeches were delivered in the overflowing chapel.[18]

Four years after women first entered UK, eighteen-year-old Leonora Hoeing became the first woman recognized at commencement when she received her Normal Department certificate. A newspaper reporter noted that the 1884 ceremony had a "new and extremely pleasant feature to it" in that "one of the graduates wore a white dress and a blush that was as daintily pink as the inside of a sea-shell from the Indian Ocean. Yes, one of the graduates was a young lady, and when his Excellency Governor Knott handed her diploma to her he looked as if he wanted to welcome her into the ranks of the wise with just a touch of his gray mustache to her velvet cheek." Highlighting the greater access that UK offered to white women from the working class, the reporter added that Hoeing was "none of your bilious blue-stockings either."[19]

This first generation of women students at UK were the daughters of some of central Kentucky's most elite families, but most were the daughters of shopkeepers and tradespeople firmly rooted in Kentucky's expanding middle class. For example, Hoeing's father, Joseph, and mother, Rebecca, had both emigrated from Germany. Joseph worked in Lexington as a silversmith, and Rebecca was a hairdresser. We may never know the multitude of factors that motivated these families to support their daughters' educations, but we know the role their daughters played as educational pioneers and that their lives were changed. But to dispel any notion of higher education's negative impact on women, the reporter concluded that Hoeing "was a fresh, healthy young woman, with an eye as full and bright as a dove's, and the head of a Greek Venus on a neck like a lily-stalk" and was "a happy, wholesome, appetizing creature, with an expression of frank good-fellowship about her, well mingled with a becoming and maidenly modesty."[20]

Finally addressing Hoeing's academic accomplishments, the reporter wrote that she "had taken a double course of study this year, but it seemed to have agreed with her." He also noted that, even though she was awarded a normal certificate and not a bachelor's degree "like they did the boys," her accomplishments are "all the same though, for she knows as much as the others, has taken the same course, won the first prize in mathematics over every rascal of them, and if she is not a 'Mistress of Arts' she is the first woman I ever saw that wasn't. The boys didn't seem to be envious of her at all, but cheered her every chance they had with hearty good will."[21]

The entrance of women into other academic disciplines and programs had already begun. Patterson later recalled that it became "expedient" to no longer confine women students to the normal school, but to open all the departments of the institution to them. In order to enter any department of the college except the Normal Department, however, graduates of the Lexington Female Academy were required to "pass a satisfactory examination in at least two of the studies required for entering the freshman class, one of which shall be Mathematics."[22]

Even as women students expanded their academic opportunities into other areas of the college, male students still outnumbered them on the campus by nearly five to one and, from outward appearances, UK remained a male domain. The college required every male student to wear a cadet uniform and participate in military-style drills. Among the 176 myriad rules governing student behavior during this period, one required that students "walk in the halls and pass up and down stairs in study hours in a soldier-like and orderly manner." However, the pres-

Professor James White's calculus class, 1906–1907. While men outnumber women five to one in the class, the presence of four women represented their ability to move into all areas of the curriculum, including mathematics. (UK glass plate negative collection.)

ence of women students on the UK campus, and continued lobbying by women leaders in the community and the commonwealth, soon forced President Patterson and the all-male faculty and board to devote more attention to the women's needs, both academically and in regard to student life.[23]

By June 1887, the board authorized the college "to employ a lady . . . to do assistant work in the Preparatory Department for the Normal School and College classes and to preside in the girls' study room as matron." A Miss Bullock filled the position for only one year at $35 a month before the board named Lucy Berry Blackburn, a fifty-five-year-old widow, matron and assistant in the Preparatory Department at a salary of $500 annually. A year later the board raised Blackburn's salary to $750, including $550 for "her services as instructor" in the Preparatory Department and $200 for her "services as Matron."[24]

Mrs. Blackburn
Monitress.

The early women students remembered Lucy Blackburn not as the first woman instructor at UK but more for her work as monitor of the women students. (*Kentuckian*, 1900.)

Gertrude Renz Gordon, class of 1904, remembered Blackburn as "always so correct, so persnickety." She tried her best "to keep her young ladies in the assembly room from looking out and flirting with the young gentlemen on the campus." Gordon recalled that the men students nearly "shocked her [Blackburn] to death one Halloween" when they built a full-size outdoor toilet and set it at the southwest corner of the old Main Building just outside the women students' assembly room. Since women students "had very inadequate toilet facilities," the men students hung a large "To Let" sign on the improvised privy. As Gordon remembered, "Poor Aunt Lucy! She almost had heart failure trying to keep her charges from looking out the windows." Occasionally women students skipped a class to stroll over to the adjoining Maxwell Place with their "young gentlemen." But Blackburn, always on the lookout, would hurry after the couples and bring the girls back. Moreover, Blackburn made all women students sign a pledge that they would not use tobacco or profane language while on the campus. Nevertheless, this pioneer generation of Kentucky college women behaved like typical students of any generation, male or female, despite the ever-watchful Blackburn.[25]

Even though Blackburn appears by today's standards as overly strict and intrusive into the women students' lives, one must also consider the real concerns that others had about sexual harassment and even sexual assault as real possibilities. The young women would have been susceptible to unwanted sexual advances from their fellow male students and even from the mostly male faculty. However, these issues are difficult to discern from the existing historical records.

Women students reached another milestone on June 4, 1888, as the college faculty reviewed the candidates for degrees and concluded that "Cadets George G. Bryan, Henry. E. Curtis, Robert T. Payne, Fred V. Bartlett, and Miss Arabella Clement Gunn" had "creditably finished the course prescribed for the degree of Bachelor of Science." Nineteen-year-old Belle Gunn became the first woman student at UK to earn a baccalaureate degree from UK.[26]

A Lexington native, Gunn spent much of her childhood on a farm near Shelbyville, Kentucky, where she attended the highly regarded Science Hill Academy for girls. Her family later moved back to Lexington, where Gunn finished her precollege education at Sayre Institute. Classmates at UK remembered Gunn as "well above average in scholarship, but not so brilliant as to inspire envy and jealousy." She participated fully in the social life available, including the literary societies.[27]

Prior to the 1888 commencement, President Patterson called Belle Gunn to his office. He asked the only woman graduate, "I suppose you will not want to sit up on the platform with the young men on Commencement Day, will you, Miss Gunn?" Gunn replied, "I've been through four years in classes with them and I don't see why I shouldn't sit on the platform with them now." At commencement President Patterson was reportedly "most gracious" to the first woman graduate, whom he referred to as the "Eldest Daughter of the Institution."[28]

Three years later a woman graduate was still a source of fascination. Callie Warner, one of five graduates in 1891, walked into the college chapel for the commencement ceremony at the front of the four men students. Once again a woman graduate's clothing and physical attributes

Arabella "Belle" Clement Gunn, 1888. (UK portrait print collection.)

were highlighted when a reporter noted that "she looked very sweet and modest in her soft, fine India silk gown, made at the neck with a baby frill exposing the white throat. Her brown hair was simply arranged in a loose coil with natural rings clustering on her brow. Suede gloves of stone color, same tone to the dress."[29]

Women increasingly made their presence felt at the school, and women's enrollment rose noticeably in 1888, increasing from 74 the previous year to 106 out of a total student enrollment of 408. The board voted in June 1889 to enlarge the men's dormitory to accommodate an additional forty men students and "to have a College Home erected for ladies attending the Normal School eligibly situated with a capacity to accommodate near fifty students to cost not exceeding $6,000."[30]

The *Lexington Daily Press* reported that seventy-five women students were enrolled in the fall of 1889, and "their admission to the college has never been regretted." At the September 1889 board meeting George Kinkead stressed the need for increased lodging and boarding facilities for students, especially those who matriculated in the Normal School, meaning most of the women students. However, Philemon Bird moved to spend $8,000 on an additional dorm for the men. Judge Kinkead offered a compromise, stating that "the Executive Committee be authorized to provide additional boarding accommodations for students male or female either upon the college grounds or elsewhere to the extent of $12,000." The motion passed 6–3. Six students signed a resolution in honor of Kentucky legislators J. Embry Allen and William Klair for their "zealous, efficient, and successful work" in support of a women's dorm at UK.[31]

The compromise motion resulted in no dormitory for women for another fourteen years. The delay in dormitory construction may have resulted from a lack of commitment by the all-male board and was likely exacerbated by a sharp decline in enrollment in 1893, which in turn may have been due in part to the Panic of 1893, which brought serious economic hardship to Kentucky and elsewhere. That year women students numbered only 34 out of a total student population of just 130. The percentage of women at the college continued to decline, and by the turn of the century the number of women students averaged fewer than 60, with their percentage of the student body declining to an all-time low of only 14 percent by 1904. In the interim, women whose families

Carr Boarding House, 1903. The delay in construction of a dormitory for women students may have resulted from a lack of commitment by the all-male board and was likely exacerbated by a sharp decline in enrollment in 1893. That year women students numbered only 34 out of a total student population of just 130. The percentage of women at the college continued to decline, and by the turn of the century the number of women students averaged fewer than 60, with their percentage of the student body declining to an all-time low of only 14 percent by 1904. (UK glass plate negative collection.)

did not live in Lexington made do with boardinghouses throughout the city.[32]

Undoubtedly, many out-of-town families would not have allowed their daughters to live in boardinghouses. For example, the student newspaper reported in March 1893 that "Miss Lunette Tompson" would soon be leaving the college because of her family's move from Lexington to Louisville, noting that "Miss Tompson is very popular" and "would have graduated next year and her many friends are sorry to lose her." It is impossible to calculate how many young women were "lost" to higher education because of the constraints of money, family attitudes,

It is unknown what prompted this group of forty-six women to gather on the steps of the Main Building in 1892, but this portrait represented roughly half of all women students at UK that year. (UK general photographic prints.)

and administrative planning and policies that did little to assist women students.[33]

In May 1902 one hundred women from Lexington and the surrounding area sent a communication to the UK Board of Trustees. They called first for the "immediate erection of the girl's dormitory for which the Legislature appropriated $60,000." In addition, they reminded the board that the legislation for the women's dormitory also called for "the appointment of three women to act as a Board of Supervisors over the dormitory for young women."[34]

Even though still relatively small in numbers, women competed and succeeded academically with the men students as never before. In an essay read to the graduating class of 1892, Irene I. Hunt exhibited the seriousness that she and other women students brought to their college work:

> Today we have finished our college course and tomorrow we begin our life work, for we all, I suppose without exception, will take up some vocation and follow it faithfully. For what would our lives be without some such purpose? An aimless life is an empty life, an idle, dissatisfying pastime. On the other hand, how much better will it be to have some noble work to perform, some goal to strive for. In the choice of a profession what nobler work could one undertake than that of the teacher?[35]

But despite Hunt's professional ambitions as a college graduate, by 1910 she had married Peter F. Downing, a dairy farmer, and was the mother of three children.

By and large, women students at UK prior to World War I shared a common purpose with college women nationally. They attended college to seek a career, most often teaching. While a majority of the women graduates of UK during the 1880s and 1890s eventually married and became homemakers, many did not. According to Helen Lefkowitz Horowitz, at least nationally, half of the women college graduates between 1880 and 1900 never married, while only 10 percent of women in the general population remained single. The marriage rate would climb until by the 1940s nearly 75 percent of women college graduates married.[36]

As early as 1882 women students founded their own literary group, the Philosophian Society, which quickly became a prominent campus organization. Pictured above is the *Old Maids Convention*, a play staged by the Philosophian Society in 1898 depicting spinsters being "renovated" into beautiful young women to find husbands. (UK general photographic prints.)

Women students at UK succeeded beyond most expectations, and the men took notice. Women students in the Normal Department founded the Philosophian Society "for literary improvement and social pleasure" as early as 1882 with seventeen charter members. Belle Gunn served as vice president of the society in 1885 and made opening remarks at its December 1885 meeting, which was attended by President Patterson. The society had a "well-equipped" hall for the meetings and events. In addition to its weekly meetings, the Philosophian Society provided public events consisting of declamations, essays, criticisms, and orations once every year. Writing in 1892, Fielding Clay Elkin, alumnus editor for the campus newspaper, urged students to become more involved in campus literary societies. He noted, "We have no fear but what the young ladies will acquit themselves as they have always done, with all

A physiology classroom, circa 1897. Visiting several classes, a Board of Trustees committee found "in most if not all of the section rooms a mingling of the sexes, and an expression of companionship" that they believed to be inappropriate in the college. (UK glass plate negative collection.)

honor to themselves and friends. But the boys need to be urged to better work, to do that of which they are capable." *The Cadet*, an early campus newspaper, reported in 1893, "The young ladies of the Philosophian Society have met and commenced work in earnest. Entertainment [oral presentations] given by these young ladies have always ranked among the first of the college."[37]

Still, the climate for women on the UK campus remained challenging. The absence of a women's dormitory limited enrollment, and women students still had no designated space on the campus to congregate for casual conversation or for formal socializing. Outside of class, men students gathered in White Hall, the men's dormitory, or on the parade ground during cadet drills. They were generally free to come and go as they pleased. Between classes college officials required women

UK class of 1895. From left to right, back row: Nellie Reynolds, Nettie B. Foster (salutatorian), Lucy Fitzhugh, John Bryan, Elizabeth W. King, John Vick Faulkner, Mary Didlake (valedictorian), Mary Atkins, Mary McCauliff; front row: Paul I. "Pi" Murrill, Joseph Milton Downing, James McConathy, Henry S. Bush, Rufus Lee Weaver, Richard C. Stoll, Lannes Spurgem Barber. Class members absent: Roberta Newman, John Webb Wilmott, John Joseph Woods, and Thomas Stone Lewis. (UK general photographic prints.)

students to report to a "well-appointed study room" next to President Patterson's office in the Main Building, where they were "under the constant and strict supervision" of the ever-watchful Lucy Blackburn.[38]

During an 1897 inspection of the campus grounds, a Board of Trustees committee found the only women's restroom more "respectable" than those provided for the men, yet "totally insufficient." The committee added that "more even than in the male" restrooms, "the walls were covered with pencil inscriptions, the names of the students, their preferences and dislikes among the male students, and the wit that belongs to such ill kept places." More importantly, the investigating committee reported that some board members remained opposed to coeducation of the sexes.[39]

The committee found "a mingling of the sexes, and an expression of companionship which in our opinion is not appropriate." They specifically cited one instance in which a male and a female student shared a book when they should have been listening to the instructor. The committee recommended that the women's and men's desks be arranged on opposite sides of the classroom and that conversation between men and women be forbidden during classes. As far as can be determined, such draconian measures were not enacted.[40]

In 1895 Mary LeGrand Didlake became UK's first woman valedictorian. She was the daughter of Nannie Bain Didlake and George Ware Didlake of Lexington. Nannie Didlake, who had completed the eighth grade, participated actively in the Kentucky Equal Rights Association; and George Didlake, a Confederate veteran, was a bank teller and insurance salesman. Mary Didlake came to UK well prepared, as she had attended Sayre School for primary grades, Miss Butler's School, and Hamilton College in Lexington for prep school. After earning her bachelor's degree, Didlake earned a master's degree from UK in 1897. She then studied at the University of Chicago, receiving another master's degree in 1901 at the same time Sophonisba Breckinridge was completing her PhD in Political Science there.[41]

Also for the first time, women received both first and second academic honors in 1895, as the college recognized Nettie Bell Foster as salutatorian of the class. Unfortunately, neither Foster nor Didlake was permitted to present her prepared remarks to the commencement audience. The day before, President Patterson's only surviving child, William Andrew "Billy" Patterson died at the age of twenty-seven. A graduate of the college, he had become an instructor in history. It was decided to keep the commencement ceremony simple and solemn out of respect for the Patterson family. A reporter noted that "the great majority of those present at the meager exercises felt deprived of an expectant pleasure, and that it was an unnecessary privation as the delivery of the Valedictory at least could not have shown any want of sympathy in the great sorrow of [President] Patterson and his heart-broken wife."[42]

Three years later, the only two women in a graduating class of twenty again swept top academic honors at commencement when Lila Beatrice Terry delivered the valedictory and Margaret Isadora King, the salutatorian, offered the welcoming address. King, "one of the youngest of her class," had "applause, quantities of flowers, and presents showered upon her" at the conclusion of her presentation. After a brief stint as a legal secretary, King became President Patterson's secretary and also served part-time as the college's registrar from 1905 to 1910. In 1910 she became the college's first librarian and oversaw the development of a modern university library until her retirement in 1947. Like Foster, King remained single until her death in 1966.[43]

At first glance it might appear that women were gaining equal recognition academically and finding their voices within the college. A closer reading of their environment, however, reveals negative undercurrents still prevalent. Of the two men who spoke at the 1898 commencement, William Thomas Carpenter, representing Mechanical Engineering, was recognized for "his manly bearing, his familiarity with his subject and its appropriateness to the times." Meanwhile, it was noted that "Miss Jennie Willmott," representing the scientific department at the 1899 commencement, "read her essay with a girlish grace and a distinctiveness of expression." The following year Lula May Cox, representing the scientific department, "read an essay that abounded in attractive phraseology and there was through it all a strain of girlish thought."[44]

Even taking into account the accepted language of the late nineteenth century, women's academic successes were often placed in a gendered context. "Manly bearing" and "girlish thought" had real and significant implications for the graduating women, just as did campus humor at the time. The December 1893 student newspaper featured what would become a long-standing, pernicious tradition of humor directed against women:

Lilli: Why didn't Miss W. have anything to do with Mr. H. when he came? She said she was going to.

Emma: Yes, but during their first talk he said he had never met a pretty woman who had any brains. So she dropped him, considering it a personal insult.

Lilli: (amiably) Why? Which does she think she has?[45]

Women's academic achievements and recognitions likely precipitated a change of university policy in 1900. No valedictorian or salutatorian was recognized at commencement because the faculty changed the awarding of honors so that each department would be represented

UK freshman class of 1900 on the steps of the Main Building. Twenty years after first entering UK, women were still vastly outnumbered by the men students. (UK general photographic prints.)

by its own "honor man." The all-male faculty argued that it was "not fair" for male students in disciplines like engineering and physics to have to compete with women students in education and such disciplines as English, where "it was perhaps easier to attain a high average." After several years of having mostly women speak at commencement, by 1902 only one woman graduate, Leola Ditto, who was receiving a Bachelor of Pedagogy, spoke on the topic "Woman and Science," while six male students spoke on various topics.[46]

For several years afterwards, men dominated specific disciplines. For example, in 1900 engineering enrolled 163 men and no women. Other academic units, such as law, agriculture, and commerce, also remained essentially all-male enclaves. These segregated academic areas virtually assured top academic honors for men students without fear of competition from women in arts and sciences, where women comprised half of UK's students in 1900.[47]

Women students found themselves navigating uncharted academic waters. Seemingly no one could determine where the bounds for women would be drawn academically or socially. At the 1902 meeting of college alumni, "Miss Charlotte Bliss, class of 1901, spoke representing the Alumnae," a tradition that had begun at the previous meeting so that "one of the daughters of the college" could speak. It was reported that Bliss's "clear, sweet voice delighted those present no less than her thoughtful and beautiful speech." Increasingly, it seemed, women students were being restricted. While not completely separated, like women at the University of Chicago and Stanford University, UK women were most often not recognized at public ceremonies and lacked a voice within colleges. This systematically diminished and compartmentalized women's role on the UK campus.[48] That is not to say that all women students at UK felt themselves totally muted or significantly marginalized. To the contrary, in some ways the women embraced their developing separate spaces and organizations. In November 1901 the Faculty Senate reviewed the "applications of certain young ladies to establish a chapter of Chi Epsilon Chi Fraternity." Professor Alexander St. Clair McKenzie "reported that his committee believed that the organization would be harmless and recommended that permission should be granted for its organization." The Faculty Senate voted to approve.[49]

In 1902 women graduates inaugurated an annual Alumnae Luncheon "exclusively for the lady members of the Alumni Association." Poking obvious fun at the men, the women graduates reported that "the sterner half of the Association" organized in opposition to the "For Men Only" alumni "smoker," which the men proposed to have but that never occurred. According to the women, "rumors circulated by certain jealous male graduates" that "moonshine was used in the punch and that Turkish cigarettes were passed" at the women's luncheon were "indignantly denied."[50]

However, women leaders in the community were doing more than merely entertaining themselves at men's expense. Women's rights activist and onetime student at UK Laura Clay fought steadily and persuasively for women's issues in regard to UK. In 1894 the Kentucky Equal Rights Association petitioned the governor to appoint a woman to the UK board. The association contended that UK's women students still did not receive equal opportunity.[51]

Chi Epsilon Chi in 1906. Women students refused to be excluded or marginalized. To the contrary, many women embraced separate women's social space. In November 1901 the Faculty Senate approved the establishment of a chapter of Chi Epsilon Chi fraternity. Professor Alexander St. Clair McKenzie reported that the new women's fraternity "would be harmless." (UK glass plate negative collection.)

Two years later the Kentucky General Assembly debated proposed legislation allowing women to serve on the UK board. President Patterson, who continued to take credit for the admission of women to the college, unabashedly appeared before the legislature to vigorously oppose the change. He argued that the education of 99 percent of women did not prepare them to serve on the board. Laura Clay, seeing the contradiction in Patterson's position, shot back that since most Kentucky women received their college educations at UK, if they were not qualified to serve on the board it meant that their education had been inferior. Some members of the legislature stressed that since women made up 35 percent of the student body the board should have similar representation, but a majority disagreed and the proposed legislation failed.[52]

Former UK student Laura Clay, holding an umbrella mid-frame, and other women marching for the Madison, Fayette, and Franklin Kentucky Equal Rights Association at the Democratic National Convention in St. Louis in 1916. Laura Clay fought steadily for women's equality at UK and beyond. (Laura Clay photographic collection.)

Nevertheless, during the Progressive Era prior to winning suffrage, Kentucky women began to make substantial gains. Margaret Ripley Wolfe, in her overview of Kentucky women's history, notes that "females cast ballots in school board elections and that thirty women were elected school superintendents between 1889 and 1897." Moreover, 1894 Kentucky legislation allowed married women to own property and make wills. By 1900 women gained control over their own earnings and a decade later rights to their own children. Wolfe notes that "all of this suggests an undercurrent of feminine unrest if not outright agitation, for such legislative action from an all-male body did not come easily."[53]

Kentucky women leaders continued to push for reforms at UK. A delegation representing the Equal Rights Association and led by its president, Laura Clay, met with the UK board at its June 1902 meeting. After being ushered into the second-floor boardroom in the newly constructed Alumni Hall (now Barker Hall), Laura Clay called first for the board to construct the long-anticipated and much-needed women's dormitory. Second, the women's rights activist demanded equity for the women students who came to UK as county appointees. She requested that until such time that the college built a women's dormitory, the board owed the women county appointees a modest weekly allowance that would offer some equality with the men county appointees, who had access to free college housing.[54]

Moreover, Clay urged the board to proceed with naming a Board of Supervisors for the women's dormitory, as required by state statute. In addition, she called "for the appointment of a woman on the faculty, with an equal voice in the faculty, with the title of Dean of Women," as well as for the establishment of a Department of Domestic Science, "in which all subjects pertaining to the domestic duties of women should be taught."[55]

The perseverance of Clay and her colleagues finally began to pay dividends. The 1902 Kentucky legislature appropriated $30,000 to build the long-awaited women's dormitory, which opened in January 1904. The board chose to name the new dormitory Patterson Hall in honor of President Patterson, but it may have been more appropriate to name it for his brother, Walter K. Patterson, the head of the Preparatory Department. Walter Patterson played a key role in securing funding and a site for the dormitory. Moreover, he gave up active teaching for a year as he supervised the construction of the new women's dorm.[56]

Patterson Hall became the first UK college building constructed apart from the central core of the original campus, on the "Pepper property" just north of campus across Winslow Street (Euclid Avenue). The legislature stipulated that the dormitory could not be constructed on the existing campus. Patterson Hall's location reinforced the prevailing separation of women students both physically and intellectually. Each day the women students made the trek from Patterson Hall, crossing Winslow Street and over a bridge spanning a small body of water fed by Maxwell Springs, up a hill to the main campus. Undoubtedly legislators, who only a few years earlier had bemoaned women and men students sitting next to each other in classes, apparently worried about the women students sleeping too near the men on the campus.[57]

As requested by Clay, the board established a Women's Board of Control to administer Patterson Hall. The board also appointed three "prudent, discreet, intelligent" women who were "members in good standing of one of the religious organizations." The male trustees instructed the new board to give them advice regarding women students and to "generally run the place."[58]

Accordingly, in June 1903 the Board of Trustees appointed three local women to the Board of Control. Nannie B. Didlake, mother of Mary Didlake, was appointed to a six-year term. Elizabeth B. Bradley, the mother of six, received a four-year appointment. Her spouse, Lee Bradley, was a Lexington banker and a well-known Confederate veteran of the Kentucky Orphan Brigade. Roberta Atkins was appointed for a two-year term. Her only child, Mary Lyons, graduated from UK in 1895; Atkins's spouse was a wholesale grocer in Lexington.[59]

As a top priority the new Board of Control sought an administrator for the new dormitory. President Patterson advised the board members that the person should be "a discreet, capable, experienced woman—a woman of dignity and culture." Moreover, she "should be selected for housekeeping and business, a woman who would know when to talk and when to be silent." Prone to overstatement, Patterson stressed that the future of women's education in Kentucky depended on their choice. He stressed that "merit, dignity, capability, and culture alone should determine the choice."[60]

Under intense pressure, the Board of Control chose widower Caroline Embry (Allen) Wallis from among one hundred applicants as the first matron of Patterson Hall. Described as "a woman of culture and education," Wallis likely owed her selection, at least in part, to the fact that her brother, state senator J. Embry Allen, served on the UK Committee in the legislature and had "fathered" the appropriation bill for the new women's dormitory. Despite her political appointment, Wallis served commendably as dormitory matron until 1911, earning $50 a month and board for her three children.[61]

In addition to the new women's dormitory, a new gymnasium was built in which "certain hours were set apart two days in the week when the girls were given exclusive possession of the building and a special instructor was provided for them." It was reported that the women "enjoyed their privileges to the utmost and did excellent work." Initially, the women students received physical education instruction from William H. Kiler, "a young lawyer" who held "a certificate from a summer

A women's physical education class, 1906. In addition to the dormitory, a new gymnasium on campus offered women students another gathering place. Two days a week, women had exclusive access to the gym. They participated in mandatory physical education during the hours set aside for the men's military drills. The Board of Control further stipulated, "no boys shall be allowed in the gymnasium proper, or baths or locker rooms etc., during the times set apart for the girls." (Louis Edward Nollau F series photographic print collection.)

school of physical education" and who also coached the college's football team for two years. A student, Olivia Elizabeth Henderson, assisted Kiler, and the women's classes came under the surveillance of Lucy Blackburn. Kiler's physical education instruction was judged to be so inadequate that he was forced to resign his position by June 1902.[62]

In December 1901 the college employed Florence Offutt to serve as Assistant Physical Director of the Gymnasium in charge of women's instruction. Offutt was the daughter of Ben and Florence Graham Offutt of Louisville. Her mother died during her birth, and she and her three older brothers lived with her maternal grandmother, Sallie A. Graham in Louisville. Upon Graham's death, the children went to live with their aunt, Mrs. Maurice Satterwhite. Florence Offutt was a cousin of Henry Stites Barker, future president of the University of Kentucky, in whose home she spent a great deal of her youth. She recalled her close relationship with Henry's wife, Kate Barker, as a "silver thread woven into the fabric of my entire life. I supplied the lack in her life—the child. She represented to me all that was exquisite and lovely in personality." After graduating from Louisville Girls' High School in 1896, Offutt studied physical education for a few months at the University of Chicago before completing a two-year degree in Physical Education at the highly regarded and coeducational New Haven Normal School of Gymnastics.[63]

Offutt recalled that while living in Lexington with her Uncle James and Aunt Ella Offutt Pepper in 1901, she waited for her chance to "uplift" the public with her "specialty," female physical education, which was new to Kentucky. She also made note of the recently completed "handsome new gymnasium" at UK, which had no woman director of physical education. Offutt secured a meeting with President Patterson to discuss a possible teaching position. Patterson told her "courteously but firmly" that "no vacancy existed or would." However, only six months later, at the December 1901 meeting, the university Board of Trustees voted unanimously to hire Offutt as the Assistant Physical Director of the Gymnasium in charge of women's instruction at a salary of $800 per year. Offutt took great pleasure in pointing out that, due to illness, President Patterson missed the meeting at which she was hired, thereby losing the opportunity to argue against her employment.[64]

Soon after Offutt's appointment to the faculty she "happened to see" a letter written by President Patterson to the board harshly criticizing her employment. But Offutt did not shy from a possible fight; and, noting that "she loved his courage," she went to see Patterson. She recalled that because she and the president were both Scottish, they each "liked a good fight for something we believe in." She eventually won the president's grudging respect and support despite telling him at one point, "I love to think of your being older than my grandfather." According to Offutt, the elderly president replied to such remarks "with a lack of enthusiasm." She also noted that Patterson worried about her first appearance before the faculty senate's "solemn enclaves," since "no weak female" had been there before. Offutt admitted that she "enjoyed" her "scraps" with the other faculty, which were at times "quite colorful, if a little strenuous." She considered having Patterson's support in such skirmishes "inspiring in the extreme."[65]

During her first two years on the faculty, Offutt continued living with her aunt and uncle at their home, Meadowthorpe, located just west of downtown Lexington. The Peppers, prominent members of Lexington society, were involved in distilling, farming, and raising horses. According to her biographer, the new twenty-seven-year-old faculty member "looked like a fairy princess as she rode to school each morning in a carriage drawn by big black horses and driven by a coachman in full livery." Two years after joining the UK faculty, Florence Offutt married Robert Lee Stout, who later served as judge of the fourteenth judicial district and as a member of the UK board. But unlike most women of her generation and social class, she continued her professional career.[66]

Stout's influence soon extended well beyond the UK campus. In 1903 Governor J. C. W. Beckham appointed her as a trustee of the Kentucky House of Reform. Later the Kentucky Education Association elected her president of the Department of Physical Education of Kentucky. Stout also spent several summers studying at the Yale Summer School of Physical Education and at the Chautauqua School of Physical Education. In her postgraduate work, Stout primarily studied "the theory and practice of classic dancing, as an artistic and intellectual means of physical development, and its revival as a fine art."[67]

Stout took her teaching very seriously because most educators considered physical education central to women's higher education in the late nineteenth and early twentieth centuries. Her view of physical education exhibited a fundamental belief in the physical capacity of women and the freedom that good physical development brought to women. Regarding physical education in Kentucky, Stout wrote:

> There is in women of all nations and all climes a barbaric disregard of the body's health and laws. She pierces her nose and her ears. She crushes her feet into sickening deformity. In America she exceeds her pagan sister. She squeezes into a space of 20 inches a body measuring 30 inches, and jerks herself through the world on exceedingly high heels. And yet she declares that she is a more superior product than her grandmother, whose especial pride was an anemic look and a power to faint when called upon.[68]

Florence Offutt Stout, circa 1910. (UK portrait print collection.)

Women's physical education received much attention on the campus, but not always in the manner that Stout would have preferred. One student proclaimed that the "modern gymnasium" offered "equal opportunities to girls" for it is in the gym where "the girls their beauty to enhance, are taught to do the classic dance."[69]

To the administration's dismay, but to the surprise of few, women's physical education especially attracted the attention of the male students.

Women's gym class in Buell Armory, 1906. The women's demure pose suggests the discrepancy between physical education for men and women. (UK glass plate negative collection.)

Writing in 1903 to William W. H. "Musty" Mustaine, Physical Director in the Department of Gymnastics, President Patterson warned that "the presence of male students in and about the gymnasium buildings while athletic instruction and practice for the girls are going on has become a matter of notoriety and is subjecting the college authorities to unfavorable criticism." He labeled the men's presence "a gross impropriety" and demanded that Mustaine prevent it from happening again. Mustaine responded that the boys didn't seem to be interfering any more than usual and that it was "practically impossible" to keep the boys out of the gymnasium without keeping the doors locked. He promised, however, to "keep closer watch during the practice of the girls," identify the "offenders," and report them to Patterson "promptly."[70]

Patterson, of course, did not place all of the blame on Mustaine and the unruly boys. In a letter to Florence Offutt Stout, Patterson noted that he had been told that young women were loitering around the gymnasium "during hours when they are not undergoing instruction." He warned Stout that he was bringing this to her attention so that she "may take the necessary steps to correct the evil." Always ready to give advice, the president said that he had "been advised that girls undergoing training for physical culture and practice wear garments of a decidedly masculine character to and from the gymnasium. In our physical training we undoubtedly spoil the women and yet fail to make men of them."[71]

President Patterson's sarcasm revealed more than he perhaps realized. He and the faculty seemed to be caught off guard not so much by the obvious and natural interaction developing between the sexes, but by the women students' overt interest in gaining the men students' attention. Patterson had grudgingly accepted the periodic rowdiness of his male cadets in matters not involving women students. But he seemed to maintain a rather limited understanding of what it meant to be a woman on the UK campus and was unprepared to handle inevitable relationships between the women and men students, and the women's public demonstrations of their attraction to the opposite sex.

In 1902, upon President Patterson's urging, the Board of Trustees restricted the twice-monthly dances on campus to just one a month. Patterson said, "it has been reported that they [dances] distracted the attention of the students, occurring too frequently, and they thought it better not to have so many." But in addition, the faculty went even further, wanting to prohibit vehicles on campus during dances and suggesting that males should be discouraged from sending women flowers prior to dances because the "student body is so ill able to afford" such extravagances.[72]

Patterson's comments, and his unwillingness to support women board members, demonstrated his limited view not only of what it meant to be a woman on the campus, but also of the direction in which gender relations were generally headed.

Writing in her diary for October 9, 1910, Virginia Clay McClure captured the spirit of a changing student culture on the campus when she wrote, "After supper all girls gathered in the parlor and yelled everything from, 'Well, well, well' to 'Rickety-rackety-russ.'! Then had a parade from first to second, to third floor, then down, and out in the yard, singing, 'Well it looks like to me 'tis a shirt-tail parade.' Got on the steps and gave all the yells, and a few boys down in the yard answered us. In a little while the 'Night Shirt Parade' came—500 boys, more or less, in night-shirts and caps, yelling, singing, beating the drum. Everybody wild with joy." College was becoming fun.[73]

Later that year, Lucy Blackburn wrote directly to the board regarding the problems in the gymnasium. She argued that coeducation "even under the most favorable conditions" continued to be fraught with "difficulties and responsibilities," creating problems only "augmented" by the building of the gymnasium on campus. She claimed that even though women students were forbidden to enter the gymnasium building "except when under instruction by the directress of Physical Culture or for other legitimate reason," the rule was being violated constantly and that men and women students skipped classes and chapel exercises to rendezvous in the gymnasium to "chat and waltz together."[74]

Blackburn reported to the board that at least one woman caught violating the gymnasium ban had been expelled from the college. In November 1903, Professor John Henry Neville called a special meeting of the faculty to report on the activities of Edna Parker Hibler of Paris, Kentucky. Previously suspended from college for "neglect of class work and other irregularities," Hibler had been reinstated following an "earnest solicitation" on her behalf by her mother. However, Hibler had been seen on two occasions waltzing with a young man in the college gymnasium during a time she should have been in chapel or in class. Upon hearing the evidence against Hibler, the faculty requested that Hibler's father withdraw her from the college. In comparison to the many incidents of destruction and physical harm brought about by the activities of the male cadets, Edna Hibler's proclivity to "waltz" in the gymnasium seemed quite tame. Nevertheless, the administration obviously used her as an example in their attempts to contain what would become a transition of college life to greater and greater emphasis on relations between the sexes.[75]

Additionally, Blackburn suggested to the board that women's physical culture classes be transferred to Patterson Hall. She acknowledged that the dormitory did not provide the same provision for "athletic training" as the gymnasium; but, following Patterson's lead, she argued that the college should "promote physical culture in the girls" and not "make athletes of them." Several women's physical education activities were transferred to Patterson Hall and to an antiquated maintenance building located near White Hall on the central campus. Although by then women had been present on the UK campus for nearly a quarter of a century, a consensus had yet to be reached in regard to why women were obtaining higher education and what their future might be.[76]

In 1903 the board appointed Elizabeth Shelby Kinkead "Lecturer of English Literature" to deliver a weekly talk on literature to the senior class. A member of the first cohort of women to attend UK, Kinkead had become a well-known local lecturer and authority on English literature, and in 1896 she had published a history of Kentucky. Probably not coincidentally, she was the daughter of former board chair Judge William Bury Kinkead and a sister of George Kinkead, a member of the college's board at the time of her appointment.[77]

Informing the faculty of Kinkead's employment, Patterson insisted that her lectures not interfere with regularly scheduled classes. Professor Joseph Hoening Kastle suggested that Kinkead's lectures would appeal to both students and to "the more cultured members" of the Lexington community. He proposed that Kinkead deliver her lectures in the evenings so that the "more cultured people in our community" would have an opportunity to attend. The public did take advantage of Kinkead's lectures, especially Lexington women, who thought Kinkead to be "earnest, capable, and learned." Whether for UK students or the Lexington community, Kinkead sought to inspire in her audience an appreciation for "a broader culture" as well as "a loftier ideal and a deeper understanding" than could be obtained from standard textbooks.[78]

Still, Elizabeth Kinkead held no formal faculty position, and in 1904 her status on campus came under review by the board. Board member Henry Stites Barker supported her lectures and offered a resolution to make them compulsory for sophomores and juniors and open to any other students. A successful substitute resolution, offered by board member Cassius M. Clay, Jr., and seconded by President Patterson, instead passed 7–2. It "resolved that Miss Kinkead be given the hour for chapel on the days for her lecture, without any compulsory requirement."[79]

Barker then moved that "for the advancement of Miss Kinkead's work in the college that she be made a regular member of the Faculty." The resolution failed on a 3–6 vote with President Patterson voting with the board members opposed to faculty rank for Kinkead. Even with the support of prominent board members such as Judge Barker, R. W. Nelson, and Judge Robert Stout, the denial of faculty rank for Kinkead

Elizabeth Shelby Kinkead, circa 1908. (UK glass plate negative collection.)

demonstrated that Patterson and other UK leaders still opposed women faculty in the general curriculum.[80]

Most women holding staff positions at UK had previous connections with the college, either as former students or as relatives of faculty members. Mary LeGrand Didlake, who earned highest academic honors in 1895, later earned a master's degree from UK and a master's in entomology from the University of Chicago. As one of the first women to be appointed on the staff of instructors, she served for years as first assistant to Professor Harrison Garman in Agriculture. By 1912, fourteen women worked at the college as either teachers or research assistants. Even though Ezra Gillis is still listed as the university's first registrar from 1910 to 1937, Mary Hodges was recognized as registrar by the Board of Trustees as early as 1901. Harriet Claiborne Hodges served one year as registrar in 1905. From 1905 until 1910 Margaret Isadora King held the position.[81]

UK evolved slowly from an austere, cadet-dominated campus to something more akin to a modern college. Just one year after a student had been expelled for waltzing in the gymnasium, a student delegation secured permission from the board to hold "Cadet Hops" every other Saturday afternoon in the college gymnasium. UK administrators and faculty came to see dances on campus as a way of exerting more control over student activities. A faculty committee reported in November 1909 that "too close restriction of dances upon the University grounds leads to the frequenting of dancing places in town where the students are removed from our supervision." The committee asked for more discretionary power from the board regarding the number of dances offered annually. As a result, Patterson Hall became the scene of even more dinners, teas, speakers, and an array of social events.[82]

Expansion of women's influence continued in the athletic arena. Despite President Patterson's vigorous opposition, men's football grew in popularity during the 1890s. Those who had endured college pranks over the years saw organized athletics as an alternative way for the cadets to vent their frustrations and act manly. Baseball also became a fixture on campus each spring. Both of these men's activities contributed to a campus environment in which sports played an increasingly central role in student culture. Initially lacking a comparable athletic outlet, women students embraced the growing sports culture as spectators. Florence Stout designed her gymnastics instruction to maintain women's health

UK women's basketball began to garner their share of athletic attention, both on the campus and in the community. Teams were successful nearly from the start and began to bring home championships with regularity. (UK general photographic prints.)

and physical development, but her classes did not promote competition or the teamwork offered by men's team sports. That soon changed.[83]

In 1902 women students began organizing their first basketball team and played their first intercollegiate game against crosstown Kentucky University on February 21, 1903. There were generally no spectators at the earliest women games, and no men were allowed. The women's teams were successful nearly from the start and began to bring home championships with regularity. In January 1904, Bess Shaw, representing the Young Women's Basket Ball Team, petitioned the faculty for permission to play a high-school team in Columbus, Indiana. The Faculty Senate denied the request. The following month, the women's team again petitioned the faculty for permission to schedule games with nearby college teams. In addition, they expressed their "desire to be governed by the same rules that apply to the other athletic associations of the college; that is to be under the supervision of the Athletic Committee of the College." The faculty agreed to allow the women's basketball team to compete against nearby institutions, provided that chaperones accompanied teams and that they return, if possible, the same day.[84]

The women's team's access to the gymnasium for practice brought complaints from some of the male students. However, the student newspaper argued for the right of the women to equal access and called upon the college either to expand the present facilities or to build a new gymnasium so that both women and men would have sufficient time and space for basketball.[85]

The Alumni Association took notice of the women's basketball successes. Since the 1903 men's basketball team lost so often, the editor for the Alumni Association Annual Report argued that it became the "privilege, if not the duty," for the women's teams to uphold the college's athletic reputation. After the "plucky little band of girls" comprising the UK basketball team won a hard-fought victory over its crosstown rival Kentucky University, the campus and the city of Lexington witnessed an "enthusiastic demonstration" in support of the women's team. That 1903 victory brought a new level of interest in the women's team from students, alumni, and the Lexington community.[86]

Control over women's basketball fluctuated between Florence Stout and the University Athletic Committee. Stout was not enthusiastic about women's intercollegiate basketball and tried to limit the number of games the team played and keep strict control over the sport. The women athletes much preferred the oversight of the Athletic Committee. In November 1909 the women's basketball team and seventy-three other women students petitioned the faculty to return control of women's basketball back to the Athletic Committee. This was eventually accomplished over Stout's strenuous objections. At the March 4, 1910, faculty meeting, Stout told those assembled that physical education experts supported her belief that the game of basketball invited injury to those women participating in it. She further argued that the transfer of authority over women's basketball from her had reduced her influence among the college's women.[87]

Team captain Bessie Hayden attended the faculty meeting and explained that "any disregard of the directions of Mrs. Stout was due to the fact that she [that is, Hayden] supposed that in matters pertaining to athletics the Athletic Committee was the official superior of Mrs. Stout." Students fueled the growth and development of women's intercollegiate athletics despite the opposition of other women on campus. However, Stout's opposition to women's participation in competitive basketball games would have serious ramifications for the future of women's athletics at UK.[88]

Even as women's athletic successes grew, women's roles in commencement exercises continued to diminish. By 1904 the program billed Nannie Susan Tucker, who was to deliver her essay "The Awakening Power," as the "Representative of Women." Six male students had the opportunity to speak that year on a wide array of subjects either representing specific departments or the graduating class generally. The male presentations were referred to as "orations," while Tucker's was called an "essay." But as women students sought to redefine their presence on campus, the Kentucky Equal Rights Association and women leaders throughout Kentucky continued lobbying for the appointment of a Dean of Women and the establishment of a Department of Domestic Science for the women students. At its 1903 meeting, the Alumni Association voted to endorse those demands.[89]

In June 1904, Laura Clay again led a delegation of forty women representing various women's organizations in an appearance before the board. They reiterated their early call for the creation of a Department of Domestic Science under the direction of a woman dean. The next year the board, responding to continuous pressure from Laura Clay and others, created a Department of Domestic Science and directed the college administration to find space for the program.[90]

The women's groups that had successfully lobbied for a domestic science program at UK worked to make sure it received the support needed to be successful. At its December 1905 meeting the UK Board of Trustees received a report from women leaders regarding the development of the Domestic Science Department that included "a list of utensils needed for the operation of the Department." Women knew from experience that only continued pressure on male administrators and board members would lead to proper support for women's programs within UK.[91]

President Patterson characteristically expressed caution in regard to the development of the Domestic Science Department. In his report to

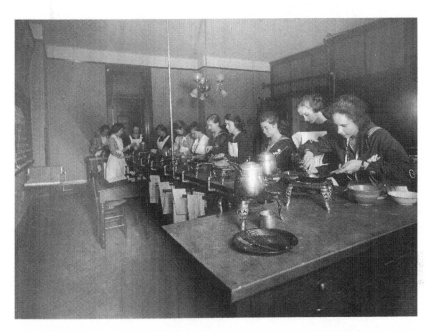

Home economics class, 1908. The establishment of a Domestic Science Department followed a curricular trend throughout the United States that had been gaining momentum since 1900. Domestic science, or home economics, provided college-educated women an opportunity to secure post-college employment as teachers and nutritionists. Simultaneously, it offered women who wished to attend college an opportunity to make higher education more compatible with future marriage and motherhood. Contrary to President Patterson's suggestion, Domestic Science was not made part of the Department of Agriculture. In time, home economics came to be viewed, even at UK, as an essential preparation for life in the home. (UK general photographic prints.)

the board he noted that he recently attended a meeting of the Association of Land-Grant Colleges where they discussed Domestic Science. He came away with the distinct impression that "Domestic Science, whatever it may mean and whatever I may comprehend, is as yet ill-defined, and in what might be termed a formative state." Noting further, "no two persons agree upon what it should include or exclude," he argued that Domestic Science at UK "ought to begin upon a relative tentative and experimental scale" in connection with the Department of Agricultural Science.[92]

By 1912 an alumni publication fully embraced Domestic Science and its contribution to women's higher education and their future. Noting that even though it had been "heard" that "colleges educate girls away from domesticity, marriage and the home . . . anyone who visits the classes and practical work carried on in the Education Building under the Department of Home Economics will be convinced that the contrary is true." Arguing that "if the girls carry home what they learn and put it into practice, the next generation will be blessed with better systems of digestion, simpler and more wholesome diets, cleaner and healthier homes and smaller bills for clothes and food and the merchants and grocers will have to look more intelligently to the quality and correct measurements of their wares."[93]

With the establishment in 1908 of the Dean of Women position, the college pressured Florence Offutt Stout to serve as the first women's dean. Although Stout had taught women's physical education at UK for seven years, she did not gain full faculty rank until her appointment as Dean of Women. The board predicted that Dean Stout would have a "splendid influence" on the women students. Because of her closeness to the women students, it was thought that Dean Stout could understand better the problems of the women "as few others could." In apparent agreement with the women who had long fought for the Dean of Women position, the board stressed that under Stout's direction the student life of women at the university would become "more attractive and more effective than ever before." In fact, some considered Stout's views as dean quite radical, as when she proposed to do away with the rule that prohibited boys and girls from walking together on the campus.[94]

However, despite glowing praise from the board and high expectations for her, Stout had a short-lived tenure as dean. Following the arrival of her lifelong friend Henry Stites Barker in 1910 and a continuing fight over control over women's basketball, Stout resigned her duties as dean to devote full time to physical education. In a letter to Barker, Stout vividly described her displeasure with the Dean of Women position. She told Barker that the dean's title impaired the distinctive quality of her academic specialty because she was most often introduced as "dean of women, rather than physical director of women."[95]

In tendering her resignation as dean, Stout concluded that "in being relieved of the very ornamental title of dean of women, I seek a greater usefulness in physical education, which is my life work and from which fact I do not wish the attention of the public diverted." Stout also added that another reason she was relinquishing the duties of dean was that she and her Circuit Judge spouse moved throughout his judicial district during the year, making "the meeting of extra office hours inconvenient."[96]

Stout's discomfort with the Dean of Women position seemed to result from the often-noted incongruity between faculty and administration. Stout viewed herself as a teacher and not someone who administered programs for women students or worried about discipline. With some consistency over the next several years, UK administrators wanted individuals to serve as Dean of Women who might successfully combine both an academic background with strengths as an administrator.

President Barker recruited Anna J. Hamilton to serve as Dean of Women and Assistant Professor of English. Like Stout, Hamilton was a Louisville native, having served the previous ten years as principal of Semple Collegiate School. Before that she had been head of the English Department of the Louisville Girls' High School. She had also served as president of the Kentucky Federation of Women's Clubs, vice president of the Jail Matron's Board, and vice president of the advisory board of the Juvenile Court.[97]

Unlike the married Stout, Dean Hamilton was single and took a suite of rooms in Patterson Hall. Some on campus felt that her very presence would be an inspiration "to those girls who are trying to become . . . The Ideal Woman." Barker expressed his pleasure with both Stout and Hamilton, whom he described as "brilliant women," adding that he "expected great things from their work in the university," noting that "their very presence will be an inspiration to the young women who have the good fortune to be associated with them."[98]

But at least one student offered a less flattering description of Hamilton. Writing in her senior journal, Maude Creekmore called Hamilton "a fat, easy going old maid who put herself up as cultured" and "curled her hair in a most peculiar manner." Creekmore did concede, however, that Hamilton had "many good ideas and always had the good of the school at heart." Perhaps Creekmore's negative impression of Hamilton can be dismissed as merely youthful overstatement or generational conflict, but it does call attention to the limited number of women on campus who could serve as role models for the women students.[99]

Anna Jackson Hamilton, Dean of Women and Associate Professor of English. (UK portrait print collection.)

Junior class of 1914. President Patterson's retirement in 1910 and Henry Stites Barker's move from the Board of Trustees to the presidency ushered in a new era in student culture at UK. Between 1910 and 1915, the UK campus gradually took on a more modern look. Women's visibility on the campus increased both as students and in faculty and administrative roles. (UK glass plate negative collection.)

Both Hamilton and Stout were "progressive" women who participated actively in women's organizations and helped expose UK women to these organizations, both within Kentucky and nationally. In 1909, for instance, former student Sophonisba Breckinridge, an assistant professor of social work at the University of Chicago, spoke at the Alumnae Luncheon regarding the Association of College Women. Since leaving UK without a degree, Breckinridge had completed an undergraduate degree at Wellesley College, taught school in Washington, DC, for two years, passed the Kentucky bar examination, and earned master's and PhD degrees in political science and a law degree from the University of Chicago.[100]

Between 1910 and 1915 UK began to take on a more modern look and feel. Women's visibility on campus increased as they gradually extended their presence into faculty and staff positions. By 1912 fifteen women were involved in some aspect of instruction or administration. In addition, with a growing prominence of social events, women students gained more individual freedom. The campus newspaper noted in September 1910 that "the senior girls have made quite a sensation this year. They are the first class which has obtained senior privileges [expanded hours] until after Christmas, and we hope it will become a precedent." This, along with a "Senior Table," apparently aroused the envy of the other women students.[101]

But these and other changes did not escape the attention of administrators and faculty, who continued to fret about student behavior. At the March 1911 meeting of the Committee on Entertainments, for instance, issues regarding dances arose again. Clarence H. Richardson, president of the sophomore class, answered questions regarding a recent dance sponsored by his class at which "the lemonade served had been liberally treated with intoxicants." According to Richardson's testimony, "the refreshments served had been provided by a committee who admitted that a quart of whiskey and two gallons of wine had been added to the punch, but he himself had not observed any flavor of liquor." After the committee discussed the issue at length and considered different punishments, they determined that the class would not be allowed to sponsor a dance during their junior year.[102]

If spiked punch was not a big enough concern, faculty also weighed in on the type of dancing evolving among the students. W. T. Lafferty, dean of the law school, successfully proposed at the February 7, 1913, faculty meeting that "no such dance known as the Turkey Trot, Drag, or any other unconventional dance shall be allowed" at any college function. The faculty instructed the Entertainment Committee to make the resolution known to all organizations and to enforce it vigorously.[103]

While student behavior generally continued to concern the administration and the faculty, "control" over women remained perhaps the most troublesome issue. President Barker, who began his presidency as much more supportive of students than his predecessor and seemed to take a more lenient view of their activities, urged the women's Board of Control to exert more influence over the women students. He called upon the board to "put the ax to the root of any evil it should find and do it vigorously."[104]

In 1915 UK's enrollment included 181 women students, comprising 19 percent of the student body. Of 154 total graduates in 1915, 32 were women. Women had also expanded their presence within the curriculum, as two women attended the law school and two studied engineering. Seven more women were enrolled in graduate degree programs. Even so, an overwhelming majority of women graduated with degrees in either education (15) or home economics (8), with the rest (9) receiving BA degrees in the liberal arts.[105]

Even as women students expanded their presence at the University of Kentucky, the classroom remained central to their education. And in the classroom real and fundamental problems for women remained. Rexie Brooks, a student in Harold H. Downing's astronomy class, said years later that she would never forget that he "didn't like girls." Upon first entering his class with six of her women classmates, Downing said to them, "What are you doing here? I told them not to send me any fool girls in here. I never thought girls had any sense and I certainly don't want any of them in my class." Brooks thought that was not "a very good welcome." But, according to Brooks, before the year ended "he proved to be one of the nicest people as I knew. He just hadn't gotten acquainted with any girls. He taught astronomy all the time and none of them has seen fit to take it. So he just hadn't had any girls and he didn't want any. We got along as well as any of them [boys] and better than some of them."[106]

Despite such problems, between 1880 and World War I UK women established a framework for coeducation during a period of experimentation and change. During this period women students, while under sometimes oppressive regulations, still experienced more freedom than any previous generation of women. According to historian Melba Porter Hay, "Increasing industrialization and urbanization brought more women into the workforce, especially in non-domestic labor. Out of this emerged the image of the 'new woman' –not only freed from the restrictive clothing and social practices of the Victorian era, but also educated, independent, and able to earn their own living."[107]

Within UK, women challenged men in the classroom and each other in oratory and athletics. They moved freely and successfully between the Normal School, Arts and Sciences, and Home Economics. They even ventured successfully into more nontraditional areas, such as law and engineering. Women enjoyed college, and a developing student culture provided social activities both on campus and in the larger community. Even if men students did not yet fully respect their women counterparts in certain academic areas, they appeared to welcome them as fellow students within the university. Andrea Radke-Moss suggests

The first *Idea* staff, 1908–1909. Women had been represented on the student newspaper, *The Idea*, since its inception. But even by 1911, although several of the nineteen members of the student staff were women, they were listed only as "social editors," keeping stereotypes in place. (UK photographs.)

that coeducation during this period at land-grant universities "is a story of the negotiation of gendered spaces—at times toward greater inclusion of women, and at times toward separation. Women took an active part in the process of achieving inclusion, but sometimes they chose to segregate themselves from the male sphere." Thus, the story of women at UK is not only about access, but how the women students and faculty attempted to control their own experiences and destinies in a still male-dominated environment.[108]

Yet women still remained outsiders in a postcollege world that did not fully embrace them except as future homemakers and teachers. This view of women students was still prevalent among a majority of faculty and administrators and often in the students' own families. Women at UK had gained confidence in their academic abilities and had undoubtedly broadened their horizons. But it remained to be seen how, or if, a coeducational university could provide equal opportunities for women students and continue to be an avenue for the advancement of the next generation of Kentucky women.

2

Frances Jewell McVey and the Refinement of Student Culture

Writing to her mother from the Baldwin School in the spring of 1908, Frances Jewell evoked images of women's paradoxical lives. At the elite, all-girls boarding school in Bryn Mawr, Pennsylvania, Jewell secured one of the principal parts in the school play: that of a man. She enthusiastically confided to her mother that after appearing in the play *The Junior Prom*, she was "still alive" and "neither fainted, nor died in a fit nor ran off the stage weeping." But Jewell confessed to her mother that she made a terrible mistake with one of her lines during the performance. Instead of saying, "I've never been in any danger in my life that I haven't wished I was a woman," Jewell, playing the part of a man, said instead, "I've never been in any danger in my life that I haven't wished I was a *man*" (emphasis added).[1]

Perhaps Jewell simply suffered a momentary memory lapse. Or maybe she subconsciously knew that any woman in trouble would want to be a man and that no man in trouble would ever truly wish to be woman. Jewell shrugged off her mistake as "awfully funny."[2] Perhaps, though, the innocent mistake foreshadowed Jewell's and her fellow women students' contradictory lives as gender roles continued to evolve in the first decades of the twentieth century. Jewell, a teenage girl of privilege, came of age at a time when society began to offer young women of her social class unprecedented opportunities for an education. She came to move easily within women's traditional social roles, while seemingly poised to step into a new era of greater opportunities outside of the home. Jewell represented a growing segment of American

Scene from the play *The Junior Prom*, in the 1908 Baldwin School yearbook. Frances Jewell is seated second from the right. (Frances Jewell McVey papers.)

women who straddled an expanded middle ground between the women reformers of the late nineteenth and early twentieth centuries and, as suggested by Annette Baxter, the "overwhelming majority of their sex who contentedly played out their conventional roles or suffered in silence." College-educated and ambitious women like Jewell brought a new dynamic to women's public higher education. Not necessarily content to live a life almost exclusively focused on the home and family, they moved cautiously in demanding still more comprehensive freedoms and opportunities.[3]

Jewell's youthful scrapbook, in which she places herself in a photo next to three US presidents, suggests that she aspired to make a difference through her life and career. Perhaps she understood that many women of her generation would have more freedom and more opportunity than any preceding generation. Her generation of college women faced continuing challenges as well as more choices. They made decisions about their education in the context of traditional social and cultural expectations for women and under the constant oversight of a male-dominated cultural hierarchy. Some women chose the path described by Geraldine Joncich Clifford as that of a "lone voyager," resisting the traditional limits to their sex.[4]

When Frances Jewell made this collage and titled it "Among the Presidents honored of the land behold I, Frances Jewell stand," she put herself alongside male leaders. Placed within one of her early diaries, this collage challenges traditional expectations for women. (Frances Jewell McVey papers.)

Other women, at least outwardly, seemed to accept the minimal opportunities available in higher education, while still others embraced and welcomed the status quo. Within this context, an increasing number of women, like Jewell, sought to assimilate the traditional expectations of women into the new and expanding sphere of public coeducation. This trend influenced the lives of thousands of University of Kentucky women over several generations. Frances Jewell's story is central to understanding the history of UK.

Mary Frances Jewell, born December 23, 1889, to Asa and Lizzie Berry Jewell, grew up in a home in Lexington, Kentucky, with an older brother, John, and a younger brother, Robert. Her family's rural, farming background spanned several counties in central Kentucky. However, Asa's business acumen and horse-trading abilities soon afforded the Jewell family rapid upward mobility and entry into the business and social elite of a still small but bustling Lexington community at the turn of the twentieth century.[5]

The Jewell family lived most of each year in their Lexington home on Ashland Avenue, part of Lexington's expanding suburbs, which encompassed the front acreage of Henry Clay's former estate of Ashland. Streetcars provided the residents easy access to downtown Lexington. The family spent summers at Pleasant View, their farm located twenty miles south of Lexington on Harrodsburg Pike near Wilmore, Kentucky. Life on the farm afforded Jewell the opportunity to absorb family stories and legends of her pioneer relatives and instilled in her a sense of place and southernism that she embraced her entire life.

Jewell attended Sayre School, a private girl's school in downtown Lexington. Like other girls of her age and social status, she became involved in a busy social world of dances, teas, and parties. But her world also included a growing social awareness, which led her as a teenager to women who were engaged in national and regional social causes, including the Appalachian Settlement School movement. After attending a lecture by well-known Appalachian activist Katherine Pettit, Jewell wrote, "I expect to be a missionary in the mountains someday." It is not surprising that Pettit influenced Jewell so strongly. Twenty years her senior and a Lexington native, Pettit had also attended Sayre School. From an early age Jewell exhibited tremendous empathy for others. Moreover, Pettit's example of becoming a "missionary to the mountains" provided what many considered a proper outlet for establishing one's independence and good work at the same time.[6]

Lexington provided a comfortable environment for Jewell's youth. There is no documentation as to why her parents wished to send her to boarding school in the northeast. It may be as simple as that an upwardly mobile Kentucky family thought it provided their daughter the best opportunities for her future. But, without question, Jewell's horizons expanded tremendously beginning in the fall of 1907 when she travelled by train to the Baldwin School. The elite boarding school thrust her into contact with both new people and challenging ideas. As a woman who celebrated southern culture her entire life, Jewell found herself in an unfamiliar environment surrounded by young women with very different backgrounds and experiences. Jewell's academic and social journey through the Baldwin School dramatically changed her life. Popular at the boarding school, she was elected the senior class president, and she participated in drama and a myriad of other school activities.

Frances Jewell in the Baldwin School yearbook, 1909–1910. (Frances Jewell McVey papers.)

"The ideal hostess," as captioned by Jewell, from a scrapbook she kept during her Baldwin school years. (Frances Jewell McVey papers.)

Though successful in her schoolwork, Jewell had serious doubts about her academic future. Writing to her mother she confessed, "My desire to go to college is gradually slipping because I want to stay at home and read and study along with you but I reckon I will go one year—perhaps." Yet Jewell's senior class prophecy predicted that within a decade she would earn a doctorate and return to Lexington as head of Sayre School, making it as good as the Baldwin School. By the spring of 1909, Frances Jewell left the Baldwin School with an acquired ambition.[7]

Frances Jewell's parents encouraged her ambition, and the following fall she left Lexington again, this time to study at Vassar College. Quickly accepted by her classmates at Vassar, Jewell was asked to be on the missionary committee, but she refused. She was also nominated for class treasurer but declined to run, concerned that she might not win the election. She wrote to her mother soon after arriving in Poughkeepsie that it made her "tired (literally) to think of doing any-thing." She added that, "if the class or college needed me . . . that would be different but there are so many just as capable as I. So let them do the 'dirty work.'"[8]

In her first year at college, Jewell seemed to enjoy remaining in the background. Moreover, she struggled with the feeling that she was, and always had been, too large and unattractive. As a young woman, she became even more self-conscious of such things. She confessed to her mother how much she enjoyed being a first-year student because "I am . . . fairly gloating over being made a baby of." Jewell explained that "somehow I was always so big that people (except for you and Father and my own family) didn't think of petting me."[9] In a subsequent letter, Jewell told her mother about meeting a young man with whom she was quite taken. But, she confessed, "He thinks that I'm a fine girl and he likes me a lot, an awful lot I think but not one bit emotionally—it's the same old thing. F. Jewell certainly is a fine girl. She is so big hearted. . . ."[10]

Never far from Jewell's thoughts while she was away at college was the question of her future. Besides dealing with the usual first-year tensions of college, Frances hoped that she would "take advantage of . . . opportunities and bring them home with me so that I really can be of some use to everybody," but she worried that she would "probably be too lazy to do anything." Still, Jewell found Vassar personally satisfying and enjoyed the intellectual challenge, even if she did worry about failure. By her sophomore year she won election as class president, and she remained an active student leader until graduation.[11]

From the time that she attended Sayre through her Vassar years, Jewell developed close friendships with other young women. At Vassar she came to know independent women professors who combined scholarship in the classroom with social life in their homes in a way that Jewell emulated the remainder of her life. Without question Vassar did for Jewell what private women's colleges did for many other women at that time: it instilled closeness with other women and a confidence to act independently.[12]

In her playing a man's role in a school play out of necessity at an all-girls school, Jewell perhaps subconsciously reflected a changing world view that she shared with other educated women regarding their dependency on men. At women's schools, authorities grew increasingly concerned not only about women adopting male attire, but also that higher education might be changing young women in unanticipated ways and making them less feminine. At Vassar and other similar colleges, some women not only abandoned their perceived femininity; they also began taking on roles formerly reserved for men, breaking down the conventional notions of womanhood.[13]

Vassar afforded Jewell an opportunity to begin to balance traditional female norms with her desire for new opportunities as an independent young woman. Approaching graduation from Vassar in 1913, Jewell expressed disappointment that she would not graduate with honors. Jewell's mother consoled her by reminding her that she had gotten from college what she wanted. Jewell viewed college as both academic and social. She refused to abandon the broader experiences available at college for the sake of better grades. For Jewell, the school plays, the teas at professors' homes, and organizational work played a central role in her college experience.[14]

With her college degree in hand, Jewell considered an offer from Sayre School to teach English. But Jewell's mother advised her to take the year off and rest—advice she took. During the next two years Jewell lived with her parents in Lexington and at Pleasant View, returning to her active social and volunteer life. She experienced the contradictions of being a college graduate in a relatively small community where, for single women of her class and generation, the two primary activities were volunteer work and parties. Writing to a former Vassar classmate in the fall of 1913, Jewell admitted that she must be a "bitter disappointment" to her parents because "I just can't be and do everything they expect." She noted that her father was happy if she did not attend so many parties because then she would have time "to do Sunday School work." She confessed that her father thought she had "no stability." Conversely, "Mother thinks I'm queer not to enjoy the good time of youth." She added that, "I do enjoy them you know but I get tired and I become unbearable because I am always being pushed to death by crowding events so that I haven't time always to spend hours dressing and yet be on time." The previous week she "went to four dances straight counting the Country Club until 12 o'clock Saturday night and a dozen parties."[15]

Jewell immersed herself in parties, social affairs, and volunteer church and social work. Women's rights leader Madeline McDowell Breckinridge, who had studied part-time at UK between 1890 and 1894 without earning a degree, encouraged Jewell to succeed her as president of the Fayette County Equal Rights Association, but she declined. Nevertheless, Jewell actively participated in other women's reform activities and even gained some notoriety. In the spring of 1915 she inspired newspaper headlines and editorial comment following a speech in Louisville attacking the state's inadequate reform-school system. That same year the Fayette County Equal Rights Association reported that a "committee of amateur thespians" chaired by Frances Jewell offered a suffrage play, *How the Vote Was Won*, in the ballroom of Lexington's Phoenix Hotel.[16]

Jewell's interest in reform activities met with mixed reviews within her family, especially from her younger brother Bob. While attending Williams College in 1915, Bob wrote to his mother that he was looking forward to an upcoming visit from Frances, adding that he had selected a potential husband for his unmarried older sister. The prospect, a senior at Williams, according to Bob, was "the finest fellow in the college." Bob believed Frances and his classmate made a perfect match, since both seemed concerned with "social uplift." However, Bob added facetiously that the best part about getting these two reform minded souls together—the marriage would not "spoil two households."[17]

Frances's two-year hiatus after college to find herself or, probably more accurately, to find a husband, was not unusual for young women of her class and educational background. According to Barbara Solomon, it was in this "post graduate apprentice stage of adulthood" that "college women faced both private questions of identity and the competing influences of family and college." Many women college graduates, like Jewell, "did not know what they actually really wanted to do even when they were permitted choices." Jewell and her fellow women graduates had been groomed for a world that did not yet fully exist, especially in the South. As Solomon concludes, "Some stayed home, some took paid jobs, volunteered in charities and settlements, studied or travelled; some combined a variety of these choices." Teaching remained Jewell's most obvious option. But the ambition she had acquired from the Baldwin School and Vassar College made teaching English at Sayre or some other local school seem less appealing than before. Certainly, Jewell and others like her had choices, but they were limited and often difficult to choose among.[18]

While Jewell was attending private eastern schools, the University of Kentucky expanded its curriculum offerings to correspond with its new status as a university. In the fall of 1915, Jewell took advantage of the opportunities at her local university, enrolling in the new graduate program in English. However, she would not complete a graduate degree because the following year the university employed her as a full-time instructor in English. At the same time that Jewell entered the graduate program at the university, a high school in Danville, Kentucky, offered her a position teaching English. By choosing to teach at the

University of Kentucky faculty, 1894. (UK general photographic prints.)

public coeducational university rather than the high school, Jewell followed a typical path for an educated woman of her generation. The fact that land-grant colleges with their low salaries found it difficult to compete with businesses in attracting male faculty did not hurt. With only her undergraduate degree, Jewell benefited from that trend.[19]

The increasing number of women teaching in higher education still did not result in a dramatically higher percentage of women faculty at institutions like UK. Lucy Blackburn had become the first woman to join the instructional ranks at UK in 1888 when she accepted the position of monitress and assistant in the Preparatory Department.

Ten years later Miriam Gratz Clay became an assistant in drawing. However, these women were never accepted as full faculty by their male colleagues, and did they not participate in any of the faculty deliberations. Even though Lucy Blackburn appears on a list of faculty in the 1894 yearbook she is absent from the faculty group portrait.[20]

With her decision to teach at UK, Jewell abandoned her career interest in separate women's education in favor of embracing the

In the early 1900s, women entered the faculty ranks with the appointment of Florence Offutt Stout in women's physical education and Elizabeth Shelby Kinkead as a lecturer. The addition of a dean of women and the opening of a home economics department also created opportunities for women faculty. Nevertheless, only two women are among the faculty in this 1907 photograph. (UK general photographic prints.)

growing presence of women at public colleges. She may not have remembered her senior class prophecy at the Baldwin School in which was predicted her return as principal to the all-girls Sayre School in Lexington. However, in accepting the position at UK she made an important change in the trajectory of her life and career. Possibly, she viewed the UK position as a temporary detour in her career. Or perhaps she was consciously committing herself to the idea of helping to construct a women's environment, similar to the women's culture she had found so fulfilling and inspiring at Sayre, Baldwin, and Vassar, at a public coeducational university.[21]

An important addition to the UK faculty occurred with the hiring of Marguerite McLaughlin to teach in the newly created Journalism Department. A Lexington native and a 1903 graduate of UK, McLaughlin reportedly "did not have any particular work in mind" when she spent most of the first decade following graduation traveling widely,

UK faculty, 1911–1912. The fifteen women who were faculty members by 1915 represented only 9 percent of the faculty; the student body was 21 percent women. Even though the number of women faculty members was slowly increasing, their appointments continued to be at lower academic ranks and they earned less for their services than did men. (Louis Edward Nollau F series photographic prints.)

both abroad and in the United States. Feeling the "call of the West," McLaughlin eventually settled in Enid, Oklahoma, where she worked for the *Enid Morning News*.[22]

Returning to Lexington around 1912, one day she happened to meet Madeline McDowell Breckinridge, a leader in women's reform efforts, who asked McLaughlin, "Young woman, what are you doing to justify your existence?" That question motivated McLaughlin to "take part in various civic campaigns in Lexington," which brought her into contact with other women reformers and social activists. In late summer 1912 McLaughlin was introduced to Madeline Breckinridge's spouse, local newspaper editor Desha Breckinridge. He asked her, "Aren't you the girl my wife has been telling me should be working on my paper? Go out right now and get me a story on the opening of the schools." After submitting a story that ran on the front page of the newspaper, McLaughlin was hired as a reporter to cover "educational matters." She later recalled also covering labor strikes, murders, and election news for the newspaper. At one point she even served as the newspaper's "farm editor," but kept her identity as a woman hidden for a time in that role.[23]

Marguerite McLaughlin when she graduated in 1903 with her BA degree.
(Marguerite McLaughlin papers and awards.)

In 1914 UK created a Journalism Department, hiring Enoch Grehan, a local veteran newspaper editor, as the department's first director. He in turn hired McLaughlin, his former colleague at the *Lexington Herald*, as assistant director of the department and instructor. Over the next nearly four decades McLaughlin became one of the most popular professors in UK history. As a teacher she was said to have had "a sparkling Irish wit [both of her parents were Irish] and a deep interest in almost anything," but especially travel and the theater. She was also well known for her support of UK athletics and for wearing her mink coat on the campus. She enjoyed telling people, "I haven't taught all of the good newspaper reporters in Kentucky, but those I have taught are good." She helped establish the Chi chapter of Theta Sigma Phi (women's journalism honorary); served for many years as a faculty advisor to the Mortar Board Leadership Society; founded, along with Enoch Grehan, S. A. "Daddy" Boles (UK Athletics Director), and Frances Jewell, SUKY (the university pep club); and organized the Lexington chapter of the UK Alumni Club. McLaughlin, who never married, epitomized how single women during her time could be economically independent. At the time of her death, her estate was valued in 2019 dollars at over three quarters of a million dollars.[24]

Coeducation at the University of Kentucky continued to evolve. Margaret Ingels made history in 1916 when she became the first woman to earn an engineering degree from UK and one of the first in the United States in mechanical engineering. Ingels had become interested in the process of condensation as a young girl in her hometown of Paris, Kentucky, and set out to learn as much as she could about science and engineering even before entering college. The *Kentucky Alumnus* in 1916 reported that "Miss Ingels completed the entire four years of the course, taking her turns in the forge shops and machine shop and doing the other duties of the engineer with the rest of the 'boys,' never shirking a duty, however irksome."[25]

Ingels was a source of fascination to many as a woman engineering major at the university. During her sophomore year, while working in the blacksmith shop along with her fellow engineering students, a reporter observed her work. He noted that "over her daintily embroidered, open-necked waist and her white skirt, she wore a very businesslike leathern apron, which dropped to the top of her gunmetal pumps;

University of Kentucky 1916 engineering graduates. Margaret Ingels became UK's first woman engineering graduate and one of the first women in the United States to earn a degree in mechanical engineering. (UK general photographic prints.)

pulled tightly down over a goodly quantity of wavy, dark brown hair, which persisted in peeping out, was a black sateen workman's cap." The reporter hastened to add that Ingels was not of the "mannish" type. Like others, this writer felt obliged to evaluate whether women in historically male endeavors were "ladylike," and also noted, "She is medium height (about five feet two inches) and of slender figure. She is really pretty; has large, intelligent gray eyes, the slightly tanned complexion of the out-door girl and the long upper lip that denotes a poetical temperament and a love of ease and luxury. But this feature is given the lie by the strength of her chin and the way she closes her mouth as she works."[26]

Machine shop instructor Joseph Dicker said he tried to exempt Ingels from the heavy parts of engineering work, "but she would not hear of it." He added, "She keeps pace with the best of her classmates and asks odds of no one. The contour that her tanned arm displays when she grasps the sledge handle shows that she can suit the deed to the will." When asked whether she supported women's suffrage Ingels reportedly replied, "Yes, don't you?" However, the reporter concluded the article by asserting that Ingels seemed "too absorbed in her work to worry about Votes for Women."[27]

71

Margaret Ingels at work on her forge, circa 1916. (UK glass plate negative collection.)

The following year Lena Madesin Phillips also made history when she became the first woman to earn a UK law degree. Phillips grew up in Nicholasville, Kentucky, where her father practiced law. She became an accomplished musician at a young age and attended the Woman's College of Baltimore (now Goucher College) but left due to ill health. After recovering, she entered law school at UK and became involved in local and Kentucky politics. Phillips graduated from the he UK law school in 1917 and opened her own law office in her hometown. Phillips's work with the Young Women's Christian Association (YWCA) took her to New York, where she began organizing businesswomen, eventually founding the National Federation of Business and Professional Women's Clubs of the United States in 1919 and serving as its first president. In 1930 Phillips helped found the International Federation of Business and Professional Women, becoming its first president, a position she held until 1947.[28]

The University of Kentucky celebrated its Golden Jubilee in the fall of 1916. Alumnae marked the occasion with a dinner at the Phoenix Hotel, which was attended by over eighty women graduates and former students. Lucy Berry Blackburn, former monitress of women, served as the guest of honor. Elizabeth King Smith, class of 1895 and secretary of the Women's Board of Control, presided at the dinner. Only a few months earlier King had been a candidate for a seat on the school board with the support of the Fayette County Equal Rights Association. She garnered 2,500 votes, losing the election by only 115 votes. Several women spoke, including Martha White Blessing, vice president of the UK Alumni Association; Ella K. Porter Green, class of 1913; Belle Gunn Kays, class of 1888 and the first woman graduate; Lucy Berry Blackburn; Rebecca Smith, "coed editor" of the Kernel in 1916; and Mary Cottell Gregory, class of 1906.[29]

Even as the women graduates celebrated their contribution to the university's history, this era proved to be a crucial turning point in the lives of women at UK. Inseparable from the suffrage drive and the impending world war, women's activities on the campus changed quickly and in diverse ways. Most young women entering UK in 1915 were not even born when the university first admitted women. In their world view, there had always been a state college where white women could seek a higher education. Once on campus they saw women teaching in

Golden Jubilee parade in downtown Lexington, 1916. (Louis Edward Nollau F series photographic prints.)

the classroom and providing important support services across the campus. This generation of women students would experience even greater changes than their predecessors due in part to the war in Europe. Lynn Gordon, writing about women at the University of California at Berkeley, noted that "World War I brought increased publicity and prominence to women students, further straining the male-female campus relationships." John Thelin suggests that once college women proved they could withstand the mental and physical challenges of higher education, "The new insight was that their presence was harmful—or rather threatening—to college men." Moreover, "Women students' battles to claim their rights extended into the social realm during the 1910s, as standards for clothing, makeup, and courting behavior changed dramatically." Women entered into new and, heretofore, closed academic areas such as engineering and law. Simultaneously, more moved into the "traditional" fields of home economics and library science, and the development of these academic areas had a dramatic effect on the incoming women students.[30]

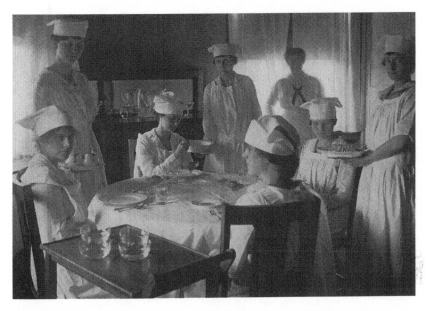

Home economics students in their practice house, circa 1919. (Austin Lilly papers and photographs.)

For example, Austin Lilly arrived on campus in the fall of 1916, the same year that Frances Jewell began teaching at UK. Lilly was the only daughter of Anna D. Lilly and Grant E. Lilly. Anna Lilly was active in civic affairs and the women's movement in Kentucky, and was editor of the *Richmond Register*, which her family owned. Austin later recalled attending the last meeting of the National American Woman Suffrage Association Convention with her mother in Chicago in 1920.[31]

A friend influenced Austin Lilly to major in home economics, one of the fastest-growing departments in the university, rather than chemistry. Still, her new major required that she complete four years of chemistry with the male students. She recalled, "Some of us were better students than some of the men in chemistry. We weren't taking a back seat!" Austin thought that during her student days women were well on their way to equality within American society. Lilly remained single and spent her career teaching at the high school and college level. When asked on a 1938 alumni questionnaire to give the full name of her husband or wife, Lilly wrote in large letters across the page, "neither-nor."[32]

Junior-year chemistry students, likely a class taught by Franklin E. Tuttle. Professor Tuttle's daughter, Margaret, graduated from UK in 1919. (Margaret Tuttle papers and photographs.)

UK women faculty faced a steep climb towards equality with their men colleagues. As an instructor in English, for example, Frances Jewell received half the pay of comparable male faculty in her department. In 1917, Professor Lehre L. Dantzler, head of the English Department, requested a salary increase for Jewell. Regarding Jewell's $600 salary, Dantzler noted her excellent work and recommended a $250 increase, still $250 less than her male colleague, E. U. Bradley, who, like Jewell, was an instructor in the department. In Journalism, Marguerite McLaughlin received only $750 for her work as an instructor. Sarah Marshall Chorn, instructor in Modern Languages, earned $900, while Mabel Hardy Pollitt, instructor in Ancient Languages, earned $800, all less than men's salaries in their respective departments.[33]

Despite the financial inequity, Jewell's students and colleagues considered her an excellent instructor. Austin Lilly vividly recalled Jewell's sophomore English class, in part because Jewell reminded Lilly of the teachers from the northeast who had taught at her earlier school, the

English Club, 1916–1917. Number 2 is Margaret Tuttle; 17 is Frances Jewell. (Louis Edward Nollau F series photographic prints.)

Madison Institute in Richmond, Kentucky. She added that Jewell's classes were "jovial" and that Jewell regularly posed questions to the class that "brought out a whole lot of things" other than just about English; she also encouraged students to express their thoughts and feelings. She was "just an excellent person" whom everybody liked and who did not act "high and mighty"; she allowed students to get to know her as a person.[34]

Men students enjoyed Jewell's classes as well. W. Hugh Peal graduated from UK in 1922 and received a Rhodes Scholarship to study law at Oxford University. He remembered Jewell as "one of the nicest people" who "had something which brought her right in my whole ken of enjoyment." They shared a mutual love of books, and Peal emphasized that "we really loved them. We could sit around, and I remember chortling for an hour with her." Jewell often recommended books for Peal to read and once suggested that he read Max Beerbohm's *Zuleika Dobson*, "probably because I was going to Oxford, or maybe she hoped I was. We had so much fun out of it."[35]

For Jewell and other women faculty members, college teaching meant more than classroom instruction. Jewell helped organize the English Club and supported student theater productions. She participated in YWCA work and attended most Patterson Hall social functions. She was an active and willing role model for the women students, as were many other women faculty. For example, Florence Offutt Stout offered additional swimming classes for women in the local community. Dean of Women Anna Hamilton, who lived in Patterson Hall, became heavily involved in the expanding social lives of the women students. As Austin Lilly recalled, "We were all active . . . the attitude about what women did then has just been lost. I don't know why. We knew what we were doing and we were going after it."[36]

Examples of women graduates' successes during this period abound, and the *Kentucky Alumnus* highlighted their stories. A 1917 issue reported that Mary C. Love Collins, a 1916 graduate of the law school, had become director of the Southern School of Social Science and Public Service in New Orleans. Collins later served several decades as president of the National Chi Omega Sorority, and the sorority created a scholarship in her honor.[37]

Another issue highlighted the ongoing success of Margaret Ingels, who was "proving that a woman may be a success even in work that is considered strictly a man's work." Ingels, employed by the Chicago Telephone Company in the switchboard department, made drawings of new layouts for additional lines. In addition to her engineering work, the phone company placed Ingels in charge of a portion of the welfare work for women employed by the Chicago Telephone Company. And in still another issue, in May 1917, the magazine reported that Rebecca Paretz and Lucille Cruikshank had become the first women members of the Henry Clay Society, an honorary organization within the law school.[38]

Even while attitudes on campus toward women's present and future possibilities were evolving, more measurable changes were occurring in regard to women's enrollment. For example, during the 1910–1911 school year only 82 women attended the university as compared with 500 men students. By 1915, the number of women students had risen to 206 in a student population of 986. The following year the number of women increased again by an additional 50. At the end of World War I the number of women students on the campus rose to 34 percent of the

Margaret Ingels holding a sling psychrometer, which reads the relative humidity of the air, an instrument she helped to perfect while working at the Carrier-Lyle Corporation around 1931. (Margaret Ingels papers.)

The freshman class, 1910. (UK general photographic prints.)

student body. By 1924, there were three times as many women students on campus as there were in 1915. However, the number of men students also rose sharply as well during this same period, and the percentage of women students on campus remained at roughly 30 percent.[39]

The increasing number of women students forced the university to focus greater attention on women's issues. Dean Hamilton reported in 1917 that women students participated in every activity in the college, including physical education and athletics. She added that even though the percentage of women compared to men remained small, their presence on the campus demonstrated that the "consciousness of women" had been "awakened to the value of higher education and to the value of vocational study." Hamilton predicted that, as a result, the university would add "other vocational studies in the industrial arts and the fine arts" as well as "a more extended course in home economics." Moreover, Hamilton called for a Woman's Building to house women's academic programs and for the enlargement of the "overcrowded woman's dormitory," noting that such improvements would be "a wonderful stride forward."[40]

The freshman class, 1924. (*Kentuckian*, 1924.)

Even though women students made inroads in academic areas like engineering and law, their numbers remained low. Women faculty and administrators, and women leaders statewide, continued lobbying hard for expanded opportunities for women in home economics and other areas considered women's "vocational studies." While this effort seemed to point toward a future where women's education might become equal to men's, creating separate academic areas for women actually represented a movement toward separate institutional spheres for women on the campus. Kentucky women awakened to the opportunities for higher education, and women's enrollment escalated rapidly in Kentucky, especially considering the growing number of women attending the commonwealth's two normal (teacher training) schools that were established in 1906. So many women entered higher education during this time across the United States that some men began to worry that women would soon become a majority and might begin to dominate.[41]

UK officials did not fear that women would reach the majority of the student population because of an unofficial, yet effective, enrollment cap for women students. By 1917 the university stipulated that all women must live in Patterson Hall, approved off-campus housing, or at home. Men, by comparison, were free to make whatever living arrangements they could find.[42] Dean Hamilton expressed her growing concern about the lack of adequate housing for women on the campus. In 1917, she noted that Patterson Hall provided adequate living space for women

Home economics students marching in a parade, circa 1919, carrying brooms, pots, and skillets. (Austin Lilly papers and photographs.)

students when it opened in 1904. However, since 1915 women's enroll-ment had increased to the point that that Patterson Hall could not house all the women who wanted to attend UK. The university placed women applicants who could not find approved housing in Lexington on a wait-ing list for Patterson Hall. Unless they were able to secure housing in the dormitory, they could not enroll in the university. Housing restrictions on women students were not unique to UK. In her study of women at Cor-nell University, Charlotte Conable noted, "The fact that women were regarded differently from men was implicit in the decision that female students must be protected and supervised in university-approved hous-ing, a ruling which confined them as a numerical minority."[43]

The Patterson Hall Board of Control, a group of three local women appointed by the president to oversee the women's residence hall, con-curred with the dean's call for new housing facilities. But with the growth in women's enrollment, a shift began in regard to how women's lives on campus should be regulated. As dean of women, Anna Hamil-ton lived in Patterson Hall, but a review of university administrative practices in 1917 recommended that the dean move out of Patterson Hall. At the same time, the university Board of Trustees made a distinc-tion between the Women's Board of Control, which supervised women's "home life," and the Dean of Women, who oversaw women's "education life." The distinctions between women's public and private lives that were being worked out in American society generally were also being renegotiated on the UK campus, mostly by men.[44]

To operate Patterson Hall, the Board of Control sought to hire someone with a home economics background who would establish more control over the women students. They chose Adelaide E. Crane, a graduate of Teacher's College at Columbia University who had previously served as a house director there. The Board noted, "She is therefore qualified not only to be a leader, but an inspiration and example to the young women under her charge." The Board felt the need to give the new house director some entree into the academic side of the campus. Thus, in addition to her responsibilities in Patterson Hall, she was expected to teach in the Department of Home Economics, which, according to the board, would give her "standing in the University" and dignify her position. Arriving on campus in September 1917, Crane announced that she hoped "to operate with tolerance and little rules."[45]

But as the 1917 fall semester began, a world at war brought new challenges to the university. Many male faculty and students left for military service or other activities to support the war effort. President Barker reported that "the war and its exigencies have taken from us a large number of our students. I think as many as 450 have left, most of them going to the farm to produce extra crops of food stuffs needed for the country and some going to the army and navy." Ultimately, several women faculty and staff, including Frances Jewell, also left during the war for other types of service and to pursue other opportunities.[46]

During her first two years at UK, Jewell maintained close contact with her Vassar classmates. They discussed social life, suffrage, and future plans. Jewell considered pursuing graduate work at the University of Chicago, where another Kentuckian, Sophonisba Breckinridge, had become a prominent member of the faculty; but instead, she chose Columbia University. Jewell knew that she needed a graduate degree if she hoped to improve her academic standing in an era of growing professionalism within higher education. Her decision to attend Columbia was not unusual for a Kentucky educator. So many Kentuckians pursued graduate work at Columbia's Teacher's College during the first three decades of the twentieth century that a vibrant Kentucky Club of Columbia alumni flourished in the commonwealth. However, while Columbia attracted most Kentuckians for graduate work in education at the Teacher's College, Jewell chose instead to pursue a master's degree in English.[47]

Jewell wanted to be involved in major events, and she must have felt that the war provided an opportunity for her to get away, earn a degree, and contribute to the war effort. While attending graduate school in New York City, she became heavily involved in war-related work, serving on the Public Education Committee of the Associates of Collegiate Alumnae at the Red Cross Institute for Crippled and Disabled Men. Nevertheless, she completed her degree in English Literature within the year. She wrote her thesis on the literature of the Shakers, most likely because the Jewell family farm and summer home outside Lexington was less than ten miles from the Shaker Village at Pleasant Hill.[48]

While completing her degree at Columbia, Jewell received an offer from the Baldwin School to join its English faculty, but she chose to return to Kentucky. Jewell felt a strong bond to her Kentucky roots and her family, and that may have been the deciding factor in her return to the Bluegrass State. Additionally, she may have preferred college teaching over secondary education. Finally, it is also possible that she viewed coeducation as the best avenue for future professional opportunities.[49]

Upon her return to Kentucky, Jewell resumed teaching while continuing her war work. She served as chair of the Kentucky Food Administration for the National War Garden Commission, a position that coordinated activities in nearly every county of the state and expanded Jewell's network outside of Lexington. In addition, she continued her involvement with the Lexington suffrage movement and later the League of Women Voters. She founded the local chapter of the American Association of University Women and became an active member of the University of Kentucky Woman's Club. Jewell also served as Kentucky chair of the Southern Association of College Women and did volunteer work at local YWCA summer camps.[50]

Other UK women faculty during this period also expanded their influence, both on campus and beyond. The growth of home economics brought to the forefront the work of Professor Mary E. Sweeney. After completing her undergraduate work at Transylvania University in 1899, Sweeney earned master's degrees at both UK and Columbia.[51]

Sweeney taught physics and chemistry at Campbell-Hagerman College before being hired by UK as a specialist in Home Economics

Professor Mary Sweeney, circa 1916. (Austin Lilly papers and photographs.)

Extension. She spent five years working in rural Kentucky to improve residents' nutrition and life skills before being named in 1913 head of the Department of Home Economics in the College of Agriculture. Home Economics became a separate college in 1916, with Sweeney serving as its first dean. In 1917, the Board designated Sweeney Professor of Nutrition and Sanitation in addition to her duties as head of the Department of Home Economics. Like Frances Jewell, Mary Sweeney's activities extended well beyond the UK campus. In the summer of 1917, she was called to Washington to aid Herbert C. Hoover's efforts in food conservation. She served as state chairwoman of the Women's Organization of the Council of National Defense and as state chairwoman of Home Economics in the Kentucky Federation of Women's Clubs. The following summer, Sweeney and her sister Sunshine were chosen from a list of more than 700 specially trained women to serve a year in France working in food canteens. Mary Sweeney also prepared a *War Cook Book* for the Committee of National Defense. Still other UK women entered war work. In January 1919 Adelaide Crane, Director of Patterson Hall, left the country to work in an Armenian orphanage.[52]

For many of the women students who remained in school the war seemed to have little immediate impact on their personal lives. Their goals remained, in large part, to get to the university, find a place to live, and acclimate to the new world of college. In the fall of 1918, Dean Hamilton continued her push for more women's housing on campus. Even with recent renovations to Patterson Hall, inadequate space existed to house the number of women who wanted to enroll. The Patterson Hall Board of Control reported in the fall of 1919 that all the rooms in Patterson Hall were filled and more girls were applying. At that point the administration rented a home near campus behind Patterson Hall for additional living space for the women students. (This building, which became known as Maxwell Hall, was located at 343 Harrison Avenue, now Martin Luther King Boulevard.) Ironically, new UK President Frank LeRond McVey announced that beginning in fall 1918 male students would need to find off-campus housing for at least a year until another "first-class" men's dormitory could be acquired. The two existing dormitories for men were being renovated for academic space to accommodate new academic departments at the university.[53]

Once arriving on campus women students encountered a world of contradictory signals. Less openly discussed than housing and social regulations were the academic expectations for the women. The dean of women, whom the Board of Trustees directed should be most concerned with the educational life of the women students, served as secretary of the university Senate Entertainment Committee and was in charge of the much of the social activities of the university. Nevertheless, the *Kentuckian* reported in 1918, "Through vocational talks and personal advice Dean Hamilton is endeavoring to impress upon the women to make more of their University opportunities, and devote less time and energy to the more superficial social life, emphasizing the need to develop a spirit of unity in social life and to create a more democratic loyalty to the university."[54]

According to Helen Horowitz's study of student culture, UK was following a national trend. The most important work of the dean of women, Horowitz noted, "was to make college life compatible with the administration's goals." Like other universities, UK witnessed the rise of student government, the expansion of fraternities and sororities, and the increased institutionalization of students' publications and activities.[55]

But Dean Hamilton's influence on UK women students soon ended. The university named a new president in 1917, and at a June

1918 meeting of the board President Frank McVey recommended that Dean Hamilton be given a one-year leave of absence with pay, after which time "her connection with the University shall cease." McVey offered no reason for Hamilton's leave of absence and departure from the university, though it may have been health-related, considering that she died within a very short time of her leaving the university. The new president took advantage of the change in the dean of women's office to revamp the responsibilities of the office. A special study of the university's operations recommended that the dean of women relinquish most of her teaching responsibilities so that she would have more time to "look out for the conduct, welfare and guidance of the women students."[56]

Despite the expanded influence of some women faculty and the success of women students in academics, women's progress toward equality was the exception and not the rule, as exemplified by the case of Mary Beall. She graduated from UK in 1919 with a degree in mathematics. The *Kentuckian* described her as "one of those rare co-eds who has a positively masculine intelligence in math and kindred subjects. During her years at the university, she has certainly upset the tradition that these subjects could be really managed only by the superior sex."[57]

While some women chose to compete directly with men on the campus, others chose not to emulate men. Rather, they established different priorities and areas of influence. Frances Jewell's approach to her work at UK was to advocate for a women's culture by creating women's organizations. It was a social construct she learned at Vassar and one that she believed would work best for UK women.

Although Jewell generally pushed for separate women's academic and social organizations, she did not hesitate to push back against unfair policies or practices that disadvantaged women, including herself. She demonstrated this vividly in her resignation letter to Lehre L. Dantzler, chair of the English Department, at the close of the 1919 school year. After seeing her teaching schedule for the next academic year that included three Freshmen Composition sections in a seventeen-hour teaching load, Jewell concluded that "in justice to my students, in justice to the university and to the English Department, and in justice to myself, I cannot possibly carry the proposed schedule." Jewell explained that the "interesting, but most tedious" reading of student essays and the student conferences required in the first-year English classes took so much time away from her other classes that she would have to "teach in such a manner that I should not be satisfied with the results of the year's work."[58]

Again demonstrating that she viewed university teaching as more than classroom instruction, Jewell added that the proposed schedule would leave her no time for committee work or for extracurricular activities, which, "I feel, are of undoubted benefit to the university and to the Department of English." Moreover, she would have no planning time and would "inevitably lose elasticity of mind and breadth of vision." While noting that she had enjoyed her work in the English Department, Jewell concluded, "I regret deeply that the above mentioned conditions have compelled me to offer my resignation." The surviving records do not indicate whether Jewell ever sent the letter, changed her mind, or Dantzler met some of her demands, because she remained an instructor at the university. Regardless, Jewell articulated her vision of a university, one that included rigorous academics alongside social and cultural activities important to a well-rounded life.[59]

With the end of World War I and the achievement of suffrage by American women, the lives of women students at UK began to take a subtle turn. Influenced by the creation of League of Women Voters chapters across the nation, students founded a Woman's League at UK in the spring of 1920, whose purpose was to bring "dormitory" women together with "the town girls." Additionally, the League hoped to "bring to the university certain notable experts on vocations for women."[60]

On still another front, women students reacted positively to the national suffrage campaign. A YWCA-sponsored women's self-government organization began in 1918 in Patterson Hall, and by 1920 the association brought forward demands by the women students. Not surprisingly, the first issues centered on the personal freedom of at least some of the women students. As the *Kentucky Kernel* reported in May 1920, "A petition presented by a representative of the senior class asking that the seniors be given the privilege of having dates on week nights for the rest of this year, that they be allowed to stay out until 10:45 without late permission . . . , and to use the telephone during quiet hours without permission, was granted by a unanimous vote of the association."[61]

Women nevertheless still held a precarious and ambiguous position within the university. Elizabeth King Smith and the Patterson Hall

THE WOMAN'S LEAGUE

The Woman's League. Every UK woman was eligible to be a member of the Woman's League. The annual dues were twenty-five cents; the funds were used to support vocational guidance work. The League sponsored monthly lectures by UK professors. (*Kentuckian*, 1923.)

Board of Control reported that fall 1919 marked the largest enrollment of women in UK's brief history. Smith quickly added that the fear often expressed by many that women would come to dominate on the campus was "extremely remote" because of the still low percentage of Kentucky women taking advantage of their access to a higher education. However, Smith believed that Kentucky women were slowly realizing the educational opportunities available at UK and that women's attendance would double "in the next few years."[62]

But even so, the demands on women's housing at the university continued to cause hardship on both current and prospective women students. In the fall of 1919, with all of the women's living spaces filled to capacity, the school telegraphed several prospective women students "not to come as there was no place for them." Since the university policy opposed housing women students "separately, through the city," university-approved rooms off campus proved difficult to find. Women administrators stressed that renters preferred men because "they are not so much at home and require less in the way of parlors and service." Part of the problem came from the women administrators themselves, who expressed the belief that women students at the university were "as a rule young and immature" and thus needed to be placed "where by wise guidance, a proper balance can be maintained between the social and academic side of college life, and ideals of study upheld."[63]

As problematic as the housing challenge facing UK women was, the tendency grew to separate women not only physically but also intellectually. President McVey announced the appointment of a new Dean of Women in the summer of 1919. Josephine Simrall, a native Kentuckian, had graduated from Wellesley College in 1893. She later did graduate work at both Johns Hopkins and the University of Cincinnati. She came to UK from Sweet Briar College, where she had served as head of the Department of Psychology and Dean of Women. The Chancellor of the University of Cincinnati wrote in Simrall's behalf that "she is possessed of marked literary talent, that she was active in women's organizations and has a charming, sympathetic manner."[64]

Like Jewell, Simrall strongly supported separate women's organizations. When a newly established student government on campus did not include women, the *Kentucky Kernel* editorially expressed concern. But the student editor explained that the decision to include only men came only after consulting with Dean Simrall and being assured that the women students preferred a student government council of their own. Writing about the history of women's student government in higher education, Kelly C. Sartorius argues that "women's governance resulted from the efforts of deans of women to extend into coeducation the citizenship preparation that originated in women's colleges." These efforts ended when male administrators appropriated and shifted the women's governance system, essentially ending "the links between student government and feminist activism."[65]

Even though the establishment of separate activities and organizations for women began when women first entered UK, some student leaders, and perhaps even many students, generally supported full equality for women and men together. At least the 1921 *Kentuckian* took that position. The yearbook dedication best illustrates the perceived roles of men and women even when equality was the goal. The dedication proclaimed, "We the Class of '21, dedicate this annual to the manhood and womanhood of Kentucky, as they stand for the first time in the history of our commonwealth as equal in the eyes of the law." Noting the historical contributions of women to the commonwealth, the editors concluded that "we, the Class of '21, consecrate our lives to do our utmost as true Kentuckians to bring about the realization of this ideal."[66]

In the midst of the equality-versus-separatist struggle, Simrall resigned as Dean of Women to take the same position at the University of Cincinnati and perhaps to be closer to her family who lived there. President McVey promptly named Frances Jewell UK's new Dean of Women. Students reacted positively to Jewell's appointment, at least according to the campus newspaper. Calling her "one of the outstanding figures in the university faculty," a *Kernel* editorial noted that Jewell brought to the dean of women's position "a rare knowledge of student life and problems and a personality that begets confidence and elicits admiration and respect. So happy a combination of those characteristics, which makes it possible for one to perform well the exacting duties incident to the position she has accepted argues well for the future of the education and culture of women in the University of Kentucky."[67]

As dean, Jewell continued to create a robust women's culture on the campus. She and her colleagues sought to offer women opportunities equal to that of the men students, while also establishing parallel

DEDICATION

The dedication in the 1921 *Kentuckian* was inspired by the Kentucky state seal, which carries the state's motto, "United we stand, divided we fall." (*Kentuckian*, 1921.)

organizations for women. For example, women students announced in April 1922 the founding of their own Women's Athletic Association. Up to this point, women's sports had not been as rigidly divided, and women athletes were members of the K-Men's Club, an organization of athletes who lettered in sports at the university.[68]

As the nation continued to debate the pros and cons of coeducation, the *Kentucky Kernel* noted that "from the viewpoint of the University of

Frances Jewell as Dean of Women. (Louis Edward Nollau F series photographic prints.)

Burton Prewitt Irene McNamara Gerald Griffin
BUSINESS MGR. MANAGING ED. EDITOR IN CHIEF

Kentucky Kernel editorial staff, 1922. (*Kentuckian,* 1922.)

Kentucky the whole question seems absurd" since "smoking certainly is not in the list of the faults of our girls, and indifference in athletics cannot justly be laid to their door." Finally, "as to moral standards, a careful observer cannot fail to see that our co-eds have exercised a salutary influence. Partly due to their intervention it is not considered the 'correct thing' to be a roue or a drunkard. We are not among the enemies of co-ed education."[69]

In May 1922, Irene McNamara became the first woman editor of the student newspaper. But for every exception like Irene McNamara, there were hundreds of other women at the university who took more traditional paths. During Jewell's tenure as dean she actively advised women students on future vocations. The responses to a student questionnaire showed that most of the women chose majors that led to traditional women's employment. Moreover, other programs suggested that university administrators believed that women students had particular needs that differed from those of men. A lecture series for the women students dealt with such topics as health, personal etiquette and social contacts, training for leisure, citizenship, university women and the community, and university women and the university. Women affiliated either with the dean of women's office or the Patterson Hall Board of Control provided the speakers. Former UK student and faculty member at the University of Chicago Sophonisba Breckinridge gave the keynote talk at UK's 1923 women's vocational conference.[70]

As Dean of Women, Frances Jewell chose not to push for women to be more like men or even to compete equally with men in all facets of life. But neither did she call for a return to male authority. Rather, she promoted a theme of consensus and consolidation. Jewell advocated a higher education that prepared college graduates for social responsibility. That society embraced preconceived gender roles did not seem to trouble her as much as it did women who pushed for complete equality. Jewell believed that women had passed through the open door of higher education and now should take advantage of the opportunities that education offered within the context of existing society.

Despite her northeastern education, Jewell combined a southern conservative world view with progressive notions regarding suffrage, progressive social views, and a basic belief that students, given the freedom to do so, could make good life choices. In a 1922 newspaper interview, Jewell stated, "Youth best understands its own problems and is best qualified to deal with them," noting that "the whole philosophy of the young woman had undergone a radical change within the last ten years and the old idea that a dean of women was an official chaperone or monitor had disappeared and, in the more progressive institutions, the dean is looked upon as an advisor and friend of the students. In order to advise youth one must live in the world of youth oneself and not in a world of scholarly seclusion."[71]

Jewell expanded on her philosophy of education during a talk to a nearly all-male engineering fraternity by suggesting that academic learning is for "knowing human nature and understanding people." She believed that the university develops a person mentally, spiritually, physically, and socially. She suggested that a university represents more than buildings and professors; a university is "a spirit" that helps people learn and develop what she called "The Art of Living." This "Art of Living" had always been central to Jewell's thinking, but now it pressed upon her with an even greater immediacy. In 1922 Jewell entered a crucial juncture in her personal life that would greatly alter her professional life as she faced an important and difficult decision.[72]

In April 1922, Mabel Sawyer McVey, wife of President Frank McVey, died unexpectedly after a brief illness. Jewell, a personal friend of the McVeys, saw them often, both at university-related events and during informal social occasions. Like Jewell, Mabel McVey actively participated in the University of Kentucky Woman's Club and served as president of the Fayette County League of Women Voters and as vice president of the American Association of Collegiate Alumni. In November 1921 Mabel McVey and Margaret McLaughlin, assistant professor of journalism at UK, had participated in a meeting in Louisville of the Executive Committee of the League of Women Voters. The group adopted resolutions calling on the state legislature to eliminate certain state laws that restricted the civil status of women. The group also asked that the age of consent in Kentucky be raised from sixteen to eighteen years of age.[73]

Less than six months after Mabel McVey's death, the friendship between Frances Jewell and Frank McVey developed into an intimate relationship. Twenty years younger than the president, Jewell enjoyed all types of social events. Many considered McVey, by contrast, reserved and socially awkward. She aspired to become a writer and loved the theater; he was a father of three nearly grown children, an administrator, and an economist who, between writing scholarly articles and books, worked at becoming a landscape painter. Yet, early in their relationship, something stirred, and it quickly became obvious to both that each wanted and needed the other.[74]

A delicate courtship by necessity, lists of persons attending presidential luncheons or dinners increasingly included "Miss Jewell." Secret correspondence between the two progressed from mutual interests and admiration to unveiled passion. Yet the question of how their relationship would affect Jewell's future hung over their courtship like a cloud. They faced some difficult choices. Undoubtedly, if she married McVey it would end her independent career. Jewell's range of choices mirrored the contradictions apparent in so many women's lives generally: marry and become a man's wife or stay single and retain one's independence and a professional career. Many women before Jewell faced this choice, and women would face similar decisions for generations to come.

In December 1922, Jewell and McVey exchanged letters that listed what each would do if offered several lives. Jewell wrote:

My lives are not so grand and noble as are yours. With one life—even if I have told you them, I want to tell you again—with one life, I should write and write—Please God I should be a *great* writer. With one life I should teach English in a college or University—please God I should be a *great* teacher. With one life I should be Dean of Women at the University of Kentucky (with some teaching of English) until the University of Kentucky was all the things it *should* be—And please God I should be a good, "fitten" dean. With one life I should have a settlement school in the Kentucky Mountains, and work for *good* rural public education in Kentucky. With one life I should have (manage, build up) a beautiful book store and finally a wonderful publishing house. With one life I should be a lovely daughter in the home, just be with my family and my friends, forever and forever. With one life I should travel, "For to admire and for to see, For to travel the world so wide; It ain't never done no good to me. But I couldn't drop it if I tried." With one life I should have married and had nine children, five boys and four girls.[75]

It is likely no coincidence that last on Jewell's list were family references. She pondered that one life would be to remain a daughter "forever and forever." And last, she would want to be married with nine children, with five of the nine being boys. Later in the letter Jewell attempted to explain to her future spouse her ambivalence toward marriage, even as she wanted everyone else to marry. She compared it to being pleased that others joined sororities while she admitted being a "gloat" for being a "non-frat." She concluded that being married is like being part of a "privileged class," and "I won't belong to a privileged class—and so perhaps I gloat over not belonging to the privileged class of those who are happily married—who knows?"[76]

Above all else McVey wanted Jewell to marry him, and he spared no effort to achieve that end. While he recognized and perhaps even appreciated her needs, there is no question where his priorities remained. He wrote to Jewell:

I know you are puzzled to know what to do. You want to go on with your work, with its press of interest and its many, many things that call for strength, patience, kindness, shrewd observation and good deeds. You do not want to retire to the drab life of a president's wife. That is because you don't know the many things that such a position brings.

It too, is busy with fun of running a house, helping the wheels go around, of making funds for the University, of entertaining men and women from everywhere and of giving an inspiration to the president thru love, sympathy, fun and exchange of comradeship in intimate knowledge of two souls that sing in attune, and many other things that I must leave to another time such as time to write, to think, to rest, as the days go on the wear of a job will lessen its attractions and you will wonder why. But I am not going to argue.

I want you dear. As you said, "You want me joyously, gloriously." Indeed that is the way, but in no sense would I persuade you if in your heart and mind you felt that you ought not to do it. Just that question of need. You said, you remember, "Is there a personal need? I know something of the others—of the position—the house, the children—but you, yourself what about you?" That is the greatest need of all. A heart crying out for companionship, for love, for sympathy. I need you so much for myself. I need you selfishly just to play with you, to read with you, to talk with you, to be with you in silence, in play, in work.

Oh! Glorious One, do you not see? You spoke of the honor that I would give you. I have not thought of that if there is any, but I have thought what you could give to me. What charm you would add to living. How together we could make any presidency a radiant thing, a joy to us and to others. Without you it will be work, but the joy will be so much less, if any at all.[77]

The importance of McVey's view regarding Jewell's decision is best illustrated in a talk that McVey gave in February 1923. McVey used these same themes when addressing the women students of the university on the "responsibilities" that they, as voting citizens, would have to bear in the future. He stressed that this new opportunity and responsibility would fall

Frances Jewell's doodles prior to her marriage to Frank McVey. (Frances Jewell McVey papers.)

principally on the country's college women. McVey added that educated women had a particular responsibility because "the family stands as the foundation of the state today and the woman is the center of the family. She has always given an element of idealism through the medium." McVey believed that women could choose to "make a great contribution" to national life or become "a great hindrance." Additionally, women could "give her high ideals about health and her high standards of morals and give a new freshness and spiritual strength to the state. The world expects from woman the things which she has gotten from life."[78]

Not only was McVey setting a course for Frances Jewell's life, but as president he could influence generations of women students. While by many standards, McVey had a somewhat progressive attitude towards women's education, it was bounded by certain constraints, and Jewell understood what she must give up to marry him. Just prior to her wedding she confided to Frank that in giving up her teaching position, "I am thinking of all the things I wish I had done."[79]

The Jewell-McVey wedding on November 27, 1923, at the Jewell family home, Pleasant View, outside Lexington exuded "charming simplicity." Only immediate family members and a few close friends attended the noon ceremony, which was officiated by the bridegroom's brother, Dr. William Pitt McVey. Following a ten-day honeymoon the couple returned home to Maxwell Place.[80]

When Frances Jewell decided to become Mrs. Frank L. McVey, she probably did not reflect on that time at the Baldwin School when she

99

played the role of a man in the school play. Yet Jewell seemed unable to come to terms fully with her generation's changing gender roles. While she outwardly advocated for a women's sphere and the further development of a parallel women's culture when possible, inwardly she seemed to long for an independent life available only to men with its many options.

Jewell's marriage to Frank McVey represented for her the best opportunity to combine her expectations of family and work. Ultimately, she decided to seek both intimacy and ambition in partnership with a man. They loved each other, undoubtedly. They were wonderful companions, yes. But in the end Frank overshadowed her. Jewell's earlier reference to the university as a "spirit" would ultimately become Frank's most notable quote.[81]

Being the president's spouse opened new doors for Jewell and allowed her to pursue many of her life goals, if not her career goals. But her independent voice became increasingly muted. She still held influence on the campus and throughout the commonwealth, but that influence derived to a large degree by virtue of her position as the president's spouse.

As young Frances Jewell closed her letter to her mother about the school play at boarding school many years earlier:

Why, Mother, I was an awfully good looking man, when I got my face browned etc. Well after the play I never had such a rush in my life. I had dances taken way ahead and when the bell rang I had to kiss such a lot of girls oh my! You see, Miss Boone says that it is the funniest thing how popular a girl is when she is dressed up in men's clothes—all the girls want to kiss her etc. I didn't know that I was going to get any flowers, or that anybody was but I got a bunch of jonquils.[82]

Assuming the role of Mrs. Frank L. McVey, Frances Jewell, in many respects, became "the most popular girl" at the university metaphorically dressed as a man, just as she had been in the Baldwin School play.

3

Sarah Blanding and the Modern College Woman

During the 1920s, Kentuckians began to confront change as modernism moved into Kentucky. Women's suffrage became law, and two new public teacher-training colleges for white students were created for eastern Kentucky and western Kentucky. By the end of the decade Lexington's population would exceed 68,000, making it an even more vibrant college town. But fundamentalism remained strong, and the commonwealth, with the help of University of Kentucky (UK) president Frank McVey, pushed back against an antievolution movement in the Kentucky legislature. The Ku Klux Klan grew stronger as racism still defined a commonwealth that was becoming increasingly nostalgic about the Confederacy and the Civil War.[1]

Like women college students nationally, the generation of women entering UK following World War I and the drive for suffrage were influenced by the educational and feminist traditions established by those who came before them. But they entered college during a period of rapidly changing student life influenced by significant shifts in American culture in what became known as the "Roaring Twenties." According to Paula Fass, the 1920s was a time when "that long-suspended ambivalence, the tension between the modern and traditional modes of thought and behavior, was finally played out and the social changes that had been remaking America for decades finally congealed into a pattern which would shape life in the twentieth century." Helen Lefkowitz Horowitz contends that many of the social changes on campus resulted from changing demographics. Unlike earlier pioneer women students, more "daughters of the middle class brought more conventional notions of womanhood into the college world and the belief that they, like college men, had come for fun." Moreover, women students "did not see college as a steppingstone to a career, but as a way station to a proper marriage." Coinciding with the new attitudes of women students was an expanding and more liberal social environment, including greater access to dance halls in Lexington, and it was noted that "Lexingtonians still loved to dance." Regarding women's changing fashions, waistlines were fluctuating wildly as hemlines became shorter; "1925 was the year of the crepe-de-chine, radium and truhu frocks—to be bought at Wolf Wiles for $15 to $25—and Balbriggan suits in popular shades of pink, orchid, tan, and poudre blue."[2]

At UK the number of women students continued to rise, the presence of women on the faculty was increasing slowly (if not surely), and the overall position of white women at the state's only public university seemed hopeful. However, Barbara Miller Solomon argues that increased access to higher education did not in turn guarantee continued general advancement toward equality. The University of Kentucky was no exception. Frances Jewell's push to build a more vibrant women's culture had succeeded in offering women a more visible and vibrant presence but had not brought about greater equity between women and men on the coeducational campus.[3]

Administrators faced the new reality of the modern college woman who would have different expectations and goals for her collegiate experience. But parents still expected colleges to regulate the activities and the morality of their daughters. The Dean of Women's office would transition into an operation that attempted to monitor and guide all aspects of women's social and academic lives in a way not seen since Lucy Blackburn ruled the "girls' room" in the Main Building two generations earlier. This new approach by the Dean of Women would not be based on trusting the women students and building women's organizations, but would instead be driven by a fundamental belief that, left to their own devices, women students would not make good decisions about their lives and their education.[4]

At the same time, a strong and widespread desire for change arose among the women students. Youth culture was being recognized as a vibrant segment of American society, and Paula Fass's and Beth Bailey's research and writings have shown that the interwar years were periods of significant shifts in the social construction of youth, in student culture generally, and in courtship patterns and rituals in particular. These changes intersected with the ambitions of the university leadership to change irrevocably the overall campus culture and, by inference, the relative position of women students on the campus.[5]

Even as Frances Jewell and Frank McVey planned for their late fall wedding in 1923, they knew that an interim Dean of Women must be named promptly. It probably was Jewell who convinced the president and her soon-to-be spouse to appoint the twenty-four-year-old recent graduate and relatively inexperienced Sarah Gibson Blanding to the crucial post. McVey probably did not need much coaxing as he had already grown fond of the intelligent, precocious young graduate. Unlike most others at UK who treated the reserved president with great deference, Blanding enjoyed arguing with and teasing McVey, and he enjoyed her company very much. Planning for the transition had begun during the summer following Blanding's graduation with her appointment as assistant to the Dean of Women. Becoming Acting Dean, and subsequently Dean of Women, dramatically changed Sarah Blanding's life and career and significantly impacted a generation of UK women students.[6]

Born November 22, 1898, on her uncle's farm south of Lexington near the Walnut Hill Pike, Sarah Gibson "Sally" Blanding began her life at the turn of a new century—one that held out great promise for both Sarah and for her generation of women. Sarah Blanding, along with her father, mother, and older sisters Ellen and Leonora (her sisters were twelve and sixteen years older), lived modestly, yet comfortably, on Central Avenue in Lexington's near east end. The family matriarch, Sarah Anderson Blanding, traced her family roots from Pennsylvania, where her maternal grandfather had served as Chief Justice of the Pennsylvania Supreme Court. She spent her childhood in rural South Carolina, where her father's family operated a plantation near Statesburg. After attending Catholic schools, first in Charleston and subsequently in Washington, DC, Sarah Anderson returned to South Carolina, where she served as governess and teacher for six children on a neighboring plantation, a position she held until she married William de Saussure Blanding, a local attorney from an established South Carolina family.[7]

In 1889, reportedly due to ill health, William Blanding gave up his law practice in South Carolina and moved the family to Kentucky. William first sold real estate in Boyd County in eastern Kentucky before securing a position as a storekeeper-gauger for the Internal Revenue Service. He was subsequently assigned to Frankfort, Kentucky, to establish tax assessments for the numerous bourbon distilleries in the area. Rather than move to Frankfort, the Blandings chose to live in Lexington, where William's younger brother, Abraham Louis "Abram" Blanding, practiced medicine. In Lexington, Sarah Anderson Blanding participated actively in the progressive reform movement. It was through her mother's activities that young Sarah came into contact with some of the leading women reformers of that time.[8]

A telephone call to the Blanding home during the early evening of July 9, 1914, dramatically altered life for Sarah Blanding. While crossing a swinging bridge at the Baker Brothers Distillery four miles southeast of Frankfort, her father fell off the bridge onto the bank of Elkhorn Creek below. Sarah and her mother hurriedly made the thirty-mile trip to Frankfort, arriving just moments before William died. In an instant, fifteen-year-old Sarah Blanding's world turned upside down, and she would face important decisions regarding her future.[9]

Blanding attended Morton High School in downtown Lexington, where she was a good student and excelled in athletics. She also participated in the Glee Club, the Literary Society, the senior class play, the senior minstrel, and took a leading part, it was said, "in everything of importance." Her classmates thought that "her jolly spirit and sweet way" made her "dear to the hearts" of her high-school classmates.[10]

Blanding aspired to become a physician like her Uncle Abram, and she often accompanied him on his medical rounds. However, her father's death, new financial constraints, and Uncle Abram's return to South Carolina may have made medical training, already a difficult proposition, now seem impossible. Her older sisters held jobs outside the home even prior to their father's death. Leonora worked as a milliner before marrying Minor E. Young, a local bookkeeper who became a dairy farmer. As early as 1909, Ellen served as principal of the Lincoln School kindergarten, and she also gave musical performances in the community and at the University of Kentucky. The Lincoln School was a progressive educational institution founded by Madeline McDowell Breckinridge, a member of one of Lexington's most prestigious families and a leading social reformer of the period.[11]

Sarah, growing up only a block from Lexington's Woodland Park, became active in the playground movement in Lexington, working as a summer recreation director in the new and expanding public parks system. During her youth she undoubtedly became knowledgeable of, if not active in, progressive educational trends sweeping Lexington. In her study of the lives and careers of southern women deans, including Blanding, Carolyn Terry Bashaw argues that Blanding's early experiences with the Lexington parks and the Lincoln School helped mold her philosophy toward women's public higher education.[12]

Following graduation from high school in 1917, Blanding chose to leave Lexington to attend the New Haven Normal School of Gymnastics in Connecticut. She later spoke of this choice as an economic decision in that she believed it would allow her to begin supporting herself more quickly than most other occupational avenues then available to young women. It is likely that Florence Offutt Stout, UK director of physical education for women and an alumnus of the New Haven school, advised Blanding to pursue her interest in physical education in Connecticut. Still, had Blanding chosen to attend UK, she could have lived at home, making college relatively inexpensive. Moreover, over half of her fellow graduates from Morton High School went on to college, a majority of them to UK.[13]

Her time in New Haven undoubtedly expanded Blanding's horizons, as she had never before been away from Lexington for any extended time. Nearing completion of the two-year program at the Connecticut school, Blanding realized that teaching high-school gymnastics probably offered the most likely employment opportunities. Dissatisfied with that option and searching for alternatives, Blanding learned that UK needed an assistant for its women's gymnastics classes. She negotiated an agreement with Paul P. Boyd, UK's Dean of Arts and Sciences, to teach women's physical education part-time while working toward an undergraduate degree.[14]

Twenty-one-year-old Sarah Blanding first met Frances Jewell while registering for classes in the fall of 1919. Blanding recalled that, like many September days in Kentucky, "it was hot and sultry," and "as the students milled around the registration desks, thumbing frantically

Casual snapshot of Sarah Blanding (in white), 1921. Blanding served as president
of the 1923 Women's Administrative Council. Founded two years earlier, the
council served as the women students' alternative to the Men's Student Council.
(Abe Thompson photograph album.)

through the gray schedule books . . . the faculty looked tired, and hot, and badgered." After a long wait, Blanding found herself standing in front of a table marked "English," behind which sat two people, "an interesting-looking man with red hair, and a woman who on first sight appeared large." A second glance at the woman behind the desk "revealed a face of great nobility, with fine aristocratic features."[15]

Reflecting upon first meeting Frances Jewell, Blanding confessed that, "to a rather bewildered, uncomfortable young woman who was both an instructor and a freshman, this first meeting marked the beginning of a new, thrilling adventure." Already excited about beginning college, Blanding felt there was "something tremendously stimulating about meeting Miss Jewell," who seemed to "radiate good will and nobility." Blanding immediately became Jewell's student and soon her protégé. She watched closely as Jewell worked to create an environment for women students on campus, both in the classroom and in the many clubs and student groups being organized.[16]

Blanding immersed herself in the expanding women's culture. Well known and popular as a student leader, Blanding served as president of the Mortar Board, president of the Women's Administrative Council, a member of the Woman's League, captain of an outstanding women's basketball team, and president of Kappa Kappa Gamma social sorority. She accomplished all that while teaching physical education each morning and working during the summers as a recreation director at the Lincoln School playground in the city's economically disadvantaged west end. Blanding's senior class yearbook, appropriately dedicated to Frances Jewell, described Blanding as one of the "all-round good girls" who could "do anything from pulling down A's to dropping the ball in the basket."[17]

While a protégé of Frances Jewell McVey, Blanding had a very different family and educational background. Divided by only nine years in age, McVey and Blanding were separated culturally and philosophically by an array of experiences. Frances Jewell McVey came of age during her family's economic and social ascent, which provided her access to Lexington's elite and private, single-sex, liberal-arts education in Lexington and at the Baldwin School and Vassar. Blanding's family, by contrast, had experienced wealth in earlier generations, but she grew to maturity at a time when her family's fortunes had diminished sharply,

Sarah Blanding's senior portrait. The entry noted, "Her presence on the campus will be greatly missed," but Blanding stayed at UK for nearly two more decades. (*Kentuckian,* 1923.)

Deans at the University of Kentucky in 1927. Front row, left to right: Dean F. Paul Anderson, Engineering; C. J. Turk, Law; Columbus R. Melcher, Dean of Men; Sarah Blanding, Dean of Women. Back row, left to right: Edward Wiest, Commerce; Paul Boyd, Arts and Sciences; Thomas Poe Cooper, Agriculture; W. D. Funkhouser, Graduate School. (UK general photographic prints.)

placing her firmly among Lexington's working middle class. Her educational experiences had been in public schools and at a utilitarian gymnastics school.

Not surprisingly, Blanding functioned much differently as dean in a post-suffrage, flapper-influenced, and subsequently Depression-era environment. Whereas Jewell had been a catalyst for the expansion of women's organizations and activities, Blanding ultimately became the prototypical dean of women familiar to most college students until the 1960s: the strict disciplinarian and guardian of the women students and their reputations.

In her first talk to the students as Acting Dean of Women, Blanding perhaps unconsciously wove Frances McVey's philosophy into her own views as she spoke to the students regarding the "splendid spirit prevailing on the campus, commending their sportsmanship, and the loyalty shown in support of all activities on the campus." But whereas McVey's relatively short tenure as instructor and dean of women is remembered for its organization building and expansion of social opportunities just for women, during Blanding's tenure as dean it became apparent that the approach advocated by McVey and others might not lead to full equality with men. Like women's protective legislation generally during the Progressive Era, special women's activities often trapped women students in a perpetual state of inequality.[18]

For example, a lack of equality for women students prevailed in athletics. Women organized their own basketball team in 1902, one year earlier than the men's basketball team. They played their first game on February 21, 1903, and women's intercollegiate basketball flourished on the campus during the first quarter of the twentieth century. Athletics provided women students a role in the growing popularity of college sports and served as a counterbalance to the rapidly expanding men's athletic teams, especially football and baseball. In her overview of the early years of women's basketball in Kentucky, Peggy Stanaland wrote that "their uniforms of dark serge and black stockings may have been cumbersome; their spectators may have been few in number; and their well-meaning protagonists may have shortened their season, but women's basketball teams did exist and were alive and well in Kentucky during the first two decades of the twentieth century. The popularity of the game could not be quashed."[19]

But quashed it was at UK, and the ripple effects spread across the commonwealth through colleges and high schools. By the fall of 1924, after years of tension on campus between Florence Offutt Stout and the male-dominated University Athletics Department, the university's Faculty Senate abolished women's intercollegiate basketball. Stout is generally blamed for the demise of women's basketball at UK. Her influence over women's athletics had waned between 1911 and 1918, even though she had maintained a long personal friendship with President Barker. With the appointment of President Frank McVey in 1918, Stout began to lobby the new president about the poor general health of many UK women students. She soon found that she also had an ally in President McVey because he too favored intramural sports for women rather than intercollegiate competition.[20]

By 1907–1908, women's basketball was increasingly seen as "good, healthy exercise." UK women players hoped that more teams would be formed around the state so that they could beat them and bring even more honor to their alma mater. The 1908 yearbook called the women "little, white angels" who were "champions of this part of the country" and a team who upheld the honor of the university. (*Kentuckian*, 1908.)

As the new Dean of Women, Sarah Blanding found herself in the middle of the ongoing debate regarding women's basketball. Blanding's role in banning the women's basketball team might seem odd for someone who just the preceding spring captained a championship basketball team for the university. Perhaps Florence Offutt Stout influenced her to change her position, or as a new dean she wanted to appease President McVey. More likely, though, it was Frances Jewell McVey's influence that caused Blanding to come to believe, or at least support, the position that intercollegiate athletics diminished attention to the "average run of women" and that women's intramural sports offered a better opportunity "to have fun " and receive "joy out of knowing how to play." While the former high school and college sports star and women's physical education instructor may have come to this conclusion on her own, the language more closely echoes Frances Jewell McVey's philosophy. By going along with the demise of women's basketball, Blanding appeased her physical education colleague, her mentor and friend, and her president.[21]

Once the proposed ban was announced, President McVey immediately defended the decision. He argued that no consensus existed as to "the type of basketball to be played by girls in intercollegiate games," adding that basketball had quickly evolved into "a strenuous sport for boys" and was "therefore too strenuous for girls." But beyond President McVey's concern for the health of women athletes, he expressed a real concern in regard to the basketball team's off-campus games. The president believed road trips to away games were inordinately expensive "because of the necessity of proper chaperonage and provision" and that "some very irritating consequences" had resulted. McVey did not advocate the abolishment of all women's athletic participation. Instead of intercollegiate games the women would participate in "inter-class games" that would "be played between the girls," which would "afford exercise, sport, and recreation."[22]

The *Kentucky Kernel* reported that "some degree of protest" against the abolishment of women's sports arose among the women students. Members of the 1923 women's basketball team asked to express their opposition to the ban to the faculty senate, and eventually over two hundred women students, representing nearly one-third of the women at the university, signed a petition calling on the University Athletic Council to save women's basketball. Their pleas were to no avail. On November 13, 1924, the Women's Athletic Association met and heard arguments from President McVey, Dean Blanding, and Florence Stout, the physical director for women, that intercollegiate basketball for women be discontinued. It was done.[23]

Blanding wrote in 1925 that in fact the UK Women's Athletic Association, "of their own volition . . . abolished intercollegiate athletics for women and instead played intramural, inter-class and inter-house games." She added that the change created much more interest in athletics among the women students and that more women were participating in athletics. Dean Blanding concluded that the Athletic Association should be congratulated for their stand.[24]

However, women students generally seemed far less satisfied with the new athletics policy than did administrators. In the place of basketball, Dean Blanding and the Women's Athletic Council established an extensive intramural athletic program consisting of field hockey, dancing, basketball, volleyball, hiking, soccer, tennis, track, and lawn-ball.

The "girls" tennis team. As noted in the yearbook, "the team enjoyed a very good season in 1925 in spite of the fact they were unable to engage in intercollegiate matches to any great extent." Pictured from left to right, Elizabeth Helm, Virginia Kelly, Eugenia O'Hara, and Dorothy Kerth were all members of the basketball team before the university prohibited it. (*Kentuckian*, 1926.)

Intramural sports had been expanding on the campus for both women and men students, but the abolishment of women's intercollegiate competition made women's intramural sports much more important, at least for the women students.[25]

By all accounts, a large number of women participated in intramurals, and occasionally the university women traveled to other cities, such as Cincinnati, to participate in multiple university "playday" programs, where UK women had an opportunity to compete against students from other universities.

All in all, however, the loss of intercollegiate women's athletics resulted in a real and negative impact on women during a period of otherwise rapid growth in college athletics for men. In 1920, President McVey organized the university's first Athletic Council, comprised of himself, the director of athletics, a representative from the faculty, and a local alumnus. The following year UK joined the Southern Conference. In 1932 UK became a founding member of the Southeastern Conference, opening the

Women's Athletic Association "playday," 1929. (Louis Edward Nollau F series photographic print collection.)

way for the university to enter the world of big-time college athletics. UK women's varsity basketball would not return until a half century later, in 1974.[26]

The changes for women in sports went beyond rules regarding participation, as rules for spectators were also introduced. The new Alumni Gymnasium opened in 1924, providing much-needed seating for students and fans. That December the university announced that men and women students could no longer sit together at men's basketball games. Men's basketball coach Clarence Oliver Applegran explained, "Young gentlemen may bring young ladies to the games but must part with them at the door and rejoin them after the game." Coach Applegran claimed "the girls and boys yell against each other, making more noise than could otherwise be gotten out of them." The seating rule, never popular with students, apparently did not survive the season, and after a 13–8 season neither did Coach Applegran.[27]

Issues surrounding UK women and athletics highlighted a situation that may have been unique to UK. Both the president's spouse and the dean of women could be strong advocates for women students and faculty. However, the actions of Frances Jewell McVey and Sarah Blanding show that having well-placed and influential women in the university structure did not always assure greater equality for women because no general consensus existed regarding women's higher education. McVey's and Blanding's greatest influence may have been as advocates for the expansion of women's dormitories and sororities. For example, in May 1925 the *Kentucky Kernel* reported that a new $150,000 dormitory to accommodate 104 women would be constructed adjacent to Patterson Hall.[28]

Also in 1925, Sarah Blanding borrowed money and took a one-year leave of absence to pursue a master's degree in political science at Columbia University. The graduate degree would provide Blanding the necessary credentials to become the permanent Dean of Women. In 1911, only six faculty held a PhD; but by 1922 there were twenty-two doctorates among the faculty. In an environment of escalating academic credentials, Blanding followed her mentor and predecessor's path to Columbia. Moreover, she realized that she had been handed the Dean of Women's position by President McVey in large part because of her friendship with him and Frances Jewell McVey rather than experience, making additional credentials even more necessary.[29]

Before leaving for graduate school in New York City, Blanding wrote to President McVey thanking him for his "consideration and judgment" and for allowing her to consult with him regularly about problems related to her work as dean. She explained her eagerness to study and of her confidence in her temporary replacement, Virginia Franke. But Blanding's own self-doubts about her abilities and qualifications for the job of dean became apparent in her closing line to McVey: "As I have said to you before, I hope you will not hesitate to tell me, if at any time during the year you find that she is better qualified to carry on the work than I."[30]

Blanding had reason to be concerned that her temporary replacement might prove to be a very good Dean of Women. Like Frances Jewell McVey, Acting Dean Virginia E. Franke, a New York City native, graduated from Vassar College and was working toward a doctorate at Columbia University. Her academic research involved the study of campus problems at large universities. Franke hesitated to take the one-year appointment at UK but realized that she would benefit professionally from the additional experience. After UK, Franke served as Secretary of the YWCA at Cornell University. She married in 1928 but died two years later at the age of thirty following childbirth.[31]

Even as she worked toward a political science degree at Columbia, Blanding seemed to reconcile herself to a career in the deanship rather than as a professor and audited some of the courses taught in the Teachers College at Columbia for "future and present" deans of women. Blanding confided to McVey that she was pleased that he expected her to return to UK and that she was looking forward to it "with renewed interest and enthusiasm." She also admitted after sitting in on some of the Dean of Women courses that "on the whole it is rather discouraging to see the kind of person into which one is supposed to develop."[32]

Looking beyond her Dean of Women assignment, Blanding wrote to McVey that her graduate work should prepare her to "possibly teach in UK's history and political science departments." But Blanding periodically reported to President McVey about his daughter, who was also doing graduate work at Columbia. She noted in another letter to McVey, "We are having an epidemic of severe colds and Virginia [McVey's daughter] is one of the victims. She was running a temperature last night so they ordered her to the infirmary. I have just come from there . . . and she is feeling better." Even away at graduate school, the dean of women's dual roles of academic and caretaker continued.[33]

Blanding was attempting to join the faculty ranks at UK during a period of professional stagnation for women faculty, even though President McVey had made hiring a better faculty one of his priorities. When Blanding became acting dean in 1923 only five women, or 7 percent of the faculty, held the rank of professor. Four of the five—Laura Maybelle Cornell, Sarah Tupper, Mary Sweeney, and Marietta Eichelberger—taught home economics. Florence Offutt Stout continued to direct women's physical education; she too held the rank of professor. No women held the rank of associate professor, while four were assistant professors. Fifteen women, or 27 percent of the total faculty, held the rank of instructor or assistant.

Elizabeth LeStourgeon, a mathematician, represented the most academically prepared woman faculty member hired during this period. A graduate of Georgetown College in 1909, she earned her PhD in mathematics at the University of Chicago in 1917. Prior to coming to Lexington at age forty, she taught two years at highly regarded Carleton

UK faculty group portrait for 1925–1926, with only five women pictured. (Louis Edward Nollau nitrate photographic print collection.)

College in Minnesota. A woman math major recalled that LeStourgeon was "an excellent teacher," but "rather staid and dignified." "You couldn't joke with Miss LeStourgeon." However, for Mary Hester Cooper, who came to UK in 1921 to become a math major, Professor LeStourgeon was her favorite professor. First intimidated by LeStourgeon's intellect and position, Cooper became impressed by "how well rounded" she was and how personable she could be in a more casual setting. In 1925 Le-Stourgeon was promoted to associate professor but was never promoted to full professor. LeStourgeon resigned in 1946. Sally Pence, class of 1914 and daughter of UK professor Merry Lewis Pence, became a grad-uate assistant in mathematics in 1927 after teaching in high schools for several years. She held the rank of instructor until she earned a PhD in mathematics from the University of Illinois. She retired from UK in 1963 with the rank of full professor.[34]

Percentages of women on the faculty remained stable but still low during the 1920s. By 1928–1929, women still comprised only 14 percent of the faculty, the same percentage as when Blanding became Dean of Women. Moreover, the women faculty remained concentrated in academic areas such as home economics and women's physical education. While women faculty sought recognition from their colleagues and from administrators, during the 1920s women students defined their own culture, evolving into what Helen Horowitz has described as "college women." They became an integral part of university life through the development of a new and distinct culture.[35]

As dean, Blanding inherited responsibility for women students who were unlike any before—and there were more of them. During the decade of the 1920s their numbers nearly tripled and their percentage of the total student population increased by nearly 10 percent. UK women students of the 1920s shared similarities with the pioneering women students who attended UK during the previous forty years. They were white, predominantly from Kentucky (particularly the central region of the state), largely Protestant, and overwhelmingly middle class. But these post–World War I women students differed from their predecessors in significant ways. They knew of F. Scott Fitzgerald, even if they had never read him. They had access to cars, cigarettes, and alcohol. They liked to dance and end their evenings with a late-night automobile ride and intimate moments. They talked increasingly openly about their relationships with men and became intent on reshaping student culture and their own futures. Universities witnessed the appearance of college women and men who were more likely to be members of fraternities and sororities and who immersed themselves in the whirl of campus social activities.[36]

But even as social mores transformed and women's equality seemed more hopeful than ever, many questions remained for women. Where did future marriage and family fit into this culture of freedom and experimentation? How did a career include a husband and a family? According to historian William Chafe, "The greatest dilemma of all involved the choice between marriage and a career," and women students at the university understood this issue in very personal terms. In the age of the flapper and the revolutionary change in women's public presence, the dichotomous issues of marriage and work outside the home still dominated the lives of young women pursuing higher educations. In 1923 they had witnessed their Dean of Women leave her own professional work for marriage. If the well-educated and talented Frances Jewell McVey could not manage career and marriage, why should they think they could? Most of the other women professors at UK remained single.[37]

A *Kentucky Kernel* headline in 1925 read, "Co-eds Hear Dr. Peters Lecture: Says That Women Can Marry and Have Careers." Dr. Iva L. Peters served as head of the Vocational/Guidance Department at Goucher College. The newspaper reported that "an interesting remark made by Dr. Peters was that women may marry and have a career as well." But what about those who still believed that having a career meant forgoing marriage and family? Women, both students and nonstudents alike, writing in *Letters,* the campus literary publication, considered this seeming paradox and often wrote about marriage and career:

Old Maid

Sarah Litsey

She caught at life with far too fragile hands.
Being well versed in patience such as hers
It managed to evade her mild demands.
Pleasurable martyrdom which sometimes slurs.
Across the prickly edge of torn conceit
Guarded her vanity. Small duties done
Rounded her hours and made each day complete.
Her life went out in dribbles. One by one
She laid the passionless, pale days aside.
Then she adopted a thin, scraggly boy;
And all the neighbors wondered when she died
If he had been a duty or a joy.
Now he is tall and gay and rather brave,
and once each year sends flowers to her grave.[38]

Sarah Blanding never married. Rena Niles, a friend of Blanding's and a Wellesley graduate, described her as "mannish" and "a truly . . . brilliant woman." But she was also "a beautiful woman, striking looking, wonderfully molded face and just a woman of tremendous charm who would have appealed to a man except that Lexington at that time did not have too many available men of her caliber." Niles added that

Blanding "was not going to marry an insurance salesman," for example, because "they would not have had anything in common."[39]

A former student recalled that Dean Blanding appeared very "business-like, although a bit mannish" and that she "didn't take any foolishness." Even President McVey often teased Blanding about remaining single. Barbara Hitchcock, McVey's niece, remembered that "Uncle Frank called her [Blanding] a 'he woman,' holding men off at arm's length because she's a coward." Blanding retaliated, joking with McVey "about [his] having been married twice."[40]

While President McVey and Dean Blanding teased each other about changing gender expectations and marriage, UK students developed their own style of rhetorical sparring. Since women first arrived on campus, competition between women and men students persisted. However, during the 1920s the competition between the sexes became more openly discussed, and it helped define gender relations on the campus. Sometimes the competition, if it were for future employment, had ominous implications for women's futures. But more than vocational and professional, the competition between men and women was increasingly social and academic. As women pushed against the bonds constraining their freedom and independence, they learned quickly that men could and would do what was necessary to maintain their privileged positions.

For example, writing in the 1925 *Kentuckian*, an anonymous student published a seemingly innocuous poem chiding men about dating and other social activities. "To the Men" specifically targeted fraternity men for ridicule. Describing Greeks as squirrels, neckers, tightwads, cavemen, dumbbells, drunkards, and roughnecks—among other things—the poem concluded by arguing that after all the dating, drinking, smoking, necking, and so forth of college life, a woman should choose a nonfraternity man for a husband:

My last love was just a good fellow—
No frat pin gleamed on his chest.
He loved me despite my flirtations,
And I found him, of all them the best.
And so, in the beautiful June-time
The church with flowers they'll trim;

For I'll walk by his side—just a shy blushing bride—
And I'll learn about husbands from him.[41]

"To the Men" illustrates a serious issue discussed in a lighthearted manner while illuminating the continuing evolution of student customs and
beliefs. Lynn Gordon, in her study of women and higher education during this period, has demonstrated the importance of students' writing in
determining their views in a way otherwise not available. This playful
poem, published in the UK yearbook, revealed the existence of serious
issues between women and men as student social customs continued to
evolve. Drinking, petting, and dating were dealt with directly, but anon-
ymously. Women students struggled to know how college social life
intersected with adult lives that still anticipated marriage.[42]

An anonymous male student replied in another poem, entitled "To
the Coeds," which appeared in the *Kentucky Kernel* shortly after publication of the 1925 yearbook. Referring to sorority women as "gold diggers"
and "neckers," the concluding stanza implies that it is not just sorority
women whom men should avoid, but all college-educated women:

I've taken my fun where I've found it,
But now I feel that I'm done;
I've learned them from Alpha to Omega,
And I'm sure I'd never marry one.
So I'll neck 'em, pet 'em and kid 'em,
Just like they try to do to me.
But 'neath the Altar, I'll kiss, an old-fashioned miss,
T'will never be a coed for me.[43]

This rebuttal received instant and harsh reactions from President McVey
and others on campus. Apparently the insinuations regarding women's
behavior on campus went too far by contemporary standards. In the
very next issue of the *Kentucky Kernel* the editors expressed regret for
publishing the poem and apologized to UK women. Explaining that the
poem's author "intended no offense," the editors explained that it was
"through a spirit of levity, and in response to a similar utterance written
by young women appearing . . . in the current Annual, this poem was
published." Both "To the Men" and "To the Coeds" demonstrate the

social complexity of the emerging student culture and the challenges for both women and men students as each confronted the future of educated and ambitious women. Women students soon realized, however, that their predicament and their futures were even more unsettled than these two student poems could foretell.[44]

Even more stringent student rules emerged in response to the new campus social life. One new rule stipulated, "Automobiling with men within the city limits is permitted until 8:00 p.m. and beyond the city limits in groups of three or more, the majority of whom are women, until 6:30 p.m. On such trips no stops may be made at places of public resort." Moreover, women students may "not lunch or dine with a man at any hotel or restaurant after 6 p.m., without permission from the house director, the University Cafeteria being an exception to this rule." Women could even be cited for "walking home from the library with a man."[45]

Perhaps more than anything, the automobile changed both the perception and the reality of college life during the 1920s. Cars offered a degree of freedom not previously experienced by women, and they quickly realized and understood the extent of this change. It also provided women a means of transportation without their having to depend on men or public transportation. Writing in *Letters* in the summer of 1930, Louise Good, a member of the university Scribbler's Club, aptly described this sense of freedom for women:

My Automobile

My automobile is a jailor's key
Unlocking my chains and setting me free
Setting me free on the open road
A gypsy song my only goad
With seven-league boots I'm swiftly shod
I'm armed with Mercury's winged rod
I step on the carpet of Bagdad and soar
Far, far away from my prison door.
No pirate, watching his foaming keel,
Feels freer than I, in my automobile.[46]

In addition to the personal freedom that automobiles offered, they fundamentally changed the ways in which women interacted with men

University of Kentucky students sledding behind a car, 1920. Frazee Hall appears in the background. The automobile brought all students more freedom, but particularly women. It changed women's social interactions with men. It took courting from the parlor and front porches of homes and dormitories and moved it to the back seat.

socially. As Beth Bailey has described, the automobile took courting from the parlor and front porches of homes and dormitories to the back seat of the automobile. The freedom from supervision that automobiles provided contrasted sharply with the general strictness of women's dormitory regulations. For example, rules regarding men's visitation stipulated that men could call Monday through Thursday from 3:30 to 6:00 p.m.; Fridays from 3:30 to 10:45 p.m.; Saturdays from 2:10 to 10:45 p.m.; and Sundays from 2:00 to 10:00 p.m. Men could only call on Sunday mornings "to accompany the women students to church."[47]

But administrators and some women's organizations attempted to extend the restrictions on women well beyond the walls of their living quarters. Under the headline "W.S.G.A. [Women's Student Government Association] Lays Down Rules for Girl Students," the *Kentucky Kernel* reported in detail the new rules being implemented "as a safeguard to community life." At a mass meeting in the school gymnasium, administrators informed women students that "dances not under the auspices of the university may be attended only by special permission." Moreover, no students could attend public dances, such as those held at the Phoenix and Lafayette Hotels in downtown Lexington.[48]

Smoking, however, fell somewhere between the cracks of university discipline. Located in the heart of Kentucky's burley tobacco belt and surrounded by tobacco warehouses, the university did not consider tobacco harmful or improper for men. The issue of women students smoking publicly remained unresolved. Acting Dean of Women Franke argued that "although there is no rule against it [smoking], tradition here makes one unnecessary." However, the *Kentucky Kernel* reported that women did smoke on campus: "one smoked at the dance in the basketball building Thanksgiving night but she was not a student." Still, several sororities established rules prohibiting smoking. Writing in the *Kentucky Kernel,* Lucille Cook, a member of the Women's Administrative Council, warned that cigarette smoking harmed women more than men and that she knew of cases of "cigarette blindness."[49]

But even as students and administrators negotiated the boundaries of social policies, women's role in academics continued to evolve. At other universities, women's increasing presence on campus occasionally created a backlash, to the point that some called for a return to all-male campuses. While this was never seriously considered at UK, the idea arose at neighboring Transylvania University, where women had attended since 1889. Leer Buckley argued in the Transylvania student newspaper that "Transy would never regain its past glory until women are sent back to Hamilton College." In their editorial "Is Coeducation a Failure?" *Kentucky Kernel* editors responded to Buckley's call, noting that, "Mr. Buckley has thus put his finger upon the exceedingly sore spot in the general plan of American higher education and we wait with interest for subsequent observations by men equipped to make them, upon this interesting subject."[50]

Questions regarding coeducation persisted in spite of, and perhaps because of, women's continued academic success. At the initiation of UK's first Phi Beta Kappa chapter in March 1926, women boasted a large percentage of the new members. Moreover, women continued to challenge men for academic recognition throughout the university. In an editorial congratulating women for again gaining a higher academic standing than the men, the *Kentucky Kernel* editors stressed, "Unless the men rally in scholarship shortly women of the institution will have ample proof to turn the tables on the men students in man's centuries-old boast of superior intelligence."[51] UK student Dorothy Stebbins continued to chide the men students for their academic standing. In the process she seemed to delight in teasing about the implications of the "Fall of Man," noting, "Men's heel no longer grinds our necks into the dust of humiliating inferiority. We have become, rather frighteningly superior. Worse luck! What have we now to reverence, to respect? What is there left in this fast dwindling, pygmy man for us to hail as hero, conqueror, protector?"[52]

While the 1920s produced no large-scale expansion of women's separate organizations, one development during the decade warranted special attention. Because the university band grew out of the all-male cadet corps, it remained an all-male band. In the spring of 1927, UK band director Elmer Sulzer casually mentioned to some women students that they should one day have a band of their own. Without further encouragement, forty-five women students met to form a brass band. Reporting this phenomenon in the *Kentucky Kernel* under the headline "Males Again Retreat," Katharine Best wrote: "Weep, men, at your loss of prestige. No longer will ye olde brass band (male) strut down the field of honor with roses and hollyhocks strewn in its path; no longer will hats be raised to welcome 'the greatest band in Dixie.' No! Its rival has appeared! And on its own campus, too. We fear the results." Obviously enjoying announcing this new women's initiative, Best added, "The only requirements for membership are a speaking acquaintance with music, and the rather restrictive quality of being a girl. Therefore, if your mamma calls you daughter and you can read music, report to practice Tuesday, state your preference as to instruments, and automatically become a member."[53]

Nevertheless, it was considered one of the highest honors for a woman student to be elected by the all-male band as their sponsor. The *Kentucky Kernel* announced the upcoming election of the sponsor in December 1927, noting that for the male band members, the fun will begin when the scrutinizing eyes of the "eighty five" will look the women prospects over and rank them according to marching ability, beauty, personality, and the willingness to work. It is also believed that the band favors a girl who is not too small. Many of the most beautiful and popular girls in the university would not make good sponsors because of their inability to keep step with the swinging strides of Drum Major Waller Jones."[54]

Barred from participation in the men's marching band, women students organized their own band, seen here in 1930. (Louis Edward Nollau nitrate photographic print collection.)

Even as women students demonstrated their academic abilities, teased their male counterparts, and established more women's organizations, the downside inherent with the creation of special women's rules and a parallel woman's culture became increasingly apparent. For example, in April 1926 Dean Blanding announced that women students' "non-academic activities" would be closely monitored and limited by the Dean and the Women's Student Government Council. Like protective legislation nationally, this move on the UK campus institutionalized "special" protective measures for the women students. What differentiates these restrictions from those of Lucy Berry Blackburn of an earlier time is the apparent role of the women students themselves in the creation of the rules and in their enforcement. Increasingly, college administrators on the campus called upon the "new college woman" to help establish and enforce rules for women.[55]

UK women students did not concern themselves with the universal pattern of women's lives so much as their own individual present and

UK's all-male marching band and sponsor, Betty Bakhaus, in the 1938 May Day parade in downtown Lexington. Each year the band chose a woman student, based on her appearance and style, to serve as "sponsor" and march at the head of the band along with the male drum major. (Louis Edward Nollau F series photographic print collection.)

future. Virginia Katherine Conroy, from Mt. Sterling, Kentucky, chose to attend UK in 1924 because it was nearby and relatively inexpensive. She became homesick and almost quit, but her father convinced her to return to school and "try it again." Conroy enjoyed the freedom of college even within the confines of women's rules on campus, later recalling, "We had very strict house rules. We weren't allowed to smoke in the house. One of our members had asthma and she had permission to smoke. Anybody that wanted to smoke would go back to her room. You weren't allowed to have men in your bedroom, but . . . it was all right to have dates downstairs." Conroy was Catholic and generally socialized with other Catholic students on the campus, although, according to Conroy, there were "very few."[56]

Conroy noted that Dean of Women Blanding "had her stool pigeons," and "the girls in the sorority houses, she kept us under wraps pretty well." Conroy did recall one evening in particular, when she and several male friends were dining at a downtown restaurant that was apparently off limits, at least to the women students, when suddenly Dean Blanding appeared in the front doorway, looking for students, as she was often prone to do. Conroy hid under a booth to keep from being seen by the dean.[57]

The social scene on campus was vibrant, and Dean Blanding struggled to come to grips with the changes in student mores. Speaking to a gathering of Kentucky deans of women in 1929, Blanding recalled a recent college dance at which the students behaved "in a lady-like and gentlemanly manner." But she added that she "remembered the 'Needs of the Girls' and with a picture of the girls limping out on their poor, tired feet, clearly before me, I concluded that the greatest need of girls today is to get to bed."[58]

Generally, the 1920s on the UK campus continued to present women with a series of contradictions regarding their status and their future. For example, each year the women's journalism honorary society, Theta Sigma Phi, produced one issue of the *Kentucky Kernel*. In November 1929 an editorial praised the work of the women's honorary. However, on the same page appeared this brief commentary: "A college editor recently stated that, 'Brains and personality were essential to beauty.' If this is the case we know a FEW girls who are automatically eliminated. Not, however, on account of their lack of beauty."[59]

Beauty, and the recognition of it, became increasingly important at the university. During the 1929–1930 school year, Cecil B. DeMille, a founder of Paramount Pictures and a leading filmmaker of the 1920s, ostensibly accepted the responsibility for choosing UK's most beautiful coed. This became major news, and the *Kentucky Kernel* editorialized about the resulting winner, Catherine Bennett Lowry, and her seven attendants, noting that, "It is essentially feminine to want to be beautiful and to have that beauty accepted as such by associates; it is feminine to be pleased with admiration." Thus, the editors concluded, "The *Kentuckian's* beauty winner, then, ought to be in a pleasant frame of mind these days with the plaudits of their friends being showered upon them. The *Kentucky Kernel* joins all those who are congratulating the most beautiful girls on the campus and expresses sincere admiration of the charms that have been recognized throughout the nation." Karen Tice, in her study "Queens of Academe," writes that college beauty contests, which gained popularity through the 1920s, "inherited the numerous debates and discord that had accompanied the growth of public exhibitions of women's bodies throughout the nineteenth century." This tension had surfaced on the UK campus well before the new emphasis on beauty pageants in regard to women's physical education clothing and women's basketball attire. The debates regarding women's bodies, proper women's clothing, and women's general appearance would continue; and, according to Tice, these debates mirrored the rapidly changing social norms that concerned some, including issues of "women's heightened sexuality, boldness, and independence."[60]

This focus on physical attractiveness coincided with how dating had transformed women's culture on the campus. Whereas men competed in athletics and other competitive activities, Helen Lefkowitz Horowitz notes that college women during the period achieved status by "being asked out by the right man. The primary contests [for women] became those of beauty and popularity, won not because of what they did, but because of how and to whom they appealed." College women increasingly had become "the consort of the college man" and "glowed in reflected light."[61]

By 1930, a half-century of women attending UK came to an inconclusive close. Without question, more women attended UK, more women taught at UK, and student life had changed significantly. But even though much had changed for women over the preceding fifty years, their quest for full equality and respect for their intellect remained elusive. The modern college woman left her mark on the UK of the 1920s, but ahead lay additional, and perhaps even more difficult, obstacles for women, as the world entered a great depression followed by yet another world war.

4

Economic Depression and an Uncertain Future

In January 1930, UK president Frank McVey reminded students about the numerous checks written by them to the university that had been returned due to insufficient funds. As the economy worsened, students found it increasingly difficult to pay for their college education, much less support the type of social life that had become popular among students during the previous decade. Even more ominous, Kentucky's governor declared a bank holiday to keep the remaining banking institutions from collapsing. Still a predominantly rural, poor state, Kentucky's economic challenges were serious and growing worse. Budget news coming out of the state capitol in Frankfort warned of hard times ahead for a university that had never been adequately funded from the beginning. Professor Martin M. White later recalled the severe impact of the economic depression on the university, including the pay cuts the faculty took during this period as well as the two months that the faculty did not receive any pay.[1]

The years following World War I demonstrated that it might take longer than many anticipated for women to achieve equality at UK. By the 1930s a women's culture promoted a decade earlier by Frances Jewell McVey faced erosion from both dramatic and subtle changes within student life, which became increasingly defined by a more liberal dating culture. But the relative position of women on the campus would not necessarily be defined entirely by the new social mores or even from the university's still-evolving rules and regulations for women. Instead, the

Great Depression would impact greatly the ever-precarious status of women students, staff, and faculty on the UK campus.

Even during difficult economic times, the growing number of high-school graduates in Kentucky caused the total number of women students at UK to increase through the 1930s. Susan Ware, in her study of women during that decade, contends that college women were "probably influenced more by broader trends affecting women's participation in higher education than by the specific dislocation of the Depression." She notes that "only a small minority of American women in the 1930s, between 10.5 and 12.2 percent, attended college" and that "while the absolute number of women enrolled in colleges increased, women's percentage of total college enrollment dropped from 43.7 percent in 1930 to 40.2 percent in 1940." Likewise, UK's enrollment continued a steady growth during the 1930s, but women's percentage of the total enrollment dropped from 42 percent to 39 percent.[2]

Beyond issues of access to higher education, women continued to confront the very real question: For what purpose? During the Depression UK women graduates began to experience what their sisters working in industry and the professions had known for several years: women's place in the workforce was tough and getting tougher. Increasingly, UK women focused not just on issues of equity on campus, but the potential for employment and a future of economic independence as they increasingly entered historically male-dominated majors.

In addition to economic woes, central Kentucky faced a severe drought during the summer of 1930, putting Lexington's meager water supply in jeopardy. Gathering in Memorial Hall for the opening convocation of the 1930 school year, President McVey advised the students that if they had been in the habit of taking a daily bath, they should instead consider taking one "every other night." If they had been "taking one every other night, take two baths a week." But if any student had been taking only one bath a week, McVey encouraged those students "for goodness sake keep that up!"[3]

The *Kentucky Kernel*, forced to cut back from eight pages to four, became just one casualty representing the broad impact of the budget crisis. Nevertheless, President McVey continued to call for a sizable increase in the state appropriation to his long-underfunded university, with a focus on new buildings. His first priority, a student union, symbolized the growing importance of the new student culture. Next on his list of priorities came dormitories, especially those needed to augment the "woefully inadequate" women's facilities. But it became increasingly obvious that even holding the line on existing appropriations might be impossible.

In this environment, Dean of Women Sarah Blanding chose to take a semester's leave of absence to study at the London School of Economics. She had considered returning to Columbia for her PhD, but President McVey, an economist, advised her to go to London instead. He personally assisted in arranging for her graduate work there and wrote letters of introduction on her behalf. While in London, Blanding boarded with friends who had strong UK connections. She stayed in contact with the McVeys during her six months abroad, detailing her graduate work and extensive travels throughout Britain.[4]

In her absence, Sarah Bennett Holmes, Blanding's assistant since 1929, administered the dean's office. Holmes, the widow of the former head of the university Hygiene Department, had completed her college degree at UK in 1929, five years after her husband's death, while raising four young children. She steadily gained respect on the campus as an able and dedicated administrator.[5]

Earlier efforts to build parallel women's organizations on campus persisted. Women's student government, women's housing arrangements, and women's clubs and organizations played major roles in the lives of UK women students. Moreover, the continuing institutionalization of separate women's academic areas or organizations was seldom challenged. In this environment, could women finally be accepted as equals to men academically and socially? Would women continue to push for equality? And, finally, what were the implications for the women students' futures, especially in such uncertain economic times?

The *Kentucky Kernel* rarely reported on women's athletics, since intercollegiate competition for women remained banned and intermural sports were generally not considered newsworthy. In September 1930 the administration informed women students that they could participate in sports activities every afternoon at 3:00 and 4:00 p.m. on the athletic field behind Patterson Hall.[6]

The women's band, founded by Elmer Sulzer six years earlier, remained active, with over thirty women participating in a group touted

Sarah Bennett Holmes, circa 1920s. (UK portrait print collection.)

as "the only organization of its type in the nation." Band members earned academic credit toward graduation by participating. But restrictions of all types remained on women students. For example, women were forbidden to travel by automobile to the annual Kentucky-Tennessee football game. Women could attend only if they traveled by train in

Women students playing field hockey behind Patterson Hall, 1930s. (Louis Edward Nollau F series photographic print collection.)

"special Pullman cars set apart for women students, under chaperones selected by the Dean of Women."[7]

"Beauty Candidates Required to Submit Measurements," head-lined the *Kentucky Kernel.* All measurements were to be delivered personally, and the "beauties" would be judged by Earl Carroll, a New York theatrical producer, director, songwriter, and composer, whose recommendations would be delivered to a committee of yearbook staff members for the ultimate decision. Carroll noted that "women with facial beauty only will not be as likely to be considered as those who have charming physiques." He added, "We have a definite standard of beauty and I could render a more solemnized decision if on the back of their photographs the young ladies would answer a questionnaire such as this: weight, height, neck, bust, waist, hips, thigh, calf, ankle, forearm, wrist, foot size, color of eyes, and color of hair." Carroll warned "measurements must be absolutely correct" or "candidates will be disqualified." The panel of judges did concede, however, that "other characteristics, as personality, etc.," would be "recorded by a committee according to instructions by Mr. Carroll."[8]

Carroll, a well-known Broadway personality, once hosted a party in New York City for several hundred people during which a nude woman sat in a bathtub of liquor during Prohibition. Carroll denied the allegation but was found guilty of lying to a grand jury and was sentenced to six months in prison. Nevertheless, by 1930 he was apparently rehabilitated sufficiently to judge a college beauty contest.[9]

While women's "beauty" continued to captivate the imaginations of men students, a more disquieting hostility toward women existed in the minds of some, as illustrated by student Harry Dent's 1932 poem:

Idealism

The death of a beautiful woman,
Or the death of a lop-eared hound,
Each a poetical subject
When they're six feet under the ground.

Either may cause inspiration,
Be sure that it matters not which,
The fickle-like love of the beautiful maid,
Or the true, tender faith of the bitch.[10]

In the classroom, some male professors provided an environment in which women could excel academically. However, others did not, and even exhibited hostility toward women. Woodrow Burchett remembered his fellow law student Mildred O. Robards as "a mighty nice little lady" whom law professor Roy Moreland "was always trying to embarrass" and "did embarrass her a lot." According to Burchett, "Every time he had an ugly rape case or an ugly case that involved sex or something that ladies didn't like to talk about he'd always call on Miss Robards. He'd get her up and ask her a lot of questions and embarrass her." One day Professor Moreland "ran in and jumped up on that desk and patted his face. We were . . . studying rape and he asked 'Miss Robards, what do you think it takes to constitute a penetration?'" She squared away real big . . . and she said, 'Dr. Moreland, I'd say about twelve inches.'" Afterward, Burchett remembers that "the class all applauded because she

Dr. Jacqueline P. Bull processing a manuscript collection, circa 1955. After completing her undergraduate degree, Bull earned a master's degree in library science and a PhD in history studying under distinguished Kentucky historian Dr. Thomas D. Clark. Bull became the first director of UK Libraries Special Collections. (UK general photographic prints.)

really lowered the boom on him that day." But even with such blatant bad behavior on the part of some, sexual harassment and even sexual assaults remain virtually undocumented in UK's history.[11]

While women professors might not have been hostile toward their women students, they could be intimidating. Jacqueline Bull, a student in Alberta Wilson Server's Spanish class in 1930, recalled, "She was a thorough teacher, and she literally scared the living daylights out of all of us," adding that "she was a sarcastic person." Bull added that Server once picked a student in the class to question about her preparedness, and "the poor girl" went "all to pieces." She subsequently failed the course. After witnessing that, Bull said that she "did stiff my spine enough to live through it and I did not take any more Spanish."[12]

Professor Server was one of only 30 women faculty members, comprising only 12 percent of the 245-member faculty, when the 1930s began. Like many early women faculty, Server had earned her undergraduate and master's degrees from UK. Having lived as a child in Mexico and being fluent in Spanish, as an undergraduate she taught Spanish and served as a lab assistant in zoology. Her senior yearbook described Alberta Wilson as "one of the brightest students in the class. . . . We predict a bright future for her." In her class of roughly one hundred fifty, Server was one of only ten students, and one of two women, to graduate "with high distinction." Studying with Professor William D. Funkhouser, she received a master's in zoology the following year (1921), while also teaching Spanish classes at Morton Junior High.[13]

To the surprise of almost everyone on campus, Alberta Wilson also got married in February 1921, during a private service in Newport, Kentucky. A week after the wedding it was announced that she had married James Milton "Big Jim" Server, one of the most popular men on campus, who had been elected football team captain for the 1921 season. "Big Jim" first enrolled at UK in 1914, but his college was interrupted by military service during World War I. A fraternity man, he played nearly every sport offered by UK and was recognized "as one of the greatest linemen that ever wore a blue jersey." The match between the cerebral Alberta Wilson and "Big Jim" Server had not been anticipated, but they were considered "one of the handsomest and most popular couples in Lexington at the time." It became an apocryphal story on the campus that "Big Jim" had taken Alberta's Spanish class and she had flunked him.[14]

In 1923 Alberta Server became a full-time instructor of Spanish and French and in 1925 was named Assistant Professor of Modern Romance Languages. According to her former colleague Daniel Reedy, in 1926 Server took the first of what would become several trips to Europe to enhance her academic credentials, eventually resulting in her earning a PhD from the Université Besançon. In 1944 Server was finally promoted to Associate Professor, but she would not become a full professor until 1960. She was only the second woman to achieve that rank in the UK College of Arts and Sciences since its founding in 1908. Following Server's second trip to Europe in the summer of 1928, she and Jim Server divorced. Jim, who worked as a salesman, relocated to Houston, Texas.[15]

Alberta Wilson Server, professor of modern languages, 1940s. (UK portrait print collection.)

Florence Offutt Stout, Statie Erikson, head of Home Economics, and Ethel Lee Parker, in Home Economics Education, were the only three women full professors. Over half (16) of the women on the UK faculty in 1931–1932 were employed in the lowest faculty category, instructor. Equity had not come to the university's faculty, and the issue of equality for UK women generally was far from settled.

A popular event in November 1930 featured a debate between two UK male students and their counterparts from Cambridge University in Great Britain. Over six hundred attended the program presided over by Dean of Arts and Sciences Paul Boyd, which was billed as a discussion of the "Woman Question," or "Resolved: that the emergence of the woman from the home is a regrettable feature of modern life." The first speaker, UK student Hugh R. Jackson, argued the affirmative, citing biological differences between women and men, adding that "the emergence of women is regrettable." One of the Britons, N. C. Oatridge, also arguing the affirmative, was said to be "entertaining" in his description of women as "stupid and selfish." UK student William Ardery held the negative, noting that the emergence of women into the workforce was a natural result of capitalism. Afterward, the *Kentucky Kernel* joined the debate with an editorial entitled "The Woman Question," noting that women should have the option of being a wife and homemaker, just as she should be able "to get out in the sphere of professional activity." The editorial concluded that "whatever course she chooses, she will contribute at least her share of life's achievement."[16]

Ardery's support for the modern woman apparently represented more than merely a debating position. A few weeks later in the *Kentucky Kernel,* he wrote about a woman student who had been confined to her dormitory except to attend classes for the supposed offense of washing her socks after 10:15 p.m. in Patterson Hall. Ardery wrote, "It seems that no washing of any kind is permitted after this hour because the sound of falling—or rising—water disturbs the other inhabitants of the prison. We live in an advanced age!" A few weeks later other *Kentucky Kernel* writers also denounced the strict rules for women students, noting that "today we are forced to accept a new order of things" because "women are, superficially at least, distinctly no longer clinging vines." Seemingly resigned to this new reality, one writer noted that, "whether we like to admit it or not, women students at the university are

Statie Erikson, 1941. Professor, 1926–1952, and Director of the School of Home Economics, 1952–1958. (Louis Edward Nollau F series photographic print collection.)

Ethel Lee Parker, Professor of Home Economics, Education, and Vocational Education, 1957. (UK portrait print collection.)

distinctly capable of taking care of themselves," so any rules based on "sex distinctions . . . therefore, are certainly questionable."[17]

Many women students did not, at least outwardly, rebel against the stricter rules. However, in regard to their future and the ongoing debate over marriage and career, their writings offer insights into the internal struggle women faced. Writing in the February 1931 issue of *Letters,* Kathryn Myrick contemplated her future:

Bonds

Before we met I thought mine was a free soul
That never could be bound by man or circumstance;
Now, looking into your eyes,
I know I will be held forever—
A crushed and bleeding flower,
In the tenderness of your love.[18]

The debate over marriage intensified. The *Kentucky Kernel* featured a story in the spring of 1930 regarding a survey of students at Northwestern University, which showed that most women students were not seeking marriage. The UK newspaper editors contended that the respondents to the survey were not telling the truth. They concluded that "the modern girl fails to see the advantage of telling the dean of women that their sole aim in attending college is to 'get her man,'" adding that "one mimeographed survey sheet cannot eradicate a nature built up from generation to generation."[19]

Whether or not to marry became a regular focus of the students' literary efforts, as the following poems by Mary Moore Davis from *Letters* reveal:

Spinsterhood

I am a book of one volume,
Pocket edition, and easy to carry around.
Yet I remain quietly upon my dutiful shelf.
But if you care to dip within my neat covers
You will find surprising things-
Great hopes, gay laughter, cruel disappointment,
And all the back and forth, that saws a heart in two.[20]

Misunderstood

I sit with the sick,
I comfort the dying—
Men look at me, and do not see.
They think I'm shy!
They cannot know that long ago
Out of a book a Knight came riding by.

These men about me
Are fat men, thin men;
They sweat in summer time.
They sell socks and ties,
And gasoline and groceries,
And have not words to charm my heart.

When I am dead.
They will write upon my tomb;
"She never know [*sic*] love"—
And will not guess
I loved myself too well to share
My own exquisiteness
With less than Lochinvar.

So I make pretense
And send abroad another self
To gossip with the world.
I sit with the sick,
I comfort the dying,
And men look at me and say:
"Pity, she never married."[21]

Yet if they chose marriage, these same women were unsure about the eventuality of such a union. Kathryn Myrick wrote:

Marriage

And then you asked, "How long will you love me?"
And in a low, choked voice I answered dutifully, "Forever,"

But even as I spoke I knew I lied.
"Forever" is too long a time for love.
Love is sharp and bright,
Love is youth and smiling eyes,
Who hums a haunting little tune
As he strolls along.
He stops only one hour
To gather fragrant blossoms to wear in his golden hair.[22]

Moreover, the women realized that the issue of marriage was not just about love, but about their freedom. Anne Luxon, an unmarried recent UK graduate, expressed these feelings in 1932:

Freedom

My husband has left me.
At last I can
Listen to the rain on the roof,
Or sit up in bed
And watch the moon.
My husband has left me.
I ought to be sad.

Luxon's poem is especially intriguing because nine months later she married.[23]

Whether women chose to marry or remain single, the consequences were substantial and long-lasting. In her study of modern marriage, Christina Simmons concludes that anyone challenging the norms of marriage in the first two decades of the twentieth century faced an entrenched institution. Most believed that marriage "was essential to social order and a civilized nation." At the same time, men knew that traditional marriage "sustained their privileges." But Simmons explains that many, if not most, women found it nearly impossible "to abandon the social honor that marriage bestowed," the protection it provided from sexual harassment as a single woman, and the "access to men's greater economic resources." Ironically, as women gained more economic independence, a man's wife was more often depicted not as a homemaker or mother but as a sexual object supporting a more sexualized masculinity.[24]

144

Even as women's college experiences continued to evolve, their future remained ambiguous. Increasingly, it became evident that the women's organization building, so prominent during an earlier era, held less allure to the women students of the 1930s. An editorial in the *Kentucky Kernel* complained that women devoted less time and attention to their organizations than did the men. Noting that although the women's organizations made excellent plans, the editorial contended that the women were "unable to carry them out because of a lack of enthusiasm." Their lack of interest may perhaps be attributed to their realization of how little control they had. Even the *Kentucky Kernel* editorial writers admitted that the women complained that because of "faculty interference" they were unable to run their organizations as they wished and thus lost interest in them.[25]

Even as they were admonished to become more involved in campus organizations, women students faced a tightening of requirements regarding the extent of their involvement in extracurricular activities. The Dean of Women required women students to keep a listing of all their activities. Points assigned by the dean's office tracked the amount of time each activity required, with the idea of putting a cap on the total time devoted to extracurricular activities. Mary Virginia Hailey, president of Mortar Board, a national senior honor society, defended the new restrictions, arguing that "the point system is devised, not to keep a girl from having honors, but to safeguard her health, to insure the organization in which she is becoming active that she will have time to serve them well, and to divide the activities on the campus among a larger group of women."[26] *Kentucky Kernel* editors supported the new policy, arguing that it illustrated the "sincere interest taken in the welfare of women students," calling it "one of the most sensible pieces of legislation undertaken by a student organization this year." The editorial also noted that the point system enabled Mortar Board to keep a "definite check on the extra-curricular affairs of women which would expose them to injurious effects on their health."[27]

Women's health seemed to be everyone's concern in the early 1930s. Reviewing the history of women's sports on campus, a *Kentucky Kernel* reporter concluded that even though women's basketball had become quite popular, "gradually the game became more and more strenuous until finally . . . it was banned on the grounds that it was

Women's intramural athletics, group photograph (field hockey, basketball, baseball, volleyball, archery, and tennis), 1935. (Louis Edward Nollau nitrate photographic print collection.)

injurious not only to the nervous and physical health of the girls but to the morals of the student body as well." The *Kentucky Kernel* also warned women students about the consequences of having too much fun in college. Dr. Ronald A. Lair, a Colgate College psychology professor, had recently warned that women students who are the "life of the party" were "destined to make a dull wife ten years later." He supposedly based his conclusions on hundreds of experiments with married couples. Lair reported that he discovered that socially active girls would burn out their thyroid gland, thus damaging their personality. The *Kentucky Kernel* noted, "In some quarters, Dr. Lair's statement has met with mild dissent; in others, it is heartily approved; and in still others, it has provoked caustic remarks at its author." Despite such dire health warnings, a vibrant campus social life flourished during the Depression years. The Greek system, while not as strong as it had been the preceding decade, still dominated student culture. And popular culture, including movies and advertisements, promoted the concept of "Betty Coed" and "Joe College."[28]

But an active campus social life could not diminish women students' concerns over their future. The opportunity to work outside the home and pursue financial independence became increasingly problematic. Barbara Harris noted that, "if the 1920s was a slowing down of the entrance of women into the professions, the 1930s spelled disaster. Under the impact of the depression, hostility to female employment reached new levels of intensity." Marriage remained a strong option.[29]

Prior to the 1931 commencement Virginia G. Gildersleeve, dean of Barnard College, spoke at UK and advised the women students, because of the economic depression, not to seek jobs "unless they are forced to earn their living." Gildersleeve contended that graduates with families that could support them or those with "a little money in the bank" should not try to find employment "in times like these." She added that girls in need should take up "honest work" and that rich girls working in an office is a "silly custom."[30]

To Dean Blanding's credit, she pushed forward with career assistance for women students. In September 1932, UK women students received career counseling from faculty and staff and assistance in the selection of suitable life work by members of the faculty and staff appointed by the Dean of Women. Conferences were held with the women students to help them select a career "most suited to their talents."[31]

Of more immediate concern, women students needed part-time work during economic hard times. By the fall of 1932 roughly 38 percent of UK's women students reportedly earned either all, or part, of their living expenses through jobs arranged by the Dean of Women's office. Jobs included waiting tables and office work in the residence halls, living with families and caring for children and helping with housework, and general office work on the campus. Student workers earned nearly $500 a year by means of these part-time jobs, which enabled many to stay in school.[32]

Despite the uncertain economic conditions encountered during the summer of 1932, Dean Blanding received some long-awaited good news. As early as 1915 women leaders in Kentucky had lobbied for a woman's building on the university campus. In that year, the Lexington Alumnae Club had written letters to Federation Clubs throughout the state as a first step toward securing the $100,000 necessary for the construction of such a building. However, the 1915 campaign for a woman's building failed.[33]

In 1932, President McVey wrote to Blanding, informing her that the death of Walter K. Patterson, brother of the former president, "releases the old Patterson house for University uses." He added, "It has occurred to me [that] Miss [Augusta] Roberts [head of the campus YWCA] might have her office in this building and provision made for some of the women's organizations to have their headquarters in it." It is no wonder that this possibility had "occurred" to McVey, since both Dean Blanding and his wife, Frances Jewell McVey, had been lobbying hard for years for just such a building. Renovations on the centrally located former president's home included plans "to remove the fence and take down the carriage shed and chicken house." The house, one of the original three buildings constructed on the campus in 1882, stood between the Main Building and the new library.[34]

Responding to President McVey's news, Dean Blanding wrote back to the vacationing "Dear Frances and Dr. McVey," once again demonstrating the value of her well-placed friend and mentor, Frances. Blanding called her letter a "combination affair," explaining, "Like the laundry you will each have to pick out what belongs to you." Obviously, Blanding wanted both Frances and Frank to read her reaction to the exciting news regarding the Patterson home.[35]

Following an inspection of the Patterson House, Blanding reported that she was "bubbling over with plans for a woman's building. I hear that J. C. [Professor J. Catron Jones] has all but established a faculty club there so I am getting my word in before he has a chance." Blanding agreed with McVey's suggestion to locate the office of Augusta Roberts, secretary of the YWCA, in the building so she "could keep an eye on things during the mornings and afternoons." The building would be especially important to the "town girls" who comprised over half of the women students. Blanding's plans included putting a "gas plate" in the kitchen so that "town girls could use it for preparing lunches and committees could have tea if they met in the late afternoon." Moreover, one room would be "set aside for the convenience of those girls who wish to rest between classes," with cots being provided. Blanding considered this "a valuable use to those women students who commute from nearby towns, and have no place in town to spend their leisure hours." Women's organizations could be housed in the upstairs rooms.[36]

Blanding estimated it would cost $300 to refurbish the old house for the women's use and informed McVey that the Women's Student Government budget could cover the renovation costs. Blanding thought that "it would be nice for the women students to feel that they had shared in getting the place ready." Both the Mortar Board and the University Woman's Club contributed funds for furnishing the building.[37]

The Board of Trustees gave official approval for conversion of the Patterson home into a Woman's Building at its September 1932 meeting. President McVey appointed a committee of faculty women, faculty spouses, and women students to supervise and made Lillian Lindenberger, former director of Smith Hall, the house director. UK student Charlotte Coffman credited Dean Blanding's "persistent work" for "realizing the dream" of a Woman's Building. Three large rooms on each of two floors provided meeting space, and women students were encouraged to use an "attractive rest room" on the second floor during their leisure time. Both Sarah Blanding and Frances Jewell McVey stood in the receiving line as more than four hundred guests attended a tea and reception at the formal opening of the Women's Building in April 1933. The house quickly became a popular gathering place, especially for those women living off campus and those who were not sorority members.[38]

In fact, during the 1930s a majority of UK women students lived off campus in approved housing. In 1932–1933, for example, 74 percent of the women students made alternative living arrangements beyond the campus. The establishment of the Woman's Building provided for nonresident students the first real space they could call their own on the campus since the demise of Lucy Blackburn's "study hall" for women years earlier. As a former "townie" herself, Blanding understood the value of the new space and reported that the Woman's Building director had "made a real place for herself in the hearts of the students, both men and women." She added that the director's "ability to see the ways in which women may be developed, has been a source of satisfaction to me. The social program with its teas and open houses has served a group of students who might not otherwise have been provided for."[39]

Having helped secure the long-coveted physical space on the central campus, Dean Blanding continued her efforts to inspire students toward better personal development and citizenship. Meeting with the Women's Self-Government Association in January 1933, Blanding

Women students on the steps of the Patterson House, circa 1935. (Louis Edward Nollau nitrate photographic print collection.)

emphasized the importance of developing leadership skills among women college students. But the code of women's behavior remained elusive. Following nineteen-year-old Mary Alice Palmer's coronation as queen of the junior prom in the spring of 1933, the *Kentucky Kernel* decreed that her election was "a lesson" for the boys "who like their girls modern and risqué" because the new queen "doesn't smoke. But don't labor under the impression that she is old-fashioned. Oh no! For Mary Alice has a funny way of handling sarcasm that makes a fellow think two or three times before talking out of turn."[40]

The following fall, women students organized a Young Women's Democratic Club, which would "work together" with the also newly organized men's counterpart. One of their first meetings was promoted as "officially a smoker." The *Kentucky Kernel* reported, "Not only is the idea of women in politics comparatively new, but also that of a smoker being opened to them presented a novel idea."[41]

The students' seemingly new interest in politics, especially Democratic politics, came as no surprise. Franklin Roosevelt's New Deal policies reached down into the colleges and universities to create much-needed employment opportunities for students. By February 1934, 233 students were on the Civil Works Administration payroll by February 1934. Under the program, 68 women worked in various departments on campus earning thirty cents an hour, for an average monthly wage of $15.[42]

Dean Blanding proclaimed 1933–1934 her most "strenuous" year since 1925, citing the large number of students that arrived at the university "without adequate means of support." She understood that women bore the brunt of the economic hard times, as there were "always fewer work opportunities for college women than for men." Particularly troubling to Blanding, during the fall semester in 1933 the Civil Works Program provided additional jobs for men students but no increase for women. However, Assistant Dean Sarah Holmes directed part-time employment for the women and obtained part-time positions for seventy women students, which helped the situation. Still, the positions held by the women all tended to be historically "women's" type of work. Of the seventy women in these jobs, seventeen were "mother's helpers," seven worked as clerks in stores, nine did secretarial work, and eight cared for children. During the 1934 spring semester an additional seventy-eight women received jobs under the Federal Emergency Relief Act. By 1937 over seven hundred UK students were employed through the National Youth Administration program, with a total payroll that year of over $72,000 for both women and men students.[43]

Additional measures assisted women students with unmet financial needs. Statie Erikson and Anita Burnman of the Department of Home Economics organized the Shelby House in 1934 "as a means of lowering college expenses for former 4-H club girls." The house, named for the state's first governor, who built it for his daughter, stood at 609 Maxwelton Court and accommodated up to twenty women students chosen on the basis of "scholarship, leadership, and outstanding service to their community." They kept living expenses low by sharing the housework and household expenses. Each resident paid roughly $13.50 per month. Sarah Blanding actively promoted the cooperative house concept and persuaded the university administration to establish three additional houses during the 1930s.[44]

Even with federal aid and creative living arrangements, Dean Blanding worried about possible declines in women's enrollment. She knew

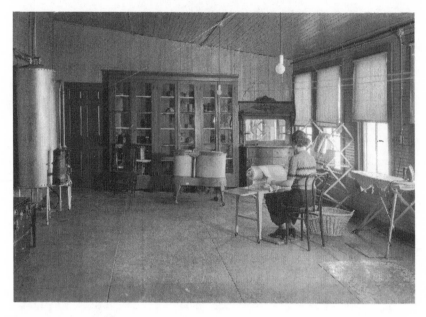

Laundry at the Shelby House, circa 1934. (Louis Edward Nollau nitrate photographic print collection.)

that during difficult economic times families generally gave sons preference over daughters when it came to a college education. Moreover,
Blanding believed that families were more likely to allow their sons to
leave for college with an insufficient means of support than they were
their daughters. Blanding's enrollment fears never materialized, as the
number of women students rose slowly through the remainder of the
decade. Still, if Blanding's suspicions were correct, then even more
women would have attended the university during the 1930s had it
been economically possible.[45]

In addition to attempting to assure that women students had
enough funds to remain in school, Sarah Blanding and other university
administrators came to believe that the university had a responsibility in
regard to women's and men's social and personal relations, beyond
merely keeping them apart as much as possible. Blanding not only continued a program of instructing women in social issues but also brought
in speakers to discuss such topics. In November 1934, the YWCA and
the Dean of Women's office sponsored a campus visit by Mildred Mor-

gan from the University of Iowa, whose specialty was "men's and women's relations." Dean Blanding noted that "we sometimes lose sight of the fact that many of our students have never had scientific sex education, that they are anxious for it and, yet do not know where to get it." She stressed that sex education on the campus could do "a great deal of good particularly with the students who have come from small schools in rural communities where sex education is not given at all." Morgan also held strong views about women working outside the home, noting that such work "gives a sense of satisfaction and achievement apart from . . . directing the lives of your children." She added that "combining home life with other interests gives a woman a sense of living in the outside world."[46]

During the 1935 spring semester, Dean of Men T. T. Jones and Blanding instituted Wednesday night dances. Blanding reported that the dances attempted "to reduce the cost of social life for our young people (a boy who takes a girl to the movies cannot do so for less than a dollar) and to have recreation that is properly supervised." The two deans deemed the dances to be "a great success" both socially and financially, as the university had "accumulated" nearly $800 profit.[47]

Mary Lee Collins's employment in 1935 as a full-time "social director" for the women's residence halls also reflected the expanding role of the university in social relations. Collins monitored activities within the resident halls, handled out-of-town permissions, kept the hall register, and worked closely with the Women's Student Government Association "in the administration of student affairs."[48]

Blanding understood that much of her influence on the campus as dean of women came by way of her close personal relationship with Frances and Frank McVey. In closing her 1935 Annual Report, Blanding offered "an expression of gratitude" to President McVey for the "understanding way" in which he dealt with problems that came before him. She added that UK's women students were "particularly fortunate" to have a president "who sees the University in terms of the women students as well as the men."[49]

Meanwhile, Frances Jewell McVey seemed to look out for everyone. For example, Clifford Amos arrived on campus from Pike County, Kentucky, in the middle of the Great Depression. A first-generation college student, he had grown up in a coal camp and arrived at UK with no more than a few dollars in his pocket. Clifford found a job waiting tables and took on a paper route, among various other part-time jobs. He remembered working up to 75 hours a week as a student just to survive.

One November afternoon in 1938, while walking along Limestone Street near the campus, Clifford fainted on the sidewalk, a result of hunger and exhaustion. Frances Jewell McVey heard about Clifford's misfortune and immediately sent word for Clifford to meet with her at Maxwell Place. After some conversation, McVey offered Clifford a place to live on the second floor of the garage in back of Maxwell Place to save money. Three other boys already lived there. Clifford's only payment for his room was to do a few chores each month.

Clifford lived in that garage until he graduated. He later recalled that "Mrs. McVey saved my life. I was too young to fully appreciate what she had done. I was just trying to survive." He fondly remembered that McVey would often walk out to the garage and ask, "Clifford, have you eaten yet?" She would then invite him into the Maxwell Place kitchen for a meal. Clifford admitted, "There I was just a little mountain boy, who didn't know straight up! Ms. McVey always asked me how school was going and if there was anything else she could do to help me. She was a leader without personal ambition. She was always there to help those in need and never seemed to be in a hurry. She was as down to earth as anyone I ever knew."[50]

The economic difficulties, the large number of students working, and the lack of extra spending money at least gave the impression that the Depression-era students were more serious and more responsible than their predecessors. A *Kentucky Kernel* editorial boldly labeled their times the "Progressive Thirties." Recalling the "gay nineties" and the "gay twenties," when money, fraternities, and jobs were plentiful, the writer noted that:

Changing values in collegiate life were inevitable. A spirit of democracy and cooperative living, a more democratic and inexpensive social life as exemplified by our Wednesday night dances on this campus, and the Student Union idea, all received a new impetus. The stress shifted from social and fraternal values to open competition in more intellectual pursuits. Scholarship has been given a new impetus. That the average boy and girl have brought these changes about is particularly encouraging.[51]

Sororities felt the stress not only of changing economics and politics, but also of the ever-watchful eye of Dean Blanding. The dean made clear her dissatisfaction with the sororities' own attempts to control student public behavior. Appearing before the Panhellenic Association in October 1935, Dean Blanding, the former president of her sorority, warned that if activities that brought public criticism did not cease, she might recommend that all sororities be abolished on the university campus. This statement, made by the former star basketball captain who helped abolish women's basketball, could not have been considered an idle threat.[52]

But even as Dean Blanding continued to emphasize rules regulating student behavior, the "serious" students of the 1930s demanded more freedom. In a scathing editorial entitled "Rules, Rules, Rules," the *Kentucky Kernel* questioned the need for the twenty-three-page booklet of women's rules produced by the Woman's Self-Government Association. The editorial assailed such rules as too numerous and unenforceable. It cited as an example a rule that radios must be silenced by 11:00 p.m., even though another rule already prohibited the playing of radios loud enough to be heard outside the room. The editorial also questioned why lights must be out by 11:00 p.m. for freshmen and by midnight for upperclassmen. It also wondered why a rule prohibited bathing after 11:00 p.m. The editorial noted that "the past decade has witnessed the passing of a large number of rules and regulations with regard to college life; students and faculty alike have come more and more to feel that the student should be given more responsibility in taking care of himself in order that college may be a training ground for life." It concluded, "The *Kernel* does not advocate the abolishment of all rules regarding life of women students at the University; it does feel, however, that worthwhile revisions of the present rules could be made and more liberal attitudes taken on a number of questions."[53]

A subsequent editorial addressed the women's curfew. Arguing it was time to abandon the "horse and buggy era," the editors wrote, "The time of vigorous discipline has passed; college now stands as a training ground for American youth in preparation for a greater college—the

Men and women socializing in the common area of Patterson Hall, 1934. (Louis Edward Nollau nitrate photographic print collection.)

school of life. The modern girl deserves and needs opportunities to prove her ability to properly care for herself." But it remained unclear what the co-ed of the mid-1930s had become. Frances Smith, writing in the *Kernel* as a "typical co-ed" on the UK campus, offered her impression:

> Although not a raving beauty, this typical co-ed is vivacious, sensible, friendly, and can lay a fair claim to what is known as "cute." She takes a great interest in the social part of college life, but is not ignorant to the fact that cultural and intellectual opportunities are knocking at her door and that she must take advantage of them. She usually dashes about the campus hatless, is always well-groomed and properly dressed. Her lipstick is vivid. Her rouge is subdued and her nails flaming or otherwise, just as she pleases. She loves dances whether formal or informal.[54]

By the end of the 1936–1937 academic year Dean Blanding reported her satisfaction with the operation of the Dean of Women's office. It had developed intricate systems for tracking every piece of information about each woman student. In her 1937 Annual Report, Blanding explained, "We keep a cumulative record of each woman student with her picture. This gives us an account of her family, test scores, scholastic achievement, health record, vocational preference, extra-curricular program, loans, money-making activities, personality ratings (made in conference with several people who know her), and various other items which we consider important."[55]

Blanding concluded that she had capable assistants, that the job program worked, and that the resident halls functioned in an orderly manner. However, she remained "concerned and worried" at the apparent increase in the amount of drinking by women students. Blanding made a distinction between social drinking and drunkenness:

When I say drinking, I do not necessarily mean intoxication, although there have been several cases of this which have come to my attention. I mean more drinking in the sense of cocktails and beer. It is difficult to know what attitude to take in this matter. When a student has cocktails at home, when her parents serve them as a matter of course, the student is likely to accept them as the normal and natural thing. It is difficult for her to see the insidious danger of this practice and for her, a cocktail at Canary Cottage is quite within bounds. I have tried to use my best judgment in this matter and have dealt with each case individually as it has come up.[56]

The mid-1930s on the UK campus witnessed a notable increase in negative comments regarding women in nearly all student publications. Student newspaper columnist Ralph E. Johnson, a self-described contrarian, argued at length against the "modern" woman. Other times, cartoons or feature stories depicted women as naive, fickle, or simply unintelligent. This trend paralleled the university's increasing fascination with the antebellum South and a glorification of the Civil War. This newfound interest in the Confederacy may have resulted in part from the popularity of Margaret Mitchell's 1936 novel *Gone with the Wind,* one of the best-selling books of all time. John Marsh, Mitchell's spouse, was a graduate of UK, and the connection was widely publicized on

Herb Hillenmeyer and Leigh Brown at the popular college spot, Canary Cottage, in downtown Lexington. (*Kentuckian*, 1939.)

campus and across the state. The turn toward myths of the Old South at UK may have also reflected the same tendencies in the larger culture in Kentucky.[57]

As the students' fascination with all things southern increased, so did their fascination with race. *Kentucky Kernel* writers increasingly sought out longtime African American UK employees, including Pierre Whiting, and wrote feature stories, which usually quoted the workers in dialect, stressing the employee's lifelong dedication to the institution. Whiting served nearly six decades as a university custodian. As a young man in 1881 he carried water and mortar during the construction of UK's original buildings. Dean Blanding, despite being a self-proclaimed "liberal" on the question of race, resisted employing African Americans in the women's dormitory food services. However, in the mid-1930s she succumbed to pressure to replace "student waitresses by negro [*sic*] girls." Blanding justified the change because it allowed students to work on other campus projects while providing jobs to eighteen African American women "who might not have found employment otherwise." Blanding found the new arrangement to be economical and "much more satisfactory."[58]

In this photograph taken at the Senior Breakfast Alumni Tea on May 31, 1934, African American servers are shown in the first row and yard workers on the truck. (Louis Edward Nollau nitrate photographic print collection.)

An effort to remodel the sitting room in Patterson Hall to resemble an antebellum parlor reflected the increasing interest in the Old South. The UK athletic teams had joined the Southern Conference over a decade earlier. Now the entire university seemed poised to become southern. UK's "new" southern woman became increasingly utilized by local merchants to sell clothes, shoes, and other merchandise. UK women began appearing in newspaper advertisements endorsing particular stores, styles, and items of clothing. Clare Piggot appeared in an advertisement for the Mitchell, Baker & Smith Company in 1938. Offering "a word of advice" for her fellow women students about "co-ediquette," Piggot suggested, "Giggle and snicker on the slightest provocation. This lends charm and glamour to the young college woman and is quite an asset in 'getting over.'"[59]

Nevertheless, UK women continued to do outstanding academic work. When Phi Beta Kappa initiated new pledges in November 1936, women comprised seven of the nine initiates. But social and student leadership remained elusive to women. The student council continued to be made up entirely of men appointed by President McVey. The president selected one student from each college and the graduate school from three nominees chosen by the dean of each college.[60]

The Association of Women Students (AWS) continued to be active during the 1930s, but it, too, gave women contradictory messages. The organization issued a rule in the fall of 1937 stating that "sophomore women with a standing of 2 or over for the past semester" were allowed "one date night a week, juniors, two nights a week, seniors, three nights a week and students with a standing of 3 every night out." Academic excellence obviously had its social rewards, at least according to the women leaders. The AWS that semester sponsored six lectures on the "Preparation of the Coed for Marriage" and also offered a "charm school for all girls who might be interested."[61]

As the number of women attending and wishing to attend the university increased during the late 1930s, housing once again became critical. Of the 3,000 students at the university in 1938, a third were forced to reside off campus. Patterson and Boyd Halls could accommodate only 220 women, and before the opening of the fall 1938 semester 50 women learned that no dorm rooms awaited them. According to Assistant Dean of Women Sarah Holmes, roughly 80 women were turned away because of inadequate housing arrangements.[62]

During her entire career at UK, Sarah Holmes criticized the inadequate housing for women students. At one point she sarcastically noted that horses in Central Kentucky could expect better housing than UK's women students. But the housing shortage affected men as well. The three men's dorms housed 260 men, and in the fall of 1938, 60 men were on a waiting list with possibly 100 turned away. However, being turned away as a man meant something much different from what it meant for a woman, in that men were not required to live in "approved" off-campus housing. Blanding pushed for more dormitories because she knew that a shortage of university housing kept women from attending the university. Moreover, she believed that dormitories offered more control over the women students.[63]

As a new Student Union Building neared completion in the spring of 1938, the Woman's Building was on its way to becoming a relic. Since it first became available, the male-dominated faculty viewed the former

Sarah Blanding, at left, and Sarah Holmes, 1939. (Lafayette Studios
photographs.)

Patterson Home and current Woman's Building as the perfect location for a faculty club, and the Board of Trustees apparently agreed. The board's all-male Executive Committee surveyed the building and proposed to make alterations, including "a large dance floor, billiard room and a library–reading room on the first floor; a card room, ladies lounge, game room, and a committee room on the second." The irony of the building's being transformed from a space totally devoted to women's activities to a space that would include a "ladies lounge" typifies the type of evolution occurring on the campus in regard to women. Women were beginning to abandon their campaign for separate women's spaces or even a separate women's culture.[64]

The long-coveted women's space on campus was abandoned in favor of a "co-ed" union. The new student union became emblematic of the growth of modern student culture. But even though Dean Blanding had spent the better part of fifteen years monitoring the rise of the new student culture, she still did not see her position as part of that change. When asked if she would be moving the Dean of Women's office into the new student union, Blanding replied, "As much as I need larger quarters, I could not consider getting far away from the business office, the registrar's office, and that of the Dean of Men." She added that she hoped "that in the not too distant future, we can have a building where all student services will be centered." Blanding's position and call for a student services building represented the rise of administrative culture as clearly as the student union represented the evolution of modern student culture. They had grown so far apart that the thought of separate student and administrative spaces seemed quite normal by the end of the 1930s.[65]

Moreover, the "sex problem" that had surfaced during the previous decade lingered. The administration announced a special convocation to discuss "Sex Problems of Youth." The featured speaker, Dr. Roy A. Burkhart, pastor of the First Community Church in Columbus, Ohio, was promoted as "an authority on sex hygiene." The students were also informed that the pastor would hold a special group interview for "steady daters."[66]

After nearly sixty years on the UK campus, women still faced inequities and ambiguities but continued to push on various fronts for greater equality. The economic depression of the 1930s highlighted their marginal economic base and the precarious foundation on which their later lives and careers might be built. While growing numbers of women attended UK, their futures were never more unsettled.

By the end of the 1930s UK, like the nation itself, seemed poised for change in a turbulent world. War in Europe and the Far East spawned uncertainty. If the economic instability of the previous decade had shaken the foundation of women's relative position in Kentucky higher education, world war would dramatically impact the status of women at the University of Kentucky.

5

World War II and the Illusion of Equality

"Sons of Kentucky have always been expert judges of feminine pulchritude" read a 1939 press release from the University of Kentucky (UK) Public Relations Office. Reviewing feature sections of UK yearbooks for the previous twenty years, the staff sought to determine if blondes or brunettes had been more popular on campus. While presenting no definitive conclusion, the story was distributed statewide to media outlets. A *Kentucky Kernel* columnist writing in 1941 asked what an upperclassman required of a first-year college woman. Fred Hill listed, "fidelity, beauty, more fidelity, more fidelity and intelligence—or rather lack of it." He suggested that the women "learn to converse easily, using all the college slang you know. Don't, above all things, try to be intellectual." Nearly seven decades after entering the University of Kentucky, women students still faced a culture that stereotyped them and questioned their seriousness as students. Moreover, their physical attributes could still be publicly debated. But life for all UK students, women and men, was about to become deadly serious and dramatically changed. Student Fred Hill soon became Lieutenant Hill and was killed in action on November 8, 1942, in the American forces invasion of North Africa.[1]

Both contemporary observers and later historians attempted to identify and explain the influences that altered the social fabric of the United States and the traditional expectations of women during the World War II years. In more recent studies, historians acknowledge that less attention has been given to the experiences of women on college campuses during the war than to women generally. Women's experiences at UK during the war years mirrored the experiences of white, middle- to upper-class American women at other universities. In contrast to previous decades, the war years offered women students expanded opportunities for employment in business and industry, and offered additional opportunities to teach at the college and university level. Not since the end of World War I had possibilities for women's employment been so promising. Nontraditional jobs and educational opportunities became available as never before, and social life changed dramatically. But would these changes and opportunities be experienced only for the duration of war, or would American higher education for women be changed permanently?[2]

Frances and Frank McVey approached the summer of 1940 with great anticipation as they planned for their retirement. Frank McVey's twenty-three-year tenure as president of the University of Kentucky, bounded by two world wars and spanning the worst economic depression in the history of the United States, received high praise from most observers. President McVey delivered the commencement address to the 1940 graduates at Stoll Field during a late spring rain. Frances Jewell McVey, an advocate for women at UK since 1916, received an honorary doctorate of letters in recognition of her long service to the university, and a women's residence hall was named in her honor.[3]

The UK Board of Trustees named agriculture dean and McVey protégé Thomas Poe Cooper acting president for the 1940–1941 academic year. Even though Cooper had broad support on campus for the permanent position, the university's board made a controversial choice in choosing Herman Lee Donovan to become UK's fourth president. Donovan, a Mason County, Kentucky, native, received his initial higher education as part of the inaugural class to attend Western State Normal School in Bowling Green, Kentucky. He later received his BA from UK in 1914. Donovan taught school in Kentucky communities before earning a master's degree from Columbia Teachers College in 1920 and a doctorate from Peabody College in 1925. He became president of Eastern State Teachers College in Richmond, Kentucky, in 1928 after serving as that institution's Dean of Faculty.[4]

Donovan and his wife, Nell Stuart Donovan, arrived at UK with dramatically different backgrounds, experiences, and personalities than the McVeys. No one thought of Herman Donovan as a scholar. His hobbies were raising registered Hereford cattle and collecting books about the US Constitution. Nell Donovan would find it impossible to move out from under the long shadow of Frances Jewell McVey's tenure at Maxwell Place. A native of Pembroke in western Kentucky, Nell Donovan was considered "soft-spoken." The Donovans had no children of their own but always had one or more students live with them each year, both during their time at Eastern and until they retired from UK. The Donovans also continued the tradition of entertaining at Maxwell Place, including hosting breakfasts and teas for the students and faculty.[5]

Donovan's appointment to UK's presidency in 1940 initially provoked harsh criticism from many of the faculty, who considered him unsuited to guide the state's flagship university. Moreover McVey, by recruiting faculty from a national pool of candidates, had built a faculty that understood the possibilities for UK's future. Many Donovan critics believed that Governor Keen Johnson, a 1922 UK graduate who as governor also served as chair of the UK Board, pushed Donovan's appointment through only so he could name his good friend, William Francis O'Donnell, Eastern's president following Donovan's departure. Some who protested Donovan's appointment disliked the political influence suspected in Donovan's appointment. Probably of more concern to the students was that the teacher's college president came with a reputation for strict student behavior, especially regarding relations between the sexes. At Eastern, he allegedly used "Donovan sticks," rulers that measured the space that should be maintained between men and women as they walked across the campus. Until 1935 Donovan enforced a rule at Eastern that required students to turn out their lights by 9:30 p.m. and ordered that "no one should be permitted to sit in dark or shadowed spots on the campus after it gets dark." Certainly, such an attitude did not fit with the modern ideas regarding student culture at the state university.[6]

The appointment of Donovan upset no faculty member more than Sarah Gibson Blanding, Dean of Women since 1923 and professor of Political Science. Perhaps no new president could have met her high expectations, given Blanding's close relationship with the McVeys. Regardless, the appointment of the meek-looking schoolman from a teacher's college made it difficult, if not impossible, for Blanding to conceal her disappointment, a sentiment she expressed freely.

During her seventeen-year tenure at UK, Blanding had received many overtures from other colleges and universities. Prominent in national deans of women professional associations, she had built a national reputation as an able administrator. In 1940, for example, Bryn Mawr College asked Blanding to apply for its presidency. Unlike her mentor Frances Jewell McVey, she had not come from an elite eastern woman's college. Blanding wrote to President McVey, "I am not losing sleep over this job but I shall take a good deal of pleasure in seeing how far a graduate of a state university can get with the committee." Even with President McVey's full support, Blanding was not surprised when the Bryn Mawr search committee passed on her application. In her study of deans of women Carolyn Bashaw notes that, like some of her contemporaries, Blanding faced economic challenges during her youth and "saw herself as an outsider among academic women." Nevertheless, she was able to "fashion a career of substantial achievement." Still, it shocked some friends and colleagues at UK when Blanding accepted an appointment at Cornell University as that university's first dean of home economics in 1941.[7]

Sarah Bennett Holmes, Blanding's loyal and conscientious assistant since 1929, seemed the logical successor. Following the death of her husband in 1924, Holmes had raised four children, finished her college degree, and served with distinction under Dean Blanding. However, she only completed a graduate degree from UK in 1939 and did not hold a faculty appointment. After some initial hesitation, President Donovan appointed Holmes Acting Dean in 1941, and a year later Dean of Women.[8]

Perhaps to add greater academic influence to the Dean of Women's office, Donovan also named Jane Haselden as Assistant Dean of Women. Haselden, a Lancaster, Kentucky, native, graduated from Transylvania University in 1926 with a degree in French. As a graduation present her parents sent Haselden to study in Paris for a year. Following her return to the United States she became a teacher, first in Beattyville, Kentucky, and subsequently in her hometown of Lancaster. While in Beattyville, Haselden achieved some notoriety for coaching the boys' basketball team at the local high school. During summers Haselden worked toward a master's degree at Columbia University, a goal she achieved in 1932. After serving as Dean of Women at both Transylvania University and Murray State Teachers College in western Kentucky, Haselden completed a PhD in Psychology at UK.[9]

167

Jane Haselden in her office, circa 1950. (UK portrait print collection.)

Along with her doctorate, Haselden also brought a pilot's license to her new position. She and her friend Anna Mayrell Johnson, also an aviator and educator, jointly owned an airplane and were known to rush out to the local airport during their lunch breaks to fly their plane over Lexington. Once Haselden flew her plane over Stoll Field during a football game between Kentucky and Alabama. Haselden and Johnson actively participated in the Kentucky chapter of the Ninety-Nines, an international organization of women pilots affiliated with the National Aeronautic Association in Washington, DC. Haselden recalled that as the war began "casual flying" came to an end because the war changed things for everyone. Johnson, who had earned her undergraduate degree from Murray State University and a master's degree from UK in 1932, joined the Navy in 1943 and served as a Navy pilot during the war. After the war, she joined the political science faculty at Murray State University.[10]

One of the first and most obvious challenges facing Donovan, Holmes, Haselden, and the university generally involved changing campus demographics. Even before the United States officially entered the war following Pearl Harbor, a decrease in enrollment among both men and women students had already begun. In 1940, women comprised roughly 40 percent of the college students in the United States; they did so at the University of Kentucky as well.

The 2,522 women students on campus in 1940 represented the largest number of women students in UK's history. Nevertheless, women's status remained uncertain even as more women nationally were attending college and obtaining degrees. Seven decades earlier most women entered UK to become teachers. By 1940, a fifth of women students at UK still followed that path. By comparison, only 5 percent of the male students sought to become teachers. The feminization of teaching had become entrenched at UK, as it had across the United States.[11]

With the United States's official entry into the war in December 1941, UK immediately experienced a decrease in enrollment. The *Kentucky Kernel* in February 1942 reported that UK's enrollment was the smallest in seven years and that the 500 fewer students would cost the university $25,000. It was the smallest enrollment since the class of 1935, and officials worried not only about a loss of revenue, but whether the university could even remain open during the war. The colleges of law, engineering, commerce, and agriculture, and the graduate school, all areas that were still made up primarily of men, sustained the most striking enrollment losses. Each of these areas would lose roughly two-thirds of its students during the war. The demographics of the campus changed dramatically, and university administrators found it increasingly necessary to initiate programs and policies to keep its women students enrolled while working to attract military training programs to the campus.[12]

In his 1942 Annual Report, President Donovan noted that because of the war, it had become necessary for women students to play a larger role in the academic life of the university and the entire nation. Writing that "liberal education must find recruits among the women," he concluded that "women have the opportunity to preserve our culture." It now seemed that during the war women not only would have more opportunities in the academic activities of the university, but also must take those obligations on as their patriotic duty.[13]

The all-women class of 1942 in the College of Agriculture and Home Economics. (Louis Edward Nollau F series photographic print collection.)

Even as women students adjusted to wartime expectations and a rapidly changing campus, university officials began planning to educate and train over one thousand soldiers in the Army Specialized Training Program (ASTP). The military required special academic programs and housing, so UK male administrators opted to displace the women from their dorms so the soldiers could move in. Writing to Frances Jewell McVey, who had retired from UK three years earlier, Dean Holmes said she had made "one last plea" to stop the new housing policy but her efforts were "to no avail." Noting that "the only students we can expect next year are women," she asked rhetorically, "How can we expect them to come if they have no place in which to live?"[14]

Trying to avert any further decrease in women's enrollment, UK issued a press release in the fall of 1943 offering prospective women students "special consideration" in both housing and programs of study. Administrators promoted "specialized fields" for women, such as medical technology, institutional management, library science, journalism, secretarial training, and general business. To assure concerned parents that the presence of soldiers on campus and the unorthodox housing arrangements would be no threat to their daughters, the release promised, "The same type of careful supervision which has always been in force at the university, and the same rules that apply to regular residence halls, will be enforced in the auxiliary living quarters under the direction of resident house mothers."[15]

The "auxiliary living quarters" turned out to be fraternity houses vacated while the men were away in the military. A house mother lived in each house that was turned over for the use of women students; the women received their meals at Boyd Hall, the one remaining women's dormitory on campus. Holmes noted, "The boys seem to think that their sacred property has been desecrated but for the first time in years the places have been cleaned up." Living in the fraternity houses required some sacrifice on the part of the women. Dean Haselden recalled that women students living in the fraternity houses experienced crowded conditions, as three or four women generally shared rooms designed for two people. In regard to the relationship between her women students and the soldiers on campus, Holmes expressed little concern, because the roughly 1,200 men were "under strict military supervision, giving them little free time except Saturday evenings and Sundays."[16]

UK women students in their dorm room, November 22, 1944. One is writing a letter to her boyfriend in the military. (Lafayette Studios photographs.)

Some of the women students remembered the war years differently. Betty Tevis lived in Boyd Hall in the fall of 1943. Her dormitory was connected by a second story enclosed walkway to Patterson Hall, one of the former women's dormitories assigned to the soldiers. She recalled that "the university had built barriers, wooden barriers, plywood everywhere, to separate them [the soldiers] from us. But we talked with them, back and forth, and got to know them, and went out with them." According to Tevis, the soldiers offered the best prospects for dates. She recalled the lyrics of a popular song at the time, "The best are in the Army, the rest will never harm me."[17]

After a "very sad time" of adjusting to the initial loss of men students, Lillian Terry recalled that after the military men arrived, the "campus blossomed out" and "every girl had anywhere from five to eight dates" and "You could choose anything you wanted to. Oh, good gracious!" For example, she and a friend would go to the Student Center to play chess and in no time "we'd be surrounded with, you know, maybe fifty GIs. You walked away with the handsomest, or the most interest-

UK students holding an item representing their academic area, circa 1940. The only woman is holding a rolling pin. (Louis Edward Nollau F series photographic print collection.)

ing, or whatever. It was sort of like heaven on earth to a girl who hadn't had that many dates up until then."[18]

The 1943 *Kentuckian* reflected the changing perceptions of women on the campus. Dedicated to "the women of today" who "have accepted the challenge of a war world by fighting on the home front in myriad ways," the yearbook included numerous silhouettes of women and men on its inside cover, with the women pictured twice the size of the men. On the title page a woman figure holds the seal of the university on her shoulders.[19]

But many on campus still had difficulty accepting any nontraditional roles for women. Student columnist Bob Ammons wrote, "All this furor about the women and the war, anyway, is rather pointless. The last word was said several years ago by a writer on the *Daily Princetonian,* who commented with startling profundity, 'Women is women is women is women . . . and nothing can be done about it.'"[20]

Student attempts at humor notwithstanding, views expressed by faculty and administrators proved more disconcerting. The student personnel office reported in 1944 that in comparison with previous classes the current class included "a larger number of ill-prepared entering students," especially among the women. Martin M. White, Assistant Dean of Arts and Sciences, concurred, noting that "more lower ability girls are coming to the university." He speculated that the decline in women students' academic standing resulted from "the disappearance of the male students from the campus," causing "superior girls" to go "in greater numbers to private schools because of the absence of regular civilian men." White cited several studies that suggested that girls do better work when boys are present. Obviously, the role of the women students continued to be challenged, whether in the area of housing, status, or academic ability.[21]

Nevertheless, Dean Holmes sought to keep the women students' activities central to the war effort. She reported in 1942 that, "impressed with the urgency of the all-out war against Axis forces and the whole Fascist degradation of life," President Donovan had appointed a faculty committee to suggest ways women could best aid in war work. The fifteen-person committee, chaired by Holmes, soon issued its report. According to Holmes, "Immediately first aid courses and war stamp sales largely supplanted golf and dances and women with PhD degrees were heard to brag of their ability in mechanics."[22]

The student newspaper chronicled the activities of women in the war effort under the headline "They Can't Shoulder a Gun but UK Girls Do Their Bit." House meetings, held throughout the campus, sought to make women students "more conscious of the effect that their thrift and industry" could have in the war effort. Taking as their motto "Every little bit helps," women signed up for Red Cross training, with classes offered on surgical dressing, home nursing, and other related topics. Forty-five women students took a home nursing course, and other similar classes filled quickly as the women students tried "to do their share while the boys are defending democracy."[23]

An article lauding former UK women students serving in the armed forces announced, "Survey Discloses UK Women Have More Courage, Bravado than Men." The article explained, "Joan of Arc had nothing on the UK co-eds. These members of the so-called weaker, daintier, more delicate, sentimental, fragile sex are not running true to their stereotyped form at this University." The conclusions were based on a campus survey conducted by the student newspaper, which found that "men indicated they would avoid the draft as long as possible" while "women indicated by 9–1 that if they were a man under twenty they would be ready to go." A *Kentucky Kernel* editorial probably expressed the mood on campus best when it commended UK women for their part in the war effort by concluding, "The University women are awake to the fact that we are at war. These are confusing days for everyone but the women are reacting admirably."[24]

Examining the war work of UK women, a *Louisville Courier-Journal* reporter observed that they were prepared to "shelve frivolity for the duration" and aid the war effort. Noting the apparent change in women's roles brought on by the war, the female reporter concluded, "The so-called glamour girl of presumably trivial interests has disappeared and in her stead is the 1942 War-Model Co-Ed, an attractive young woman quite able to do a man's job."[25]

Yet concerns lingered regarding the perception of women's activities in the war effort. Despite her positive public pronouncements, Dean Holmes remained disturbed by some women students' apathy toward the war. At one point before war was declared, Holmes had questioned how the students could be "so indifferent to something that touches their lives so deeply. The only reason for this attitude that I can believe is that the students just don't realize that world problems will ever concern them." Later, Holmes reflected that some of the students were "relatively uninformed."[26]

In a talk before the UK women students, Margaret A. Hickey, a Missouri attorney, women's rights advocate, and chair of the Women's Advisory Committee of the National War Manpower Commission, suggested that it was every woman's "obligation to render maximum service to the nation in its hour of peril" and that women students must quickly prepare themselves "for the most essential jobs available." She was disturbed that employers, both in government and industry, still thought of women in terms of women's traditional skills, which greatly underestimated women's potential. But Hickey noted that, these concerns notwithstanding, women college graduates during the war had broader career choices and fewer barriers to employment than any previous generation of American women.[27]

Dean Holmes understood this continuing paradox for women. The war had increased the nation's reliance on women workers, yet many prospective employers still considered women for work in areas using only their "traditional skills." After listening to Hickey's lecture, Holmes wrote, "Our women have a wider choice and few barriers, but there are still many prejudices. It is still 'A man's world.'" Even during these war years with unprecedented possibilities for women, the Dean of Women conceded that women still held an inferior position in the workplace.[28]

Dean Holmes needed to look no further than the university's own faculty for these inequities. Of the 339 instructional staff at UK in 1940–1941, women comprised only 18 percent. Moreover, women made up only 4 percent of the number of full professors at the university and only 10 percent of the associate professors. The percentage of women faculty members would not rise above 18 percent through the war years, and by 1950 the number of women faculty at UK actually decreased to 11 percent.[29]

Changes in the status of women on campus also affected the spouses of male faculty. Several wives held advanced degrees, making them qualified to teach at the university. However, UK policy restricted faculty spouses (who were most often women) from the faculty. Throughout the war years, as academic departments increasingly lost male faculty, President Donovan made special arrangements for faculty spouses and other women in the Lexington community to teach, but only "for the duration of the present emergency."[30]

Lydia Roberts Fischer became one of the first women hired to teach during the war. A Lexington native and a 1929 UK graduate, she also earned a master's in mathematics in 1931 after her marriage. Upon learning of her plans to marry, she recalled that professors in the mathematics department told Fischer, "Well, that [marriage] does you in. You won't get your master's." Fischer responded immediately, "Oh, I think I shall!"—and she did. Still, Fischer had no plans for a career other than "housewife and mother" until she divorced her husband in 1937. As a mother of two small children she knew she must do something "to earn a living," so she enrolled in education classes at the university. Securing a job teaching at Morton Junior High School near the university, Fischer soon learned that she did not enjoy teaching at that level and approached Paul Boyd, Dean of Arts and Sciences, about the possibility of teaching at UK. Boyd offered her a position for the summer teaching ASTP classes on campus. The dean told Fisher, "Of course, you can't be hired permanently without your PhD." For the next seven years, Fischer and her former teacher Elizabeth LeStourgeon taught all the "regular student" mathematics classes during the war while the men faculty in the department taught the ASTP classes.[31]

Fischer never felt discriminated against by the male faculty and administrators until one day, after several years at UK, she learned that men hired to do the same work as she in mathematics made $250 a month as compared to her $150. Without hesitation, she went to Dean Boyd and asked about the discrepancy in the salaries. Boyd responded, "Well, I thought you were just teaching for the love of it anyway." Fisher replied, "the money does help a little bit!" Following her conversation with the dean, Fischer's salary increased to $250 a month, the same as the men.[32]

The relative scarcity of civilian men on campus created new opportunities for women in extracurricular activities. On campuses throughout the country women were moving into leadership positions on student publications and in student government. Nontraditional areas of study in the sciences and engineering programs were also opening to women on an unprecedented scale.[33]

Women at UK made noticeable gains working on the student newspaper. Patricia Snider served as editor of the 1942–1943 Kentucky Kernel. That same year Betty Jane Pugh worked as news editor. The Kentuckian noted, "For the first time in many years a woman editor has occupied the swivel chair in the front office of the Kernel," and "despite the obstacles of war—lack of man-power in the shop, less advertising, and newsprint restriction—the press rolled twice a week."[34]

For the first time in university history, a woman, Betty Tevis, served as sports editor in 1944. She was featured in a Louisville Courier-Journal article as the first woman ever allowed into the men's basketball team dressing room to conduct interviews with the players. However, Tevis recalled that the entire article had been staged by the UK Public Relations Office. She said she went along with it because she did not have "sense enough" to say, "No, I'm not going to let you exploit me this way." She admitted that she never had access to the men's dressing room because that was "unthinkable in those times." Rather, "they just posed me down there" while "a university photographer took the picture" for the press release. Upon learning of the press release Dean Holmes called

Tevis into her office for a conference. Holmes did not appreciate the story and the photograph of Tevis in the men's dressing room. In her defense Tevis told Holmes that it was not her idea and that she "wouldn't think" of going into the men's dressing room.[35]

Also making news, if less sensational, was the fact that women made up the entire business staff of the *Kentucky Kernel*, successfully overcoming the business staff's taboo against women. The following year the women moved into the physical printing operation and "put on working clothes and began to set type and make up the newspaper themselves." Such efforts pleased at least one faculty member. Neil Plummer, head of the Journalism Department, noted that the student publications "staffed almost entirely by women" were "completing another successful year" and that relations between the Department of Journalism and the student executives "continued on a plane of mutual respect and confidence." Plummer seemed pleased to report that "both of the young women who served as editor of the *Kentucky Kernel* in the last year have been elected to membership in Phi Beta Kappa. This is in keeping with the tradition that the editorship of the *Kentucky Kernel* be entrusted to scholarly students."[36]

Patricia Snider, a reporter and later editor of the student newspaper, tracked changes for women students in the student newspaper and featured in one article three women majoring in agriculture. Billy Frances Jackson planned to work on her family's horse farm; Anne Douglas "Doug" McCown hoped to work in a veterinary lab; and Elizabeth McDowell, according to Snider, intended to become "a full-fledged farmer, not merely an ornamental farmette."[37]

Billy Jackson recalled that she majored in agriculture simply because of her interest in horses. She acknowledged being treated differently as a woman in the field, since students of her sex, for example, could be members of the agricultural honorary but were not allowed to participate in its activities. Nevertheless, she did not think that she had been treated unfairly. Upon reflection she described herself and the other women majoring in agriculture as "girls that were not primarily interested in primping and catching a boy." While still an undergraduate, Billy Jackson offered "professional riding instruction" to UK students for $1 per hour though a special contract approved by the Board of Trustees.[38]

Society of Mechanical Engineers, 1944. Margaret Wayne is the only woman. (*Kentuckian*, 1944.)

Snider also reported, "Women just seemingly won't stay put in the limited fields that for years have been considered their social and mental level. For some reason or other they pop up in the most unexpected places." In 1941 Caroline Conant studied engineering while Mary Barton, Elizabeth Gillespie, Barbara Moore, and Helen Stephenson studied law. Martha Koppius majored in physics, and Mary Wiedeman majored in anatomy and physiology. Additionally, six women declared premed majors and three women majored in industrial chemistry.[39]

Women's presence in Engineering increased during the war, and the women students attracted considerable media attention. Under the headline "Hey, This Is Really News, Engineers Have Three Girls," the *Kentucky Kernel* reported in February 1942 that "competition" for the men in Engineering "appeared in the form of Margaret Jane Wayne." Noting that she is "five feet seven" and a "brunette," she "became the third girl to invade the realm of the transit and slide rule." Focused on architectural engineering, when asked about her choice of vocations Wayne "smiled" and "replied in her husky voice" that "I think there is going to be a good field in engineering for women. It's a woman's world now and it would be foolish for us not to take advantage of it." The report concluded by noting, "Her olive skin glowed, her big eyes twinkled, and her engaging smile brightened when she was questioned about having classes with so many of the now scarce males." By the fall of 1944, ten women were enrolled in the College of Engineering.[40]

But even as women received attention for their new roles, the ways in which the media described them demonstrated that the struggle to overcome ingrained prejudices and stereotypes continued. For example, during "Campus Courtesy Week" the newspaper encouraged men to be more thoughtful toward the women students. A poem posted around campus in honor of this new thoughtfulness read: "Boys get up when a girl comes in; whether she's pretty or ugly as sin."[41]

UK also boasted a "Lone Woman Civilian Aeronautics Administration Trainee." Trainee Billy L. Dyer told *Kentucky Kernel* news editor Jim Wooldridge that "any girl would like to fly . . . if she doesn't get rattled and lose her head." Adding that "Miss Dyer isn't just any girl," the article noted that Dyer could "cook, knit, and sew with the best of them," although "that's about as far as her domestic traits go." As the only woman geology major at the university, Dyer found that her classmates called her "Bill" and told her jokes "as though she were one of the boys." Women were often misrepresented in newspaper articles, and Wooldridge may have decided to have what he thought was some fun when he added that Dyer admitted that flying gave her a "ticklish feeling" and that she found learning stalls so much fun that she nearly stalled herself "silly."[42]

In addition to changing academic and training opportunities for women, the war also influenced extracurricular life. Until 1939 separate student government organizations represented women and men students. That year the faculty approved a new Student Government Association (SGA), resulting in the election of twenty-five student representatives from the various colleges. Offices in the new SGA included a president, a men's vice president and a women's vice president. But as the number of male students on campus declined during the war it became necessary to drop the gender distinctions for vice president, and the men's and women's positions were combined.[43]

Spring 1943 witnessed the first real challenge by the women to male domination of student government on campus. Described as "the battle of the sexes," the election featured the Independent Party, which nominated all men for the top posts; and the Constitutionalists, who supported women for the positions. The men won the election again that year even though women students outnumbered the men, proving that a significant number of women on the campus failed to vote or chose to support the status quo in regard to gender on the campus.[44]

Student Union board, 1945, nearly all women. (*Kentuckian,* 1945.)

The university's long-anticipated Student Union building opened in 1938. Historian John Thelin noted that student unions were an acknowledgment by administrators "that the campus was not a cohesive residential entity but rather was characterized by diverse living arrangements, including the arrangement of commuter students." Perhaps even more important, student unions "represented an attempt by college administrators to exert some influence, perhaps control, over the patterns of student life." The push for UK's Student Union building came primarily from members of Omicron Delta Kappa, then a men's leadership fraternity, who began a fund drive to support construction. Some students were dissatisfied with the final plans for the building because it did not include a swimming pool and the ballroom was not as large as expected. In response, President McVey reminded the students of the university's financial condition, noting that UK "could not build the Waldorf-Astoria or the Michigan Union."[45]

By the spring of 1942 the UK faculty approved the formation of a Student Union organization. Initially, the Union's Board of Directors consisted of six men and three women. A month later the constitution was amended so that the board would be comprised of five men and four women, "effective for the duration of the war." By 1945 the university faculty again revised the Student Union constitution to read that "the Board shall consist of nine students with no specification as to the number of men and women elected . . . for the duration of the war." Slowly but surely, barriers to women's involvement in campus activities crumbled, but always only "for the duration."[46]

Even the university marching band did not escape the changes brought on by war, as women for the first time in university history became members of a coed band. *Kentucky Kernel* reporter Casey Goman recalled that in years past only the sponsor elected by the men was allowed in the "Best Band in Dixie." The war years, however, turned the band "predominately feminine from bass drummer to drum major," and they "speed up the tempo, but march at half-step." Goman concluded that the "band had gone coed with a vengeance, all because of the war."[47]

Women students' inclusion in the university band, however, did not come about without concern on the part of the Dean of Women. Dean Holmes wrote to the band director complaining about the hazing of some women members of the band after a basketball game in Louisville. Saying that she appreciated band tradition, Holmes argued, however, that in following tradition, band members had failed to take into consideration "changing personnel," meaning the addition of women musicians. Holmes made clear to the director that the women members should be held to the same "standards of musicianship" while also being given the "consideration due every woman on the campus."[48]

During the war, Dean Holmes remained concerned about not only the actions of the women students, but also the general public's perception of them. In an angry letter to the director of UK public relations, Holmes reacted to a *Louisville Courier-Journal* article that featured women students in glamour poses and wearing swimsuits. Holmes admitted that the article was well written and some of the pictures were interesting, but she could see "no reason" for the photographs featuring student Pat Ochs. Holmes contended that if UK had a swimming pool on campus "it might be logical to take pictures of girls in swimming suits." But UK had no such facility, and Holmes thought that including photographs of women students in swimsuits "violates good taste."[49]

But Holmes was concerned with more than just appearances and "good taste." Throughout the war years she lobbied hard for the interests of the women students and sought to reinstate the type of career counseling for women that had been prevalent during the early years of Dean Blanding's tenure. In October 1944, Holmes requested that university administrators consider adding a vocational counselor to her staff in the Dean of Women's office. She pointed out that while the university had given much consideration and planning to the vocational needs of the returning men veterans, little had been planned for postwar women students, and "women face an even greater problem of vocational adjustment than men." She concluded that she would like the university to be in a position to assist women students before major problems arose. The editorial writers for the *Kentucky Kernel* shared Holmes's concerns. A February 1943 issue noted, "What seems to be bothering the senior women more than anything else is not so much getting jobs they want when they graduate as being sure that they will have jobs when the war is over."[50]

Employment concerned not just UK women but women at colleges and universities everywhere. As early as 1942, the Kentucky Association of Deans of Women's annual meeting dealt exclusively with the issue, with such talks as "War Occupations for Women and Girls," "Women after College," "The War Training Program," and "What We May Expect in a Post-War World." Most speakers emphasized the need for women to develop positive attitudes toward work outside of the home and toward blue-collar jobs.[51]

The concern of the deans extended beyond employment opportunities. At a 1944 meeting of the association, the group discussed counseling for women students for matters other than academic. In regard to the postwar home, "The consensus was that both high schools and colleges can do much to prepare girls to 'live alone and like it' and to adjust themselves to the reaction of the particular man in whom they are especially interested when he returns from service in the army or navy."[52]

What would become of the woman student on campus at the end of the war? Several different scenarios were offered in response to that question. As early as March 1943, a woman editor for the *Kentucky Kernel* offered a prediction:

The Rosie the Riveter may be one of the girls you dated in college days who then went to dances and teas and was strictly a lady. She's still a lady even if she is doing a man's work. And she'll be a lady after the war when you come home. There will still be a home when you return and there will be the same life you knew before December 7, 1941. The change now has been a definite one but is just for the moment, for the moment we win the war. The theory of the "Amazon Woman" will disappear and she will go back to her duties in the home. The average co-ed is confident of this even in the midst of confusion.[53]

The university administration began to plan for a postwar campus by organizing a Committee on Postwar Planning, charged with reviewing major issues that the university would face following the war. While

Women bearing the weight of the Commonwealth. (*Kentuckian,* 1944.)

much of the committee's discussion pertained to returning men veterans, the group also expressed concern about the "problems of student welfare" on the part of the total student population. Members of the committee expected that the campus would change again quickly at the end of hostilities; but even with planning, they were unprepared for the scope of the changes.[54]

President Donovan told the Board of Trustees in September 1946 that while the war had ended for the nation, it was not yet over at the university. Even before the war came to its formal end, hundreds of veterans returning to UK found "girls occupying their fraternity houses [and] soldiers still in the few dormitories." As could be expected, the general concerns about postwar problems centered primarily on male students. However, women students at UK also faced serious challenges. As Linda Eisenmann explains, "women's high participation as students and their enhanced leadership roles diminished with the influx of male veterans, leading to a decade-long decline in women's participation as both students and faculty. In a nation eager to return to perceived normalcy, women's continued press for an enhanced presence in academic life fell by the wayside."[55]

Men soon outnumbered women on the campus, and as the *Kentucky Kernel* noted in a headline, "Distraught Men Outnumber Elusive Coeds Five to One." Veterans comprised nearly 80 percent of the male students (seventy-five women students were also veterans). Surveying these changing demographics, the *Kernel* writer concluded, "In a return to prewar normality the university campus is rapidly becoming a man's world." The sharp rise in the number of male students had an immediate and detrimental impact on UK women. In July 1946, UK stopped admitting additional women students because the university lacked adequate living facilities for them. After filling the available women's dormitories, only those women who could make satisfactory arrangements to live in private homes were considered for admission. Donovan described this action as "our painful duty to decline any further applications from Kentucky girls who desired to enter the University." He later admitted, "It is a tragedy in the life of any girl who may desire to come to college and not be able to do so because of the lack of a place in which to live."[56]

Dean Holmes concurred. Writing in 1946, she wondered "if the doors are closing for women students at our co-educational institutions.

JAS. M. HISLE   K. A. LENTZ, JR.   E. LIEBERMAN

COLLEGE OF
ENGINEERING·
UNIVERSITY OF
KENTUCKY~

BETTY McNAMER   W. J. DRUMMY, JR.

   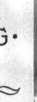

LOUIS DUSINA   G. P. MUNDRANE, JR.   GEO. R. TURNER, JR.

C. R. TIPTON, JR.   G. L. BARROW   E. M. EVANS, JR.   J. A. DEARINGER

College of Engineering class of 1946. (Louis Edward Nollau F series photographic print collection.)

It is a short-sighted policy to provide educational benefits for veterans at the expense of women." Even with more women than any time previously applying to attend UK, Holmes resented that "some people are saying let women wait their turn" but, she said, "There is no turn in higher education for women." She also realized that this was not a short-term problem because the pressure to educate returning male veterans would be "felt perhaps five or ten years" and that "women cannot wait until this pressure is reduced." Offering at least officially to give the administration the benefit of the doubt that the resulting "discrimination against women students" was "not actually designed," the negative impact on women students would be the same. She believed that, as Dean of Women, she and "other college officials" must "see that women as well as men have their chance for higher education."[57]

Dean Haselden worked hard to assure that any woman wishing to come to UK after the war found university-approved housing. She later noted that "nobody stayed away because they couldn't find housing" because she "looked at and approved all the housing." One particular landlord insisted on using forty-watt lightbulbs in his boardinghouse instead of the seventy-five-watt bulbs required by the dean of women's office. Haselden confronted the landlord and told him that if the problem was not resolved she could not recommend that the university use his facility. The landlord shot back that he would "tell what I know about you" if the requirements were not dropped, adding, "It doesn't have to be true, you know!" Haselden responded that the landlord could "tell everything you know about me to anybody that you know!" She subsequently removed all of the women students from that boardinghouse, but the pressures brought to bear upon the women administrators continued.[58]

Not only were women being challenged in the area of admissions, but their leadership roles and involvement in extracurricular activities were also under attack. It was reported in 1946 that "men are beginning to compete for positions on these publications [the *Kentucky Kernel* and the *Kentuckian*], replacing women who held all important posts during the war years." The Student Union Board experienced a similar postwar regression. The *Kentucky Kernel* reported in April 1947 that, "with the return of the campus male population, steps are being taken to return gradually to the old ratio ('six men and three girls'), and this year's election calls for the election of four of the six men."[59]

During the war, women dominated the *Kernel* editorial staff, but when the men returned, women lost their positions. (*Kentuckian,* 1944.)

Even the band, which had opened its ranks to women during the war, experienced a rapid return to "normalcy." In October 1947, the Student Government Association voted to approve a music department–instituted ban on drum majorettes. Addressing the student assembly, drum major Bill Jones argued that "the Best Band in Dixie" had earned a national reputation before the war as "an all-male group." A return to the all-male tradition, he contended, would represent "a step back up the ladder of national recognition." Jones concluded that with the band back to "normal" the emphasis for the coming year would be on "dignity and esprit de corps."[60]

Newspapers still included reminders of women's changed roles during the war, but the examples emphasized relatively insignificant

The marching band just prior to the return to a males-only policy. (*Kentuckian*, 1946.)

activities. For example, the *Kentucky Kernel* featured a photograph of a woman playing pool, noting, "A shark of a different kind of pool is Gertrude Begley, [from] Hazard, who braved the look of the campus men and invaded the Union pool room to pursue a hobby the women developed while the men were away."[61]

Women's social behavior remained very much on the minds of people as the *Kentucky Kernel*'s woman editor did not hesitate to publish an editorial in December 1946 holding women responsible for the moral climate on the campus. Asking, "Doesn't your personal privacy mean anything to you?" the editor added that "students, faculty, and townspeople again have complained about the promiscuous 'courting' which goes on day and night, Monday through Sunday, on the University campus." Pointing out that even the campus police had been called in to see what they could do about it, ultimately "everyone realizes that love flourishes on a college campus" because "most girls admit they're looking for a husband and training for a job just in case." But the editor concluded that perhaps "love" on campus had gone too far because "students are embarrassed to have their parents visit them on account of the parked cars around the

189

dorms in the afternoons." One idea from the House President's Council for stopping the show of campus passion was to forbid women to sit in parked cars on campus, but no vote on this proposal had been taken. Admitting that most students consider rules for women on campus "silly," the editor instead called for "a little good taste and discretion on the part of a few persons" to stop these "embarrassing situations."[62]

The university faculty, for its part, seemed ready to implement new rules for women's postwar behavior. In September 1947, the faculty banned women students who were living in residence halls, sorority houses, cooperative houses, and boardinghouses from participating in overnight camping parties. Additionally, women students were not permitted to swim in the river or any pool outside of Lexington without expressed written permission from their parents or guardian or approval from the Dean of Women.[63]

"Normalcy" again prevailed at UK. By the late 1940s the percentage of women pursuing higher education at UK dropped in comparison to the men. The gains women had made in leadership roles on campus were systematically reversed, both by specific rulings and by default. Women faculty members, hired to teach "for the duration," found it necessary to find postwar teaching jobs elsewhere. Lydia Roberts Fischer, who had been hired to teach mathematics during the war, knew that without a PhD degree she could not continue permanently at the university. Single and with two young children, she believed that obtaining a PhD was all but impossible. After leaving UK and taking substitute teaching positions in local public schools, Fischer subsequently obtained a full-time teaching position at Lafayette High School, where she taught until her retirement.[64]

Little evidence exists that women on campus openly resisted the return to prewar practices. Only Dean Holmes is on record as vocally opposing the most obvious discrimination. Overall, little overt protest came from either the students or the faculty. Thus, UK women once again experienced discriminatory rules regarding social life, uncertain academic potential and prospects, and steep challenges to remaining on the faculty. The changes that took place in the first half of the 1940s could have set the stage for fundamental shifts; instead, they existed only "for the duration." The steps toward equality that occurred during World War II would need to be fought again and again.

Epilogue

L ying in her bed in the early summer warmth of 1945, Frances Jewell McVey quietly, and gracefully, received friends and family who called at her Shady Lane home. The visitors found a subdued Frances. Her frantic pace had slowed and her high energy level had finally ebbed. Frances was dying, and her death seemed imminent.

Cancer had claimed a lung the previous year, and she suffered tremendous daily pain. Yet, firmly determined to beat the odds, Frances faced cancer the way she had approached her life—with optimistic determination. After seeking the most advanced treatment, she resolutely walked the tree-lined streets of her neighborhood to maintain her stamina for the ensuing struggle.[1]

Frances Jewell McVey died June 13, 1945. While a sad time for the McVey and Jewell families, it became a national summer of celebration. As Frances's life ended, so too did World War II. In less than a year, her protégé Sarah Blanding would be named the first woman president of Vassar. Frances would have been thrilled.

To Frank McVey's surprise and dismay, Frances left strict instructions not to be buried in the plot Frank McVey had purchased in the Lexington Cemetery, where his first wife, Mabel, was already interred. Instead, Frances's will expressed her wish to be buried in the same cemetery but alongside her parents next to a small, peaceful body of water. In choosing not to join her spouse and his first wife, Frances exhibited a final show of independence for a woman who earlier had sacrificed so much of that independence to become Mrs. Frank McVey. In the end, she symbolically, if not intentionally, reclaimed the Jewell name and her own history and identity.[2]

Frances Jewell McVey's life drew us to this story about women at UK. A remarkable woman by any definition, she accomplished much that should be acknowledged. She continues to this day to be celebrated and remains one of the most often remembered and most beloved women in the over 150-year history of the University of Kentucky.

Frances Jewell McVey vividly represented the possibilities, contradictions, successes, and failures that UK women confronted during their first seven decades on the campus. Although not part of the first generation of women at the university, Frances Jewell McVey proved central to their unfolding story. Born to a privileged class, she acquired compassion for the less fortunate. Naturally extroverted and socially graceful, she sympathized with those more awkward in such environs. A proponent of women's rights, she experienced and even sometimes accepted the limitations created by the sexism of her generation. A romantic for the "Old South," she supported improved race relations and better education for African Americans. In short, Frances Jewell McVey's own life and career reflects in microcosm the struggles and contradictions of women at UK between the late nineteenth century and the end of World War II, and perhaps even to this day.

Frances Jewell McVey came to UK at a time when women's hopes had never been more promising. In the wake of the advances made by women in the first half of the twentieth century, there was cause for optimism that the progress would continue. Yet when Frances Jewell McVey died in the summer of 1945 many challenges still remained regarding women's struggle for equality of opportunity. The modern women's movement still remained mostly hidden below the horizon. Only Sarah Holmes and a few women colleagues stood as strong voices against the push to educate men at the expense of women.

The hopes and dreams of an earlier era for women seemed to symbolically die that summer as Frances Jewell McVey lost her struggle with cancer. The university's tradition of sexism prevailed in spite of women's push for equality. Following World War II, women remained mostly relegated to stereotypical roles as devastating as any seen before. Progress continued in the postwar years, but the momentum for equality ebbed and flowed.[3]

Frances Jewell McVey's story, and the stories of countless other UK women students, faculty, and staff revolves not around their successes and failures, but around the struggle itself. It will soon be a century and a half since a few young women walked into President James Patterson's office and signed their names to the student ledger for the first time. But gaining access to UK was just the beginning of the struggle. Since then, these women's academic descendants have pushed, prodded, argued, cajoled, and even threatened as they sought to gain their rightful place within the institution. Without doubt, women at UK today benefited from every previous generation of UK women's participation in the struggle.

Acknowledgments

The idea for this book germinated in a gender and education class taught by Beth Goldstein several years ago. Richard Angelo provided invaluable direction and encouragement from the very earliest stages of this manuscript to the present. Richard's skills as a teacher and academic mentor are extraordinary.

James C. Klotter, State Historian and Series Editor for Topics in Kentucky History, adeptly guided the refinement of the manuscript and spent hours reading, editing, and offering valuable suggestions. Jim is a state treasure for his dedication to the commonwealth and its history. Janice Elias Birdwhistell also read the manuscript during its various stages and made important contributions.

We are also deeply appreciative of the support and guidance received from the University Press of Kentucky, especially Leila Salisbury and Anne Dean Dotson. They never stopped believing in the value of this project and have been instrumental in bringing it to fruition. Thanks also to the outside readers of the manuscript, whose comments and suggestions ultimately made the final product better.

Thanks also to the faculty and staff of the University of Kentucky Libraries for making needed resources readily available. The Special Collections Research Center's Digital Lab through ExploreUK has transformed the process of researching UK history by providing keyword access to thousands upon thousands of digital files. The Louie B. Nunn Center for Oral History is home to more than 10,000 interviews, including the voices highlighted in this study. Special thanks to Sarah Dorpinghaus, Jason Flahardy, Kopana Terry, Doug Boyd, Danielle Gabbard, and Marie Dale.

Acknowledgments

Finally, we thank the thousands of women who studied, taught, and worked at the University of Kentucky between 1880 and 1945. Your lives were, and are, important. The composite story of your journeys helps us to understand our past better and reminds us that the struggle has been long and hard. The push for gender equity across all of higher education continues today.

Notes

Introduction

1. The last comprehensive study of women at the University of Kentucky was completed nearly thirty years ago. See Carolyn S. Bratt, "Let Facts Be Submitted to a Candid World," Report of the University Senate Council Ad Hoc Committee on the Status of Women (University of Kentucky, October 1990), University of Kentucky Libraries Special Collections Research Center (hereafter UKLSCRC); *Lexington Herald-Leader*, March 29, 2001, and December 5, 2002.

2. See Geraldine Joncich Clifford, *Lone Voyagers: Academic Women in Coeducational Universities, 1869–1937* (New York: Feminist Press, 1989).

3. Barbara Miller Solomon, *In the Company of Educated Women: A History of Women and Higher Education in America* (New Haven: Yale University Press, 1985), 44; Dorothy Gies McGuigan, *A Dangerous Experiment: 100 Years of Women at the University of Michigan* (Ann Arbor: Center for Continuing Education of Women, 1970); Marian J. Swoboda and Audrey J. Roberts, "'What if the Power Does Lie Within Me?' Women Students at the University of Wisconsin, 1875–1900," *History of Higher Education Annual* (1984): 78–100; Marian J. Swoboda and Audrey J. Roberts, "They Came to Learn, They Came to Teach, They Came to Stay" (Madison, WI: Office of Women, 1980); Charlotte Williams Conable, *Women at Cornell: The Myth of Equal Education* (Ithaca, NY: Cornell University Press, 1970); Lynn D. Gordon, "Co-education on Two Campuses: Berkeley and Chicago, 1890–1912," in Mary Kelly, ed., *Woman's Being, Woman's Place: Female Identity and Vocation in American History* (Boston: G. K. Hall, 1979); Carol Sonenklar, *We Are a Strong and Articulate Voice: A History of Women at Penn State* (University Park: Pennsylvania State University Press, 2006); Carol D. Hoffecker, *Beneath Thy Guiding Hand: A History of Women at the University of Delaware* (Newark: University of Delaware, 1994); Andrea G. Radke-Moss, *Bright Epoch: Women and Coeducation in the American West* (Lincoln: University of Nebraska Press, 2008), 4–5. For women's higher

education at one university in Canada see Margaret Gillett, *We Walked Very Warily: A History of Women at McGill* (Montreal: Eden Press, 1981).

4. For southern women's colleges, see Christie Anne Farnham, *The Education of the Southern Belle: Higher Education and Student Socialization in the Antebellum South* (New York: New York University Press, 1994); Gail Kilman, "Education at Wesleyan Female College and Randolph-Macon Woman's College, 1893–1907" (PhD diss., University of Delaware, 1984); Florence Corley, "Higher Education for Southern Women: Four Church-Related Women's Colleges in Georgia, Agnes Scott, Shorter, Spelman, and Wesleyan, 1900–1920" (PhD diss., Georgia State University, 1985).

5. Amy Thompson McCandless, *Women's Higher Education in the Twentieth-Century American South* (Tuscaloosa: University of Alabama Press, 1999), 18, 50. See also Margaret Ripley Wolfe, *Daughters of Canaan: A Saga of Southern Women* (Lexington: University Press of Kentucky, 1995).

6. Shannon H. Wilson, *Berea College: An Illustrated History* (Lexington: University Press of Kentucky, 2006); Carolyn Terry Bashaw, "'She Made a Tradition': Katherine S. Bowersox and Women at Berea College, 1907–1937," *Register of the Kentucky Historical Society* 89 (1991): 61–84; Marion B. Lucas, "Berea College in the 1870s and 1880s: Student Life at a Racially Integrated Kentucky College," *Register of the Kentucky Historical Society* 98 (Winter 2000): 1–22; William E. Ellis, *A History of Eastern Kentucky University: The School of Opportunity* (Lexington: University Press of Kentucky, 2005); Lowell H. Harrison, *Western Kentucky University* (Lexington: University Press of Kentucky, 1987); Terry L. Birdwhistell, "Divided We Fall: State College and the Normal School Movement in Kentucky, 1880–1910," *Register of the Kentucky Historical Society* 88 (October 1990): 431–456.

7. For the complex history of the University of Kentucky's first fifteen years see James F. Hopkins, *The University of Kentucky: Origins and Early Years* (Lexington: University of Kentucky Press, 1951), 51–135; John D. Wright Jr., *Transylvania: Tutor to the West* (Lexington: University Press of Kentucky, 2006); Linda Raney Kiesel, "Kentucky's Land-Grant Legacy: An Analysis of the Administrations of John Bryan Bowman and James Kennedy Patterson, 1865–1890" (PhD diss., University of Kentucky, 2003). See also James C. Klotter, "Promise, Pessimism, and Perseverance: An Overview of Higher Education History in Kentucky," *Ohio Valley History* 6, no. 1 (Spring 2006): 45–60. For a history of higher education in the United States see John R. Thelin, *A History of American Higher Education* (Baltimore: Johns Hopkins University Press, 2004).

8. A.M&C Report, 1879, in Chronological Print File, UKLSCRC.

9. Annual Register, 1880–1881, p. 8, UKLSCRC; Klotter, "Promise, Pessimism, and Perseverance," 45–60. The first public institution for higher education for African Americans in Kentucky was the State Normal School for

Colored Persons, which opened in Frankfort in October 1887 and eventually became Kentucky State University. See John A. Hardin, *Fifty Years of Segregation: Black Higher Education in Kentucky, 1904–1954* (Lexington: University Press of Kentucky, 1997). For a study of African American women and higher education see Stephanie Y. Evans, *Black Women in the Ivory Tower, 1850–1954: An Intellectual History* (Gainesville: University Press of Florida, 2007). Also see William E. Ellis, *A History of Education in Kentucky* (Lexington: University Press of Kentucky, 2011).

10. Hopkins, *The University of Kentucky*, 117; *Laws, Federal and State, Incorporating, Regulating and Endowing State University of Kentucky* (Lexington: University of Kentucky Board of Trustees, 1913), 59–63. It has not been possible to determine how many women students came as county appointees during these early years.

11. Radke-Moss, *Bright Epoch*, 49.

12. See, for example, Lynn D. Gordon, *Gender and Higher Education in the Progressive Era* (New Haven: Yale University Press, 1990).

13. The use of the phrase "Me Too" to promote empowerment among women who had experienced sexual harassment or assault dates back to as early as 2006. The phrase became prominent during 2017 through social media. For an overview of current research on campus sexual harassment and assault see Leila Wood, Caitlin Sulley, Matt Kammer-Kerwick, Diane Follingstad, and Noël Busch-Armendariz, "Climate Surveys: An Inventory of Understanding Sexual Assault and Other Crimes of Interpersonal Violence at Institutions of Higher Education," *Violence against Women* 23 (2017): 1249–1267.

14. Elise Lopez and Mary P. Koss, "History of Sexual Violence in Higher Education," *New Directions for Student Services* 161 (2018): 9–19. The earliest research on the topic cited by the authors is from 1957.

15. Terry L. Birdwhistell, "An Educated Difference: Women at the University of Kentucky through the Second World War" (EdD diss., University of Kentucky, 1994).

1. First Women and the Will to Succeed

1. Lynn D. Gordon, *Gender and Higher Education during the Progressive Era* (New Haven: Yale University Press, 1990).

2. John R. Thelin, *A History of American Higher Education* (Baltimore: Johns Hopkins University Press, 2004), 84–85; Barbara Miller Solomon, *In the Company of Educated Women: A History of Women and Higher Education in America* (New Haven: Yale University Press, 1985), 53.

3. Jo Della Alband, "A History of the Education of Women in Kentucky" (master's thesis, University of Kentucky, 1934); James Franklin Hopkins, *The*

University of Kentucky: Origins and Early Years (Lexington: University of Kentucky Press, 1951), 129–131; Ellis Ford Hartford, "Highlights of Early Teacher Training in Kentucky" (University of Kentucky, Bureau of School Service, 1974), 70. Additional public normal schools would not be created in Kentucky until 1906 with the founding of Eastern Kentucky State Normal and Western Kentucky State Normal. For an overview of normal school education in other states see Pamela Claire Hronek, "Women and Normal Schools: Tempe Normal" (PhD diss., Arizona State University, 1985) and Christine A. Ogren, "Where Coeds Were Coeducated: Normal Schools in Wisconsin, 1870–1929," *Journal of the History of Education* 35 (Spring 1995): 1–26. See also John A. Hardin, *Fifty Years of Segregation: Black Higher Education in Kentucky, 1904–1954* (Lexington: University Press of Kentucky, 1997).

4. *Lexington Daily Transcript,* August 23, 1881.

5. Ibid., November 19, 1881; Helen Lefkowitz Horowitz, *Campus Life: Undergraduate Cultures from the End of the Eighteenth Century to the Present* (Chicago: University of Chicago Press, 1987), 193.

6. *Annual Register of the State College of Kentucky, 1880–1881* (Lexington: Transylvania Printing Co., 1881), 8; *Mechanical Engineering and Electrical Engineering Record* 1 (Summer 1908): 16; George Blackburn Kinkead, "Memoirs," microfilm copy, UKLSCRC.

7. William Benjamin Smith, "James Kennedy Patterson: His Career, His Achievement, His Personality," unpublished manuscript, n.d., copy in UKLSCRC, 4–9.

8. *Lexington Daily Leader,* March 21, 1900; Ellen Fitzpatrick, *Endless Crusade: Women Social Scientists and Progressive Reform* (New York: Oxford University Press, 1990), 4–9.

9. *Lexington Daily Leader,* March 21, 1900; Fitzpatrick, *Endless Crusade,* 4–5; Joan Marie Johnson, *Southern Women at the Seven Sisters Colleges: Feminist Values and Social Activism* (Athens: University of Georgia Press, 2008), 51.

10. *Lexington Daily Ledger,* March 21, 1900; Johnson, *Southern Women,* 51; see also James C. Klotter, *The Breckinridges of Kentucky, 1760–1981* (Lexington: University Press of Kentucky, 1986), 189–207; Helen Lefkowitz Horowitz, *Alma Mater: Design and Experience in the Women's Colleges from Their Nineteenth-Century Beginnings to the 1930s* (Boston: Beacon Press, 1984), 55; Leslie Miller-Bernal, *Separate by Degree: Women Students' Experiences in Single-Sex and Coeducational Colleges* (New York: Peter Lang, 2000), 3–4.

11. *Lexington Daily Ledger,* March 23, 1900. For enrollment data see Ezra L. Gillis, *The University of Kentucky, Its History and Development: A Series of Charts Depicting the More Important Data, 1862–1955* (Lexington: University of Kentucky, 1956), 20.

12. Mary Didlake File, Miscellaneous Faculty Papers, UKLSCRC. The Woodland campus became Woodland Park, a very popular public park on High Street only a few blocks southeast of downtown Lexington.

13. *Lexington Weekly Press*, March 14, 1883; Minutes of the University of Kentucky Board of Trustees (hereafter Board of Trustees Minutes), June 4, 1902; Hopkins, *The University of Kentucky*, 162–193. Hopkins makes note of the entrance of women and of the establishment of some of their first academic and social organizations. However, his descriptive and detailed chapter examining student culture on the campus during this period deals almost exclusively with the actions of, and tensions between, the men students and the all-male faculty and administration.

14. See Kolan Thomas Morelock, *Taking the Town: Collegiate and Community Culture in the Bluegrass, 1880–1917* (Lexington: University Press of Kentucky, 2008). See also Paul E. Fuller, *Laura Clay and the Women's Rights Movement* (Lexington: University Press of Kentucky, 1973).

15. Ada Coles (Mead) Saffarrans was the daughter of Cowles Green Mead, a Mississippi planter. Her grandfather had served as acting governor of Mississippi Territory in the early 1800s. Her daughter, Ada Mead Saffarrans, toured the country in musical comedies using the stage name Ada Meade. In 1917 the Hippodrome Theater in Lexington was renamed the Ada Meade Theatre in her honor.

16. *Annual Register of the State College of Kentucky*, 1880–1881, UKLSCRC, 16; University of Kentucky Matriculations Records, 1869–1881, UKLSCRC. Also see James William Thomas, "Campus as Home: An Examination of the Impact of Student Housing at the University of Kentucky in the Progressive Era" (PhD diss., University of Kentucky, 2017), 138–143; Horowitz, *Campus Life*, 195.

17. Hopkins, *The University of Kentucky*, 119–120; *Annual Register of the State College of Kentucky*, 1887–1888, UKLSCRC, 44.

18. Hopkins, *The University of Kentucky*, 133–134.

19. *Louisville Times*, June 6, 1884. Throughout the period covered in this study, examples abound of men describing women's physical appearance and characteristics. In *Unbearable Weight: Feminism, Western Culture, and the Body* (Berkeley: University of California Press, 1993), Susan Bordo notes that in the Victorian era women were often depicted as "naturally passive" and as "sweet, gentle, domestic, without intensity or personal ambition of any sort" (162).

20. *Louisville Times*, June 6, 1884.

21. Ibid. Hoeing's younger brother, Charles, also attended UK at the time. Hoeing's mother's maiden name was Kastle, and she was related to Joseph Hoening Kastle, who graduated from UK that same year. Joseph helped found the UK Alumni Association and served as its president. He later received his

doctorate from Johns Hopkins University, became an internationally recognized chemist, and served as dean of the UK College of Agriculture. Kastle Hall on the UK campus is named in his honor.

22. *Mechanical Engineering and Electrical Engineering Record* 1 (Summer 1908): 16; Board of Trustees Minutes, June 5, 1883, 46, UKLSCRC. The Lexington Female Academy was an elite boarding school for women in downtown Lexington.

23. *Annual Register,* 1887–1888, 52.

24. Board of Trustees Minutes, June 1, 1887, June 6, 1888, and June 5, 1889. Administered by Walter K. Patterson, President Patterson's brother, the Preparatory Department served students wishing to attend UK but not deemed qualified for admission at the collegiate level.

25. Gertrude Renz Gordon to Ezra L. Gillis, May 9, 1939, in "Recollections of the Class of 1904," Alumni File, UKLSCRC; *The State College Cadet* 5, no. 1 (September 1894): 6.

26. Minutes of the University of Kentucky [Faculty] Senate, March 23, 1888, UKLSCRC (hereafter Faculty Senate Minutes).

27. Recollections by John W. Gunn in the Belle Gunn File, Alumni Questionnaires, UKLSCRC. John Gunn was Belle Gunn's younger cousin and was also a graduate of UK. Belle Gunn married Charles S. Kay in 1893. They lived in Springfield, Ohio, and she was the mother of seven children, six of whom survived childbirth. She was an active member of the UK Alumni Association during her lifetime. For a history of Science Hill Academy see Deborah Eaton Richard, "Women's Academies in Kentucky: Denominational/Nondenominational Differences in Character Formation" (PhD diss., Southern Illinois University, 2000).

28. Belle Gunn Alumni File.

29. *Lexington Daily Transcript,* June 5, 1891. Warner's father, Evan Tylor Warner, a Lexington hardware merchant, had attended UK, as did her two sisters, Harriett Hocker Warner (class of 1894) and Logan Hocker Warner (class of 1897). Callie Warner married Dr. Joseph Hoening Kastle (class of 1884), a professor at UK. See *Kentucky Alumnus* 3 (1973).

30. Board of Trustees Minutes, June 6, 1889.

31. Ibid., September 3, 1889; *Lexington Daily Press,* October 3, 1889; *Kentucky Gazette,* March 17, 1900.

32. Gillis, *The University of Kentucky, Its History and Development,* 20.

33. *The State College Cadet* 3, no. 7 (March 15, 1893).

34. *Lexington Leader,* May 30, 1902.

35. *The State College Cadet* 3, no. 1 (September 15, 1892).

36. Alumni Questionnaire Collection, UKLSCRC; Horowitz, *Campus Life,* 197–198.

37. *The State College Cadet* 3, no. 1 (September 15, 1892), and 4, no. 2 (October 1893); Hopkins, *The University of Kentucky*, 175; Morelock, *Taking the Town*, 92–95. A second women's society, the Neville Literary Society, named for UK professor and vice president John Henry Neville, was founded in 1904. According to Morelock, Neville took an active role in the society until his death.

38. *Catalog of the Officers and Students of the State College of Kentucky, Lexington, Together with the Regulations for the Session Ending June 6, 1895* (Lexington, 1895), 77; *The State College Cadet* 5, no. 1 (September 1894).

39. Board of Trustees Minutes, June 2, 1897.

40. Ibid.

41. *The State College Cadet* 5, no. 8 (April 1895). Didlake's father died only a month after she received her degree from UK, and her mother died eight years later, in 1903. She began working in the Entomology Department as a student assistant in 1891 and advanced to Associate Entomologist and Botanist before retiring in 1957. Mary Didlake died in 1971 at the age of ninety-six.

42. *The State College Cadet* 5, no. 8 (April 1895). Foster's father, Patrick, was a Lexington butcher. She never married and became a teacher in Lexington. Unidentified and undated newspaper clipping in Mary LeGrand Didlake Faculty/Staff File, UKLSCRC.

43. "Annual Report of the Association of Alumni of the State College of Kentucky" (hereafter Alumni Association Annual Report), 1898, UKLSCRC, 22–23; *Kentucky Kernel,* October 5, 1928. Beatrice Terry became a teacher in Lexington and in 1928 was serving as head of the Spanish Department at Kentucky Wesleyan College in Winchester, Kentucky. She remained single until her death at age fifty-seven in 1933.

44. Alumni Association Annual Report, 1889, 5; and 1900, 11. Jennie Willmott married Arthur John Vance in 1902.

45. *The State College Cadet* 4, no. 4 (December 1893).

46. Alumni Association Annual Report, 1900, 13; and 1902, 12.

47. Gillis, *The University of Kentucky,* 16–17.

48. Alumni Association Annual Report, 1902. A discussion regarding the concerns over feminization of the universities can be found in Solomon, *In the Company,* 57–61.

49. Faculty Senate Minutes, November 1, 1901.

50. Alumni Association Annual Report, 1902.

51. *Lexington Daily Leader,* February 17, 1896.

52. Ibid., February 13, 1896. Laura Clay attended UK for one semester after having attended the University of Michigan in 1879–1880. For a full account of her life and career as an advocate for women's rights see Fuller, *Laura Clay.* See also Laura Clay Papers, UKLSCRC.

53. Margaret Ripley Wolfe, "Fallen Leaves and Missing Pages: Women in Kentucky History," *Register of the Kentucky Historical Society* 90 (Bicentennial Issue, 1992): 82.

54. Board of Trustees Minutes, June 4, 1902.

55. Ibid.

56. Charles Kerr, ed., *History of Kentucky,* vol. 3 (Chicago: American Historical Society, 1922), 29–31; Hopkins, *The University of Kentucky,* 159–160. Because Walter Patterson supervised construction of the women's dormitory and even served as assistant matron for a brief time, the students often called him "She-Pat" as a form of derision. His brother, the president, by contrast was often referred to as "He-Pat."

57. *Lexington Leader,* August 29, 1902. President Patterson had preferred building the women's dormitory on the "Graham property" a few blocks south of campus on Limestone near Washington Avenue.

58. *Laws Federal and State Incorporating, Regulating and Endowing State University of Kentucky* (Lexington, 1913), 80–82; *Mechanical Engineering and Electrical Engineering Record* 1 (January 1908): 47–50; Board of Trustees Minutes, June 2, 1903.

59. Board of Trustees Minutes, June 2, 1903.

60. Ibid.

61. *Lexington Democrat,* February 14, 1902, and June 12, 1903; *Lexington Leader,* June 11, 1903; Merry Lewis Pence, "The University of Kentucky, 1866–1936," unpublished manuscript in UKLSCRC, 1938, p. 59.

62. Board of Trustees Minutes, June 5, 1902; Alumni Association Annual Report, 1902, 18.

63. "Our Dean of Women," in Alumni Association Annual Report, 1908, 38–39; Florence Offutt Stout, "The Memoirs of Mrs. Florence Offutt Stout," in Florence Offutt Stout Papers, 1874–1960, UKLSCRC, 2.

64. Board of Trustees Minutes, December 10, 1901; Stout, "Memoirs," 17. Stout's greatest supporter on the board was most likely Henry Stites Barker. During her childhood in Louisville Stout had known the Barkers quite well and had spent much time in their home. Stout would later provide much-needed financial support for Judge Barker's widow, Kate Sharp Meriwether Barker, in her last years.

65. Stout, "Memoirs," 17–19; Mary Elizabeth Payne, "Florence Offutt Stout: Teacher of Physical Education for Forty Years at the University of Kentucky" (master's thesis, University of Kentucky, 1941), 17.

66. Payne, "Florence Offutt Stout," 17.

67. Alumni Association Annual Report, 1908, 38–39.

68. Florence Offutt Stout, "Physical Education in Kentucky," *Mechanical Engineering and Electrical Engineering Record* 1 (May 1908): 30–31; Also see

Martha H. Verbrugge, *Active Bodies: A History of Women's Physical Education in Twentieth-Century America* (New York: Oxford University Press, 2012).

69. *The Idea*, December 15, 1910.

70. Letter from James K. Patterson to W. W. H. Mustaine, March 17, 1903, and letter from W. W. H. Mustaine to James K. Patterson, March 18, 1903, Box 14, James K. Patterson Papers, UKLSCRC; H. H. Downing, "Truckles: Sixty Years on the Same Campus," unpublished memoir, 195–196, UKLSCRC.

71. Letter from James K. Patterson to Florence Offutt Stout, March 17, 1903, Patterson Papers, Box 14 (January–April 1903).

72. Board of Trustees Minutes, June 4, 1902, and June 2, 1903.

73. Virginia Clay McClure Diary, October 9, 1910, UKLSCRC.

74. Board of Trustees Minutes, December 9, 1903.

75. Faculty Senate Minutes, November 6, 1903.

76. Board of Trustees Minutes, December 9, 1903.

77. Alumni Association Annual Report, 1903, 9–15; Board of Trustees Minutes, June 4, 1903, and June 10, 1904. Elizabeth Shelby Kinkead, *History of Kentucky* (New York: American Book Company, 1896).

78. Faculty Senate Minutes, September 15, 1903; Alumni Association Annual Report, 1903, 9–15; Board of Trustees Minutes, June 4, 1903, and June 10, 1904.

79. Board of Trustees Minutes, June 10, 1904. Cassius M. Clay Jr., was Laura Clay's first cousin.

80. Ibid.

81. Alumni Association Annual Report, 1912, 9–12; Mary LeGrand Didlake Biographical File, UKLSCRC; Nancy D. Taylor, "Rise of the Administrator in Higher Education: Focus on Professionalization of the Registrar at the University of Kentucky from 1910 to 1937" (PhD diss., University of Kentucky, 2015), 105–106.

82. Alumni Association Annual Report, 1903, 14; Faculty Senate Minutes, November 12, 1909.

83. Gregory Kent Stanley, *Before Big Blue: Sports at the University of Kentucky, 1880–1940* (Lexington: University Press of Kentucky, 1996), 94–112. For a detailed description of physical education at UK see Stout, "Physical Education in Kentucky," 24–42.

84. Faculty Senate Minutes, January 15 and February 8, 1904; Rita J. Pritchett, "The Battle between Promise and Privilege: The History of Women's Basketball at the University of Kentucky, 1972–2002" (PhD diss., University of Kentucky, 2007), 18–22.

85. *The Idea*, November 18 and November 25, 1909; March 3 and April 7, 1910.

86. Alumni Association Annual Report, 1903, 14.

87. Faculty Senate Minutes, November 12, 1909, and March 4, 1910; Stanley, *Before Big Blue,* 95.

88. Faculty Senate Minutes, November 12, 1909.

89. Alumni Association Annual Report, 1904, 18.

90. Alumni Association Annual Report, 1903; Board of Trustees Minutes, June 2, 1903, June 10, 1904, and May 31, 1905. Also see Marjorie S. Stewart and Joyce Cotton Threlkeld, *Celebrating the Past, Building the Future: History of Home Economics at the University of Kentucky, 1906–1990* (Lexington: University of Kentucky College of Home Economics, 1990).

91. Board of Trustees Minutes, December 12, 1905.

92. Ibid.; Hopkins, *The University of Kentucky,* 236.

93. Alumni Association Annual Report, 1912, 13.

94. Ibid., 1908, 38–39.

95. *The Idea,* September 15, 1910; Stanley, *Before Big Blue.* Stanley contends that even though Stout had been friends with President Barker and his spouse for years, on becoming president, Barker did not support Stout and even reduced her recommended salary on more than one occasion.

96. *The Idea,* September 15, 1910.

97. Alumni Association Annual Report, 1910, 20; *Southern School Journal* 26 (May 1915): 17–18. The Semple Collegiate School was founded in 1893 by Patty Blackburn Semple and Ellen Churchill Semple, both graduates of Vassar College, who wanted to offer a more rigorous curriculum for girls. Ellen Churchill Semple became an accomplished geographer and was the first woman to receive an honorary degree from UK in 1923.

98. *The Idea,* September 15, 1910.

99. Maude Creekmore Journal and Scrapbook, UKLSCRC.

100. Alumni Association Annual Report, 1909, 35. For information regarding Sophonisba Breckinridge see Klotter, *The Breckinridges of Kentucky,* and Anthony R. Travis, "Sophonisba Breckinridge, Militant Feminist," in *Mid-America: An Historical Review* 58 (April 1976): 111–118.

101. *The Idea,* September 22, 1910.

102. Faculty Senate Minutes, March 1, 1911.

103. Ibid., February 7, 1913.

104. Board of Trustees Minutes, Executive Committee, November 15, 1916.

105. Gillis, *The University of Kentucky,* 15.

106. Rexie Brooks Raymond, interview with Terry L. Birdwhistell, May 26, 1976, Louie B. Nunn Center for Oral History, UKLSCRC. After graduating from UK in 1915, Raymond became a teacher in Corydon, Kentucky. Probably her most notable student was A. B. "Happy" Chandler, who was twice

governor of Kentucky, was elected a US senator, and served as commissioner of baseball.

107. Melba Porter Hay, *Madeline McDowell Breckinridge and the Battle for a New South* (Lexington: University Press of Kentucky, 2009), 37.

108. Andrea G. Radke-Moss, *Bright Epoch: Women and Coeducation in the American West* (Lincoln: University of Nebraska Press, 2008), 289.

2. Frances Jewell McVey and the Refinement of Student Culture

1. Frances Jewell to Lizzie Berry Jewell, April 1908, Box 13, Jewell Family Papers, University of Kentucky Libraries Special Collections Research Center (hereinafter UKLSCRC).

2. Ibid.

3. Annette Baxter in Karen J. Blair, *The Clubwoman as Feminist: True Womanhood Redefined, 1868–1914* (New York: Holmes & Meier, 1980), xiv–xv.

4. Geraldine Joncich Clifford, *Lone Voyagers: Academic Women in Coeducational Universities, 1870–1937* (New York: Feminist Press, 1989); Barbara Miller Solomon, *In The Company of Educated Women: A History of Women and Higher Education in America* (New Haven: Yale University Press, 1985); Rosalind Rosenberg, *Beyond Separate Spheres: Intellectual Roots of Modern Feminism* (New Haven: Yale University Press, 1982). Also see Rosalind Rosenberg, "The Limits of Access: The History of Coeducation in America" in John Mack Faragher and Florence Howe, eds., *Women and Higher Education in American History: Essays from the Mount Holyoke College Sesquicentennial Symposia* (New York: Norton, 1988), 107–129. For an earlier treatment of women and higher education see Thomas Woody, *A History of Women's Education in the United States*, 2 vols. (New York: Science Press, 1929).

5. Jewell Family Papers, passim.

6. See J. Winston Coleman Jr., *A Centennial History of Sayre School* (Lexington, KY: Winburn Press, 1954). Sayre School was founded in 1854 as the Transylvania Female Institute. The school was renamed Sayre Female Institute in 1885. Elizabeth Jewell Davis, interview with Terry L. Birdwhistell, January 23, 1992, Alumni/Faculty Oral History Project, UKLSCRC; Frances Jewell to Dr. Edward Guerrant, ca. 1902, Box 13, Jewell Family Papers, UKLSCRC. Katherine Pettit founded both the Hindman Settlement School (1902) and the Pine Mountain Settlement School (1913). For a critical assessment of Pettit's life and career, see David S. Whisnant, *All That Is Native and Fine* (Chapel Hill: University of North Carolina Press, 1983). For other interpretations regarding women reformers in Appalachia see Jennifer Anne Nickeson, "Transforming Appalachia: Female Reformers in the Mountains, 1900–1941" (PhD diss., State University of New York at Buffalo, 2016) and Karen Tice,

"School-Work and Mother-Work: The Interplay of Maternalism and Cultural Politics in the Educational Narratives of Kentucky Settlement Workers, 1910–1930," *Journal of Appalachian Studies* 4 (Fall 1998): 191–224. Years later Jewell wrote about Pettit's work in Frances Jewell McVey, "The Blossom Woman," *Mountain Life and Work* 1 (April 1934): 1–5.

7. Frances Jewell to Lizzie Berry Jewell, January 6, 1908, Box 13, Jewell Family Papers; Baldwin School Yearbook, 1908, copy in Frances Jewell McVey Papers, UKLSCRC.

8. Frances Jewell to Lizzie Berry Jewell, October 21, 1909, Box 13, Jewell Family Papers, UKLSCRC.

9. Ibid.

10. Frances Jewell McVey to Lizzie Berry Jewell, April 21, 1913, Box 13, Jewell Family Papers, UKLSCRC.

11. Ibid.

12. Helen Lefkowitz Horowitz, *Alma Mater: Design and Experience in the Women's Colleges from Their Nineteenth-Century Beginnings to the 1930s* (Boston: Beacon Press, 1984), 65–68, 179–197. Also see Joan Marie Johnson, *Southern Women at the Seven Sister Colleges: Feminist Values and Social Activism, 1875–1915* (Athens: University of Georgia Press, 2008).

13. Horowitz, *Alma Mater,* 163–169. For a study of Vassar in particular, see Agnes Rogers, *Vassar Women: An Informal Study* (Poughkeepsie: Vassar College, 1940).

14. Lizzie Berry Jewell to Frances Jewell, February 19, 1913, Box 8, Jewell Family Papers, UKLSCRC.

15. Frances Jewell to Lilias Wheeler, October 21, 1913, Box 13, Jewell Family Papers, UKLSCRC.

16. Robert Berry Jewell to Lizzie Berry Jewell, January 28, 1914, Box 13, Jewell Family Papers, UKLSCRC; *The Lexingtonian,* April 1, 1915; *Lexington Daily Leader,* March 26, 1915. For a discussion regarding the appeal of social work activities to women of Jewell's class and generation, see Barbara Sicherman, "College and Careers: Historical Perspectives on the Lives and Work Patterns of Women College Graduates," in John Mack Faragher and Florence Howe, eds., *Women and Higher Education in American History: Essays from the Mount Holyoke College Sesquicentennial Symposia* (New York: Norton, 1988), 155. See also Melba Porter Hay, *Madeline McDowell Breckinridge and the Battle for a New South* (Lexington: University Press of Kentucky, 2009), 18–19. Before studying part-time at UK, Breckinridge attended Miss Porter's School in Connecticut.

17. Robert Jewell to Lizzie Berry Jewell, May 23, 1915, Box 8, Jewell Family Papers, UKLSCRC.

18. Solomon, *In the Company of Educated* Women, 117.

Notes to Pages 66–71

19. Lizzie Berry Jewell to Frances Jewell, May 25, 1915, Box 8, Jewell Family Papers, UKLSCRC. Also see Rosenberg, "Limits of Access," 124–125; and Susan B. Carter, "Academic Women Revisited: An Empirical Study of Changing Patterns of Women's Employment as College and University Faculty, 1890–1963," *Journal of Social History* 14 (Summer 1981): 675–699.

20. Compiled from listings available in University of Kentucky catalogs. These figures include all individuals on campus involved in instructional activities. Women instructors did not participate in faculty meetings and other faculty related activities until Florence Offutt Stout's appointment in 1908 as dean of women. Even then, her involvement was not equal to the men on the faculty.

21. Baldwin School Yearbook, 1909, 25–26.

22. *Louisville Courier-Journal*, May 25, 1952. Prior to entering UK, McLaughlin attended the Dudley School [public] in Lexington and St. Catherine's Academy, operated by the Sisters of St. Dominic near Springfield, Kentucky.

23. Ibid.; *Kentucky Alumnus* 8 (1916): 14–15. McLaughlin may have returned to Lexington because of the death of her father in 1910. Her mother died seven years later, in 1917. McLaughlin would live in the family home near the UK campus until her death.

24. *Louisville Courier-Journal*, November 5, 1950, and May 25, 1952. In 1921 McLaughlin was promoted to assistant professor; she never obtained a higher faculty rank. Her activities outside the university included memberships in the Woman's Club of Central Kentucky, the Lexington Altrusa Club, the Lexington Business and Professional Women's Club, the National Association of Arts and Letters, and the National Conference of Christians and Jews. She also served as president of the W. S. Welch Printing Company, a family-owned business in Lexington.

25. Elizabeth Bragg became the first woman to earn an engineering degree from an American university when she graduated from the University of California at Berkeley in 1876 with a civil engineering degree. Bertha Lamme followed in 1893 with a mechanical engineering degree from Ohio State University. Margaret E. Layne, ed., *Women in Engineering: Pioneers and Trailblazers* (Reston, VA: American Society of Engineers, 2009), 5; *Kentucky Alumnus* 8 (September 1916): 28; Alice C. Goff, "Women Can Be Engineers" (first published in 1946), in Layne, ed., *Women in Engineering*, 168–173.

26. Unidentified and undated newspaper clipping, Engineering Scrapbook, 1885–1917, College of Engineering Records, UKLSCRC.

27. Ibid. Also see Margaret Ingels Papers, UKLSCRC. After graduating, Ingels stayed at UK and earned a master's degree. She pursued a career as an engineer and a successful researcher, eventually working for the Carrier Corporation.

During the latter part of her career she became a spokesperson for the corporation, advocating air conditioning for the home. She particularly made appeals to women on behalf of this modern convenience.

28. See Lisa Sergio, *A Measure Filled: The Life of Lena Madesin Phillips Drawn from her Autobiography* (New York: R. B. Luce, 1972); and Leila J. Rupp, "'Imagine My Surprise': Women's Relationships in Historical Perspective," *Frontiers: A Journal of Women Studies* 5 (Autumn 1980): 61–70. The University of Kentucky College of Law opened its doors in the fall of 1908 with a dean, two part-time instructors, and thirty law students, none of whom were women. The first woman enrolled in the college two years later in 1910, but she remained in the law program only one year. In the fall of 1913 the college's second woman student enrolled, and by 1916 a total of four women were taking law classes. See Terry L. Birdwhistell, "'Some Kind of Lawyer': Two Journeys from Classroom to Courtroom and Beyond," *University of Kentucky Law Journal* 84 (1996): 1075–1152.

29. *Kentucky Alumnus* 8 (November 1916): 11–12; *Report of the Kentucky Equal Rights Association Annual Meeting*, November 8–10, 1915, UKLSCRC. Elizabeth King Smith was Margaret I. King's older sister.

30. Lynn D. Gordon, *Gender and Higher Education in the Progressive Era* (New Haven: Yale University Press, 1990), 81–82; John R. Thelin, *A History of American Higher Education* (Baltimore: Johns Hopkins University Press, 2004), 186.

31. Austin Paige Lilly, interview with Terry L. Birdwhistell, April 3, 1990, Louie B. Nunn Center for Oral History, UKLSCRC.

32. Ibid. See also Austin Lilly Collection, UKLSCRC; and the Grant E. and Anna D. Lilly Collection, 1832–1981, Special Collections and Archives, Eastern Kentucky University.

33. Minutes of the University of Kentucky Board of Trustees (hereafter Board of Trustees Minutes), February 21, 1917.

34. Austin Lilly interview.

35. David Farrell, "A Kentucky Collector: An Interview with W. Hugh Peal," *Kentucky Review* 10 (1990): 48; W. Hugh Peal, interview with David Ferrell, October 4, 1977, Louie B. Nunn Center for Oral History, UKLSCRC.

36. Austin Lilly interview.

37. *Kentucky Alumnus* 8 (January 1917): 20.

38. Ibid. (March 1917): 20–22.

39. Ezra L. Gillis, *The University of Kentucky, Its History and Development: A Series of Charts Depicting the More Important Data, 1862–1955* (Lexington: University of Kentucky, 1956).

40. *Biennial Report of the Superintendent of Public Instruction of Kentucky for the Two Years Ending June 30, 1917* (Frankfort: Kentucky Department of Edu-

cation, 1917), 446. The Women's Building would remain on the Dean of Women's wish list until one was finally established in 1932.

41. Solomon, *In the Company of Educated Women*, 50. For the normal school movement in Kentucky, see Terry L. Birdwhistell, "Divided We Fall: State College and the Normal School Movement in Kentucky, 1880–1910," *Register of the Kentucky Historical Society* 88 (1990): 431–456.

42. Board of Trustees Minutes, May 16, 1917.

43. Kentucky Superintendent's Report (1915–1917), 449–450 (available from the UK Libraries). Charlotte Williams Conable, *Women at Cornell: The Myth of Equal Education* (Ithaca: Cornell University Press, 1977), 135. Kentucky appropriated $2,000 annually for the operation of Patterson Hall. Women students who took their meals at Patterson Hall, both those living in the hall and those lodging outside, paid $3.73 weekly. Through the end of World War II, UK deans of women reported regularly that more women had applied for admission to the university than there were dormitory rooms available to house them.

44. Board of Trustees Minutes, May 16 and June 20, 1917. The Board of Trustees also asked President Barker not to live in Patterson Hall. President Emeritus Patterson still occupied the President's Home, and President Barker apparently had nowhere else to live, at least on the campus. At the June 20 meeting Barker said that he "intended to remove from the Hall."

45. Board of Trustees Minutes, May 15, 1917; Superintendent's Report (1915–1917), 451. Caroline Embry Wallis served as the first "monitress" of the women's dormitory from 1903 until 1911. She was followed by Mary G. Fisher (1911–1916) and Elizabeth D. Pickett (1916–1917). Pickett also served for one year (1917–1918) as dietician for the women students. Board of Trustees Minutes, June 20, 1917; *Lexington Herald,* September 9, 1917.

46. For the involvement of women in war work nationally during World War I see Lettie Gavin, *American Women in World War I: They Also Served* (Niwot: University Press of Colorado, 1997).

47. See, for example, Miriam Winter to Frances Jewell, March 28, 1916, Box 8, Jewell Family Papers, UKLSCRC. For a discussion of women's access to graduate education during this period, see Solomon, *In the Company of Educated Women*, 134–140; and Rosenberg, "Limits of Access," 125–126.

48. Board of Trustees Minutes, May 16, 1917. Frances Jewell McVey, "The Literature of Shakerism" (master's thesis, Columbia University, 1918). Some of Jewell's relatives remained heavily involved with the Shaker community, which later became a historic site and tourist attraction. Letters and other materials relating to Jewell's war work in New York are found in Frances Jewell McVey Papers, Box 10, UKLSCRC.

49. See Elizabeth Johnson to Frances Jewell, March 12, 1918, Box 9, Jewell Family Papers, UKLSCRC.

50. Frances Jewell McVey Papers, Box 10, UKLSCRC.

51. Sweeney Family Papers, UKLSCRC.

52. Sweeney Papers; *Kentucky Alumnus* 9 (November 1917): 34–38; Board of Trustees Minutes, March 21, 1917; *Kentuckian* (1917): 43. (Issues of the *Kentuckian* are available from the UKLSCRC.) Also see Lulu B. Cochrane, General Secretary, Lexington YWCA, to Frances Jewell, April 12, 1918, Box 10, Frances Jewell McVey Papers, UKLSCRC; *Kentucky Alumnus* 10 (November 1917): 34, 38. Sunshine Sweeney graduated from UK in 1908 and was, like her sister, known as an independent woman. The *Kentucky Kernel* reported on May 24, 1921, that "Miss Sunshine Sweeney is a farmerette at Combs Ferry Pike, Lexington, Kentucky." *Kentucky Alumnus* 10 (April 1919): 25–26.

53. *Kentucky Alumnus* 10 (April 1919): 25–26; *Kentuckian* (1918): 33; Kentucky Superintendent's Report (1919), 294–295; University of Kentucky Press Bulletin, August 15, 1918.

54. *Kentuckian* (1918): 33.

55. Helen Lefkowitz Horowitz, *Campus Life: Undergraduate Cultures from the End of the Eighteenth Century to the Present* (Chicago: University of Chicago Press, 1987), 111.

56. Board of Trustees Minutes, June 4 and December 10, 1918.

57. *Kentuckian* (1919): 55.

58. Frances Jewell to L. L. Dantzler, June 23, 1919, Box 3, Frances Jewell McVey Papers, UKLSCRC.

59. Ibid.

60. *Kentucky Kernel*, March 12, 1920.

61. Ibid., May 7, 1920. For a study of women's student government at another land-grant university see Christine D. Myers, "Gendering the 'Wisconsin Idea': The Women's Self-Government Association and University Life, c. 1898–1948," in Joyce Goodman and Jane Martin, eds., *Gender, Colonialism, and Education* (London: Woburn Press, 2002), 148–172.

62. *Kentucky Alumnus* 11 (March 1920): 13–14.

63. Ibid.

64. Ibid. 10 (July 1919): 15–16. Simrall later returned to the University of Cincinnati, where she served as Dean of Women from 1921 to 1933.

65. *Kentucky Kernel*, May 20, 1921; Kelly C. Sartorius, "A Coeducational Pathway to Political and Economic Citizenship: Women's Student Government and a Philosophy and Practice of Women's US Higher Coeducation between 1890 and 1945," in Margaret A. Nash, ed., *Women's Higher Education in the United States: New Historical Perspectives* (New York: Palgrave Macmillan, 2018), 178.

66. *Kentuckian* (1921): 6–7.

67. *Kentucky Kernel*, May 10, 1921. See also Board of Trustees Minutes, May 4, 1921; Charles Gano Talbert, *The University of Kentucky: The Maturing*

Years (Lexington: University of Kentucky Press, 1965), 54; and *Lexington Herald*, May 5, 1921. Simrall served twelve years as dean at the University of Cincinnati. She never married and died in 1949.

68. *Kentucky Kernel*, April 20, 1922. The previous semester the student newspaper announced that "the day of equal rights arrived at the University . . . when eight girls were admitted into the SUKY," a previously all-male campus pep club. See also *Kentucky Kernel*, October 28, 1921.

69. Ibid., May 26, 1922.

70. Ibid., May 5, 1922, and February 9 and 23, 1923. Sophonisba Breckinridge received the first honorary degree given to a woman by the university in 1925.

71. Ibid., March 24, 1922.

72. Ibid., October 27, 1922. President Frank McVey used this same metaphor for a university in his inaugural speech at the University of Kentucky. See Frances Jewell McVey, ed., *A University Is a Place . . . a Spirit: Addresses and Articles by Frank LeRond McVey, President, UK, 1917–1940* (Lexington: University of Kentucky Press, 1944).

73. Eric A. Moyen, *Frank L. McVey and the University of Kentucky: A Progressive President and the Modernization of a Southern University* (Lexington: University Press of Kentucky, 2011), 123–125. Mabel Sawyer McVey died on April 19, 1922. She had met Frank McVey as a student in one of his classes at the University of Minnesota, where McVey was a member of the faculty. In Kentucky, besides her work as the president's spouse, she was president of the Lexington League of Women Voters and a strong supporter of Prohibition. See Virginia Morris, interview with Charles G. Talbert, June 29, 1972, Nunn Center, UKLSCRC; *Kentucky Kernel*, November 11, 1921 and April 28, 1922; *Lexington Leader*, April 20, 1922; *Lexington Herald*, April 20 and 26, 1922.

74. Frances Jewell to Frank McVey, December 13, 1922, Box 125, Frank L. McVey Papers, UKLSCRC.

75. Ibid.

76. Frances Jewell to Frank McVey, November 13, 1923, Jewell Papers, UKLSCRC.

77. Frank McVey to Frances Jewell, November 12, 1922, Box 9, Frank L. McVey Papers, UKLSCRC.

78. *Kentucky Kernel*, February 23, 1923.

79. Frances Jewell to Frank McVey, November 13, 1923, Jewell Papers, UKLSCRC.

80. *Kentucky Kernel*, November 29, 1923.

81. See Carolyn G. Heilbrun, *Writing A Woman's Life* (New York: W. W. Norton & Co., 1988), 11–12: "In 1984, I rather arbitrarily identified 1970 as the beginning of a new period in woman's biography because *Zelda* by Nancy Milford had been published that year. Its significance lay above all in the way it

revealed F. Scott Fitzgerald's assumption that he had a right to the life of his wife, Zelda, as an artistic property. She went mad, confined to what Mark Schorer has caller her ultimate anonymity—to be storyless. Anonymity, we have long believed, is the proper condition of a woman. Only in 1970 were we ready to read not that Zelda has destroyed Fitzgerald, but Fitzgerald her: he had usurped her narrative." Also see McVey, *A University Is a Place . . . a Spirit*.

82. Frances Jewell to Lizzie Berry Jewell, April 1908, Box 13, Jewell Papers, UKLSCRC.

3. Sarah Blanding and the Modern College Woman

1. Lowell H. Harrison and James C. Klotter, *A New History of Kentucky* (Lexington: University Press of Kentucky, 1997), 343–351. See also William E. Ellis, "Frank LeRond McVey His Defense of Academic Freedom," *Register of the Kentucky Historical Society* 67 (January 1969): 37–54; and James C. Klotter, *Kentucky: Portrait in Paradox, 1900–1950* (Lexington: University Press of Kentucky, 2006).

2. Paula S. Fass, *The Damned and the Beautiful: American Youth in the 1920s* (New York: Oxford University Press, 1977), 5; Helen Lefkowitz Horowitz, *Campus Life: Undergraduate Cultures from the End of the Eighteenth Century to the Present* (Chicago: University of Chicago Press, 1987), 201; Loretta Gilliam Brock, *A History of the Woman's Club of Central Kentucky, 1894–1994* (Lexington: Woman's Club of Central Kentucky, 1996), 68.

3. Barbara Miller Solomon, *In the Company of Educated Women: A History of Women and Higher Education in America* (New Haven: Yale University Press, 1985), 157.

4. Ibid., 159.

5. See Fass, *The Damned and the Beautiful*; and Beth Bailey, *From Front Porch to Back Seat: Courtship in Twentieth-Century America* (Baltimore: Johns Hopkins University Press, 1988).

6. Minutes of the University of Kentucky Board of Trustees (hereafter Board of Trustees Minutes), July 20, 1923, UKLSCRC. Blanding's appointment as Assistant Dean of Women began on September 1, 1923, paying a salary of $50 per month. For Blanding's appointment as Acting Dean of Women, see Board of Trustees Minutes, November 21, 1923, and April 4, 1924. Blanding retained her appointment as an instructor in the Physical Education Department and in that capacity was paid $2,000 annually.

7. See profile of Sarah Anderson Blanding by Rena Niles in *Louisville Courier-Journal*, September 15, 1940.

8. Ibid.; Carolyn Terry Bashaw, *"Stalwart Women": A Historical Analysis of Deans of Women in the South* (New York: Teachers College Press, 1999), 35.

Louis Blanding is not listed in any Lexington city directory as having a private medical practice. He likely practiced medicine in rural Fayette County.

9. *Frankfort State Journal,* July 9, 1914.

10. *Mortonian* 5 (June 1917): 21, Henry Clay High School Collection, UKLSCRC.

11. The occupations of Blanding's sisters are listed in various Lexington city directories. Blanding's desire to become a physician is mentioned in Sarah Gibson Blanding, interview with William Cooper Jr., May 23, 1976, Louie B. Nunn Center for Oral History, UKLSCRC. For information regarding the Lincoln School and the progressive reform movement in Lexington see Melba Porter Hay, "Madeline McDowell Breckinridge: Kentucky Suffragist and Progressive Reformer" (PhD diss., University of Kentucky, 1980); Hay, *Madeline McDowell Breckinridge and the Battle for a New South* (Lexington: University Press of Kentucky, 2009); Hay, "The Lexington Civic League: Agent of Reform, 1900–1910," *Filson Club History Quarterly* 62 (July 1988): 336–355; and Sophonisba P. Breckinridge, *Madeline McDowell Breckinridge: A Leader in the New South* (Chicago: University of Chicago Press, 1921).

12. Carolyn Terry Bashaw, "'We Who Live Off the Edges': Deans of Women at Southern Coeducational Institutions and Access to the Community of Higher Education, 1907–1960" (PhD diss., University of Georgia, 1992), 45–48.

13. Blanding interview; "Sarah Gibson Blanding," *Louisville Courier-Journal* Magazine (October 1915), 19.

14. Blanding interview; Paul P. Boyd to Frank L. McVey, June 13, 1919, Box 30, Frank LeRond McVey Papers, UKLSCRC. Board of Trustees Minutes, June 6, 1919, 96. Blanding was appointed an instructor in the Physical Education Department at a salary of $800 annually.

15. "Remarks by Sarah Gibson Blanding at the Unveiling of the Frances Jewell McVey Portrait in Jewell Hall at the University of Kentucky, May 14, 1946," Frances Jewell McVey Papers, UKLSCRC.

16. Ibid.; Blanding interview.

17. Blanding interview; *Kentuckian,* 1923 and 1924.

18. *Kentucky Kernel,* February 23, 1924.

19. Peggy Stanaland, "The Early Years of Basketball in Kentucky," in Joan S. Hult and Marianna Trekell, eds., *A Century of Women's Basketball: From Frailty to Final Four* (Reston, VA: American Alliance for Health, Physical Education, Recreation, and Dance, 1991), 173.

20. For a detailed discussion of the move to abolish women's basketball at UK see Gregory Kent Stanley, *Before Big Blue: Sports at the University of Kentucky, 1880–1940* (Lexington: University Press of Kentucky, 1996), 94–112. For a study of girls' high-school basketball in Kentucky see Sallie Lucille

Powell, "Constructing the Modern Girl, Kentucky Style: An Examination of Gender and Race through the Lens of Kentucky Girls' High School Basketball Prior to Title IX" (PhD diss., University of Kentucky, 2012). For a national overview of the disputes between women physical educators and those in charge of intercollegiate sports see Susan K. Cahn, *Coming on Strong: Gender and Sexuality in Women's Sport* (Urbana: University of Illinois Press, 2015), 26–27.

21. Blanding interview; *Kentucky Kernel,* October 3, 1924.

22. *Kentucky Kernel,* October 2, 1924.

23. *Kentucky Kernel,* October 3 and 24, and November 21, 1924.

24. *University of Kentucky Annual Report,* 1924–1925, UKLSCRC. In her study of Blanding, Carolyn Bashaw accepts Blanding's claims that a majority of the students agreed with the abolishment of women's basketball. However, the extent of the protests by the women students would seem to discount Blanding's claim. See Bashaw, "We Who Live off the Edges," 97–98, and Stanley, *Before Big Blue,* 94–112, for discussion of abolishing women's basketball. Also see Bashaw, *"Stalwart Women,"* 85–91.

25. *Kentucky Kernel,* November 21, 1924. Virginia Frances Cavanaugh, "Required Physical Education for Men and Women at the University of Kentucky, 1923–1933" (master's thesis, University of Kentucky, 1945); Joe Daniel Starnes, "Required Physical Education for Men and Women at the University of Kentucky, 1913–1923" (master's thesis, University of Kentucky, 1948).

26. See Eric A. Moyen, *Frank L. McVey and the University of Kentucky: A Progressive President and the Modernization of a Southern University* (Lexington: University Press of Kentucky, 2011), 180–181, 217.

27. *Kentucky Kernel,* December 12, 1924.

28. Ibid., May 1, 1925.

29. Blanding interview.

30. Letter from Sarah Gibson Blanding to Frank L. McVey, March 8, 1926, Box 28, UKLSCRC.

31. *Kentucky Kernel,* September 25, 1925.

32. Sarah Gibson Blanding to Frank L. McVey, March 8, 1926, Box 28, UKLSCRC.

33. Ibid.

34. Lydia Roberts Fischer, interviews with Terry L. Birdwhistell, October 16 and 26, 1989, and Mary Hester Cooper, interview with Cathy Cooper, September 20, 1977, both Louie B. Nunn Center for Oral History, UKLSCRC; Board of Trustees Minutes, July 7, 1920, 121; Charles Gano Talbert, *The University of Kentucky: The Maturing Years* (Lexington: University of Kentucky Press, 1965), 52; Judy Green and Jeanne LaDuke, *Pioneering Women in American Mathematics: The Pre-1940 PhDs* (Providence, RI: American Mathematical

Society, 2009), 89–90; *Kentucky Kernel,* February 19, 1926. Mary Hester Cooper also earned a master's degree in mathematics at UK and worked as an instructor for a time. After teaching at Pikeville Junior College and Lindsey Wilson College, Cooper returned to UK to work in the registrar's office and eventually the University Archives.

35. Horowitz, *Campus Life,* 203–211.

36. Ibid., 201–212.

37. William H. Chafe, *The Paradox of Change: American Women in the Twentieth Century* (New York: Oxford University Press, 1991), 109.

38. *Letters* 1 (May 1928). Sarah Litsey was born at home in Springfield, Kentucky, in 1901. After a brief career as a teacher, she married Frank Wilson Nye in 1933 and lived the remainder of her life in Connecticut writing novels and poetry, many of them about her native state. "Old Maid" was published before Litsey's marriage to Nye, while she was teaching in the Louisville public schools. *Letters,* which began publishing in 1928, was issued quarterly by the English Department, managed by the Journalism Department, and financed by the *Kentucky Kernel.*

39. Rena Niles, interview with Terry L. Birdwhistell, March 6, 1990, Louie B. Nunn Center for Oral History, UKLSCRC. See also Ron Pen, *I Wonder as I Wander: The Life of John Jacob Niles* (Lexington: University Press of Kentucky, 2010), 188–189. Niles received her BA from Wellesley in 1933 with a major in English and a minor in French. She was born in Russia, where her father worked for the czar's government. After the revolution the family immigrated to the United States and then relocated for a time to Paris, France. Rena became a writer and ultimately manager for her musician spouse, native Kentuckian John Jacob Niles, who often entertained at events at Maxwell Place, the president's home on campus.

40. Rena Niles interview; Fischer interview; Barbara Hitchcock, interview with Charles G. Talbert, August 10, 1972, Louie B. Nunn Center for Oral History, UKLSCRC.

41. *Kentuckian* (1925), 257.

42. Lynn D. Gordon, *Gender and Higher Education in the Progressive Era* (New Haven: Yale University Press, 1990), 9–10.

43. *Kentuckian* (1925), 257; *Kentucky Kernel,* May 15, 1925.

44. *Kentucky Kernel,* May 22, 1925.

45. Ibid., October 2, 1925.

46. *Letters* 3 (August 1930): 42. Louise Good was not a student but a forty-five-year-old faculty spouse. An Ohio native, she attended Wellesley College in 1903 and 1904 before marrying Edwin S. Good in 1905. A member of the Agriculture faculty, E. S. Good became head of Dairy Science at UK.

47. Bailey, *From Front Porch to Back Seat; Kentucky Kernel,* October 2, 1925.

48. *Kentucky Kernel,* October 2, 1925.

49. Ibid., December 11, 1925.

50. Ibid., March 12, May 7, and May 21, 1926; see John D. Wright Jr., *Transylvania: Tutor to the West* (Lexington: University Press of Kentucky, 1980); *Kentucky Kernel,* November 6, 1925. Hamilton College was originally established in 1869 as Hocker Female College. Renamed Hamilton Female College in 1878 in honor of benefactor William Hamilton, the college became affiliated with Transylvania University in 1889. Under Transylvania, the college became a junior college for women, and many of its graduates finished their college degrees at Transylvania University. The women's college closed in 1932, its building becoming a women's dormitory for Transylvania University.

51. *Kentucky Kernel,* October 8, 1926.

52. Ibid. During her time as a UK student, Stebbins was a member of Theta Sigma Phi, the Women's Professional Journalistic Fraternity, a member of the State Press Association, and junior editor and then editor in chief of the *Kentuckian.*

53. *Kentucky Kernel,* April 1, 1927.

54. Ibid., December 9, 1927.

55. Ibid., April 16, 1926.

56. Virginia Katherine Conroy, interview with Terry L. Birdwhistell, March 20, 1990, Louie B. Nunn Center for Oral History, UKLSCRC.

57. Ibid.

58. *Kentucky Kernel,* October 18, 1929.

59. Ibid., November 27, 1929. Negative representations of women in publications appeared at other universities as well. For example, see Helen Delpar, "Coeds and the 'Lords of Creation': Women Students at the University of Alabama, 1893–1930," *Alabama Review* 42 (October 1989): 300–301.

60. *Kentucky Kernel,* January 17, 1930; Karen W. Tice, *Queens of Academe: Beauty Pageantry, Student Bodies, and College Life* (New York: Oxford University Press, 2012), 26. For a detailed study of beauty and beauty contests in higher education with specific focus on Kentucky, see Karen W. Tice, "Queens of Academe: Campus Pageantry and Student Life," *Feminist Studies* 31 (Summer 2005): 250–283.

61. Horowitz, *Campus Life,* 208.

4. Economic Depression and an Uncertain Future

1. *Kentucky Kernel,* January 17, 1930; Martin M. White, interview with Terry L. Birdwhistell, February 5, 1979, Louie B. Nunn Center for Oral History, UKLSCRC; Lowell H. Harrison and James C. Klotter, *A New History of Kentucky* (Lexington: University Press of Kentucky, 1997), 359–361; and Eric

A. Moyen, *Frank L. McVey and the University of Kentucky: A Progressive President and the Modernization of a Southern University* (Lexington: University Press of Kentucky, 2011), 187–234. For a detailed study of the Great Depression in Kentucky see George T. Blakey, *Hard Times and New Deal in Kentucky, 1929–1939* (Lexington: University Press of Kentucky, 1986), 4–9.

2. Susan Ware, *Holding Their Own: American Women in the 1930s* (Boston: Twayne Publishers, 1982), 56–57.

3. Jacqueline Page Bull, interview with Terry L. Birdwhistell, October 6, 1977, Louie B. Nunn Center for Oral History, UKLSCRC.

4. *Kentucky Kernel*, December 19, 1930 and January 20, 1931; Frank L. McVey Papers, Dean of Women File, Box 28, UKLSCRC.

5. Sarah B. Holmes Biographical File, UKLSCRC; Sarah Bennett Holmes, interview with William Cooper Jr., February 20, 1978, Louie B. Nunn Center for Oral History, UKLSCRC; *Kentucky Kernel*, September 19, 1930.

6. *Kentucky Kernel*, September 26, 1930.

7. Ibid., November 1 and 21, 1930; and November 1, 1932.

8. Ibid., November 7, 1930. Also see Karen W. Tice, *Queens of Academe: Beauty Pageantry, Student Bodies, and College Life* (New York: Oxford University Press, 2012).

9. *New York Times*, June 4, 1926.

10. *Letters* 5 (February 1932): 33.

11. Woodrow Burchett, interview with William H. McCann Jr., April 7, 1993, Louie B. Nunn Center for Oral History, UKLSCRC. During the depression Robards found employment as a secretary for the Works Progress Administration and then as a stenographer for the National Youth Administration. She later worked as an attorney for the Veterans Administration in Lexington and Louisville, Kentucky.

12. Bull interview. Even though Jacqueline Bull never took Spanish again from Professor Server, she did manage to become one of the first women to receive a PhD from the University of Kentucky and directed the Library's Special Collections and Archives Department for over thirty years. Server may not have failed her future husband in one of her classes, but she most likely was his teacher. Jim Server graduated in 1922 after having served as captain of the 1921 football team. The two married on February 12, 1921.

13. *Kentuckian* (1920), 71; Alberta Wilson Server File and James M. Server File, Alumni Questionnaire File, University Archives, SCRC. Daniel Reedy, "The Lady in the Portrait: A Remembrance," in Alberta Wilson Server Biographical File, UKLSCRC.

14. *Kentucky Kernel*, February 22, 1921; *University of Kentucky Press Bulletin*, March 1, 1921; Reedy, "The Lady in the Portrait"; Jacqueline Bull interview.

15. Reedy, "The Lady in the Portrait."

16. *Kentucky Kernel,* November 25 and December 2, 1930.

17. Ibid., January 13 and 16, 1931.

18. *Letters* 5, no. 18 (February 1932).

19. *Kentucky Kernel,* April 11, 1930.

20. *Letters* 5, no. 19 (May 1932): 44.

21. Ibid. 4 (May 1931): 42.

22. Ibid. 5, no. 19 (May 1932): 44. Kathryn Myrick married Kenneth Roland See in Los Angeles, California, in 1934. They were married for thirty-seven years and had two children.

23. Ibid. 5, no. 18 (February 1932): 43; *Kentucky Kernel,* February 3, 1933.

24. Christina Simmons, *Making Marriage Modern: Women's Sexuality from the Progressive Era to World War II* (New York: Oxford University Press, 2009), 220.

25. *Kentucky Kernel,* December 12, 1930.

26. Ibid., March 20, 1931.

27. Ibid., March 24, 1931.

28. Ibid., October 27 and November 10, 1931; Susan Ware, *Beyond Suffrage: Women in the New Deal* (Cambridge, MA: Harvard University Press, 1981), 61; Jeane Eddy Westin, *Making Do: How Women Survived the '30s* (Chicago: Follett, 1976), 84–85.

29. Barbara Harris, *Beyond Her Sphere: Women and the Professions in American History* (Westport, CT: Greenwood Press, 1978), 141. Also see John L. Rury, *Education and Women's Work: Female Schooling and the Division of Labor in Urban America, 1878–1930* (Albany: SUNY Press, 1991).

30. *Kentucky Kernel,* May 28, 1931; also see Ware, *Holding Their Own,* 21–22. Ware argues that professional women did hold their own during the Depression in terms of numbers employed.

31. *Kentucky Kernel,* September 20, 1932.

32. Ibid.

33. Ibid., October 27, 1933

34. Frank L. McVey to Sarah Gibson Blanding, July 16, 1932, Box 28, Frank L. McVey Papers, UKLSCRC.

35. Sarah Gibson Blanding to Frances Jewell McVey and Frank L. McVey, September 5, 1932, Box 28, Frank L. McVey Papers, Box 28, UKLSCRC.

36. Ibid. Professor J. Catron Jones was head of the Political Science Department.

37. Ibid.

38. *Kentucky Kernel,* September 23, 30, November 22, 1932, April 11, 21, 25, 1933, October 13, 1933, and October 11, 1935 (Coffman quoted in the April 11, 1933, issue); University of Kentucky Annual Report, 1936–1937, 285,

UKLSCRC. The Woman's Building provided dedicated meeting space for the Woman's Student Government Association, the Woman's Administrative Council, Theta Sigma Phi, Phi Upsilon Omicron, Phi Beta, Chi Delta Phi, Mortar Board, and the YWCA.

39. Dean of Women Annual Report, 1936–1937, 7, UKLSCRC.

40. *Kentucky Kernel,* January 20 and March 24, 1933.

41. Ibid., October 31, 1933.

42. Ibid., February 16 and 20, 1934. See also Blakey, *Hard Times and New Deal,* 93–94.

43. Dean of Women Annual Report, 1933–1934, 196; *Kentucky Kernel,* July 21, 1937.

44. *Kentucky Kernel,* October 11, 1935; Dean of Women Annual Report, 1936–1937, 285; Holmes interview. Also see Dana Bush, "Plan Your Work and Work Your Plan: Home Economics and Efficient Living at Two State Funded Universities, 1900–1940" (PhD diss., University of Kentucky, 2011).

45. Dean of Women Annual Report, 1933–1934, 197.

46. Ibid., 1934–1935, 302; *Daily Iowan,* February 4, 1934.

47. Dean of Women Annual Report, 1934–1935, 303.

48. *Kentucky Kernel,* September 24, 1935; Minutes of the University of Kentucky Board of Trustees (hereafter Board of Trustees Minutes), June 27, 1935, and August 1, 1938. Collins resigned in 1938.

49. Dean of Women Annual Report, 1934–1935, 307.

50. Clifford Amos, interview with Terry L. Birdwhistell, December 5, 1991, UKLSCRC.

51. *Kentucky Kernel,* October 4, 1935.

52. Ibid.

53. Ibid., February 18, 1936.

54. Ibid., February 21 and May 22, 1936.

55. Dean of Women Annual Report, 1936–1937, 282.

56. Ibid., 287–288.

57. Ralph E. Johnson, interview with Terry L. Birdwhistell, February 6, 1984, UKLSCRC. See *Kentuckian* for 1928 and 1929; *Kentucky Kernel,* August 18, September 18, and November 3, 1936. See also Anne Marshall's excellent study, *Creating a Confederate Kentucky: The Lost Cause and Civil War Memory in a Border State* (Chapel Hill: University of North Carolina Press, 2010).

58. See for example an interview with Pierre Whiting in the *Kentucky Kernel,* October 23, 1936, and an article by Leslie Lee Jones, "Dormitory Girl Tells How Their Meals Are Cooked," *Kentucky Kernel,* February 19, 1937; Dean of Women Annual Report, 1936–1937, 282–283. Blanding's family had southern roots, and while living in Lexington the Blandings employed a live-in African American maid. Blanding's position on race was most likely heavily influenced

by her mentor, Frances Jewell McVey, who as an elected member of the Lexington school board during the 1930s supported better educational opportunities for African Americans.

59. *Kentucky Kernel,* February 18, 1938.

60. Ibid., November 24, 1936, and October 1 and 15, 1937.

61. Ibid., October 1, 1937.

62. Ibid., January 7, 1938.

63. Holmes interview.

64. *Kentucky Kernel,* March 11, 1938.

65. Dean of Women Annual Report, 1936–1937, 290.

66. *Kentucky Kernel,* October 11, 1938.

5. World War II and the Illusion of Equality

1. Press release to the *Louisville Courier-Journal,* October 8, 1939, Public Relations File, 1928–1956, University of Kentucky Libraries Special Collections Research Center (hereafter UKLSCRC), Margaret I. King Library; *Kentucky Kernel,* September 19, 1941.

2. Charles Dorn, "'A Woman's World': The University of California, Berkeley, during the Second World War," *History of Education Quarterly* 48 (2008): 536–537. For overviews of women's experiences during World War II, see William H. Chafe, *The Paradox of Change: American Women in the Twentieth Century* (New York: Oxford University Press, 1991), and D'Ann Campbell, *Women at War with America: Private Lives in a Patriotic Era* (Cambridge, MA: Harvard University Press, 1984).

3. Recollections of Barbara McVey, Alumni Publications File, University Archives, UKLSCRC.

4. Herman Lee Donovan Biographical File, UKLSCRC; Herman Lee Donovan Papers, UKLSCRC.

5. *Kentucky Alumnus* 3 (1973): 12; *Kentucky Kernel,* July 1, 1941.

6. Charles G. Talbert, *The University of Kentucky: The Maturing Years* (Lexington: University of Kentucky Press, 1965), 133–134; William E. Ellis, *A History of Eastern Kentucky University: The School of Opportunity* (Lexington: University Press of Kentucky, 2005), 67, 90.

7. Sarah Gibson Blanding, interview with William Cooper Jr., May 23, 1976, Louie B. Nunn Center for Oral History, UKLSCRC; Blanding to McVey, March 13, 1940, Frank L. McVey Papers, Box 30, UKLSCRC; Carolyn Terry Bashaw, *"Stalwart Women": A Historical Analysis of Deans of Women in the South* (New York: Teachers College Press, 1999), 38–39. Much of the surprise over Blanding's taking the Cornell position had to do with the fact that Blanding had no background, either as a student or as an administrator, in the field of home economics.

8. Sarah Bennett Holmes, interview with William Cooper Jr., February 20, 1978, Louie B. Nunn Center for Oral History, UKLSCRC; Ezra Gillis Papers, UKLSCRC; Minutes of the University of Kentucky Board of Trustees (hereafter Board of Trustees Minutes), July 25, 1941 and September 15, 1942, UKLSCRC. Holmes's spouse, Percy K. Holmes, a physician with a medical degree from Bates Medical School, served as head of the UK Hygiene Department until his death.

9. Jane Haselden, interviews with Terry L. Birdwhistell, October 17 and 27, 1989, Louie B. Nunn Center for Oral History, UKLSCRC. Haselden believed that Holmes received the dean's appointment over her because of widespread support throughout the Lexington community. According to Haselden, McVey put pressure on Donovan to appoint Holmes.

10. *Ninety-Nine Newsletter,* December 1942–January 1945, available at https://www.ninety-nines.org/99-news-magazine.htm; Haselden interview; *Kentucky Kernel,* February 2, 1943.

11. Ezra Gillis, *The University of Kentucky, Its History and Development: A Series of Charts Depicting the More Important Data, 1862–1955* (Lexington: University of Kentucky, 1956), 21.

12. *Kentucky Kernel,* February 6 and 10, 1942; Susan B. Hartmann, *The Home Front and Beyond: American Women in the 1940s* (New York: Twayne Publishers, 1982), 103; Annual Reports of the University of Kentucky, 1944 and 1945, UKLSCRC.

13. UK Annual Report, 1941–1942, 4.

14. Sarah Holmes to Frances Jewell McVey, April 29, 1943, Dean of Women Papers, UKLSCRC.

15. Public Relations File, 1928–1956, UKLSCRC.

16. Sarah Holmes to her children, October 2, 1943, Dean of Women Papers, UKLSCRC; Haselden interview.

17. Betty Tevis Eckdahl, interview with Terry L. Birdwhistell, September 22, 1989, Louie B. Nunn Center for Oral History, UKLSCRC.

18. Lillian Terry Warth, interview with Terry L. Birdwhistell, March 14, 1989, Louie B. Nunn Center for Oral History, UKLSCRC.

19. *Kentuckian,* 1943.

20. *Kentucky Kernel,* December 8, 1942. An ROTC student, Bob Ammons later entered the military and died in combat.

21. Dean of Women Annual Report, 1943–1944, 181, 337, UKLSCRC.

22. Ibid., 1941–1942, 268.

23. *Kentucky Kernel,* February 17, 1942.

24. Ibid., October 16 and 24, 1942, and January 15, 1943.

25. *Louisville Courier-Journal,* June 1, 1942.

26. Ibid., October 30, 1941; Holmes interview.

27. Dean of Women Papers, Speeches, 1943–1954, UKLSCRC.

28. Ibid.

29. Catalog, University of Kentucky, 1940–1941; Gillis, *The University of Kentucky*, 21.

30. Board of Trustees Minutes, August 20 and November 5, 1943.

31. Lydia Roberts Fischer, interviews with Terry Birdwhistell, October 16 and 26, 1989, Louie B. Nunn Center for Oral History, UKLSCRC.

32. Ibid.

33. Hartmann, *The Home Front and Beyond*, 104.

34. *Kentucky Kernel*, April 24, 1942; *Kentuckian*, 1943.

35. *Louisville Courier-Journal*, March 19, 1944; Eckdahl interview. Betty Tevis did believe that she was the first woman to sit on press row at Madison Square Garden while she was sports editor during a UK game played there.

36. *Kentuckian*, 1944; UK Annual Report, 1943–1944, 156.

37. *Kentucky Kernel*, January 17, 1941.

38. Billy Frances Jackson Bower, interview with Terry L. Birdwhistell, January 18, 1993, Louie B. Nunn Center for Oral History, UKLSCRC; Board of Trustees Minutes, March 30, 1943.

39. *Kentucky Kernel*, February 4, 1941.

40. Ibid., February 17, 1942, September 29, 1944.

41. Ibid., April 1, 1941.

42. Ibid., March 25, 1941.

43. Talbert, *The University of Kentucky*, 128–129.

44. *Kentucky Kernel*, May 14, 1943.

45. *Kentucky Kernel*, March 2, 1937; Minutes of the University Faculty, March 20, 1942, April 2, 1945, UKLSCRC; John R. Thelin, *A History of American Higher Education* (Baltimore: Johns Hopkins University Press, 2004), 192–193; Talbert, *The University of Kentucky*, 116. For a historical overview of student union development see M. Dahlgren, K. Dougherty, and A. Goodno, "The Role of Physical Space in Establishing Community," *Journal of the Student Personnel Association at Indiana University*, Special Issue, May 1, 2013: 62–86.

46. Minutes of the University Faculty, March 20, 1942, April 2, 1945.

47. *Kentucky Kernel*, May 25, 1945.

48. Sarah Holmes to Alexander Capurso, March 5, 1945, Box 3, Leo Chamberlain Papers, UKLSCRC.

49. Sarah Holmes to E. G. Sulzer, February 19, 1943, Box 3, Chamberlain Papers; *Louisville Courier-Journal*, February 14, 1943.

50. Sarah Holmes to Leo Chamberlain, October 5, 1944, Box 3, Chamberlain Papers; *Kentucky Kernel*, February 2, 1943.

51. Minutes of the Kentucky Association of Deans of Women, October 30–31, 1942, Kentucky Association of Deans of Women Papers, 1921–1950, UKLSCRC.

52. Ibid., October 27, 1944.

53. *Kentucky Kernel,* March 2, 1943.

54. Minutes of the University Faculty, 1944–1947, UKLSCRC.

55. Minutes of the Board of Trustees, September 21, 1946; Linda Eisenmann, "Reconsidering a Classic: Assessing the History of Women's Higher Education a Dozen Years after Barbara Solomon," *Harvard Educational Review* 67 (1997): 701. For a study of women students following World War II, also see Linda Eisenmann, *Higher Education for Women in Postwar America, 1945–1965* (Baltimore: Johns Hopkins University Press, 2006).

56. *Kentucky Kernel,* October 24, 1947; Herman L. Donovan to William P. Gragg, December 27, 1945, Box 3, Chamberlain Papers; UK Annual Report, 1945–1946, 4; Hartmann, *The Home Front and Beyond,* 106.

57. Dean of Women Annual Report, 1945–1946, 48–49.

58. Haselden interview; Dean of Women Annual Report, 1945–1946, 211.

59. *Kentucky Kernel,* April 4, 1947.

60. Ibid., October 17, 1947.

61. Ibid., June 28, 1946.

62. Ibid., December 6, 1946.

63. Minutes of the University Faculty, September 1947, 20.

64. Fischer interview.

Epilogue

1. Betty Morris, interview with Terry L. Birdwhistell, March 12, 1990, Louie B. Nunn Center for Oral History, UKLSCRC; Martha Elizabeth Clark, interview with Terry L. Birdwhistell, March 6, 1990, Louie B. Nunn Center for Oral History, UKLSCRC; Frances Jewell McVey Papers, Box 27, Margaret I. King Library, UKLSCRC.

2. Chloe Gifford, interview with Charles G. Talbert, November 15, 1972, Louie B. Nunn Center for Oral History, UKLSCRC.

3. In the immediate postwar era Kentucky leaders and academicians completed studies and issued reports regarding Kentucky's future. It was a time of introspection and planning that, though hopeful, failed to achieve most of the goals put forward. See James C. Klotter, *Kentucky: Portrait in Paradox, 1900–1950* (Lexington: University Press of Kentucky, 2006).

Bibliography

Oral History Interviews, Louie B. Nunn Center for Oral History, University of Kentucky Libraries Special Collections Research Center

Amos, Clifford. Interview with Terry L. Birdwhistell, December 5, 1991.

Blanding, Sarah Gibson. Interview with William Cooper, Jr., May 23, 1976.

Bower, Billy Frances Jackson. Interview with Terry L. Birdwhistell, January 18, 1993

Bull, Jacqueline Page. Interview with Terry Birdwhistell, October 6, 1977.

Burchett, Woodrow. Interview with William H. McCann, Jr., April 7, 1993.

Clark, Martha Elizabeth. Interview with Terry L. Birdwhistell, March 6, 1990.

Conroy, Virginia Katherine. Interview with Terry L. Birdwhistell, March 20, 1990.

Cooper, Mary Hester. Interview with Cathy Cooper, September 20, 1977.

Davis, Elizabeth Jewell. Interview with Terry L. Birdwhistell, January 23, 1992

Eckdahl, Betty Tevis. Interview with Terry L. Birdwhistell, September 22, 1989.

Fischer, Lydia Roberts. Interviews with Terry L. Birdwhistell, October 16 and 26, 1989.

Gifford, Chloe. Interview with Cathy Cooper, October 14, 1977.

———. Interview with Charles G. Talbert, November 15, 1972.

Haselden, Jane. Interviews with Terry L. Birdwhistell, October 17 and 27, 1989.

Hitchcock, Barbara McVey. Interview with Charles G. Talbert, August 10, 1972.

Holmes, Sarah Bennett. Interview with William Cooper, Jr., February 20, 1978.

Johnson, Ralph E. Interview with Terry L. Birdwhistell, February 6, 1984.

Lilly, Austin Paige. Interview with Terry L. Birdwhistell, April 3, 1990.

Morris, Betty. Interview with Terry L. Birdwhistell, March 12, 1990.

Morris, Virginia. Interview with Charles G. Talbert, June 29, 1972.
Niles, Rena. Interview with Terry L. Birdwhistell, March 6, 1990.
Peal, W. Hugh. Interview with David Ferrell, October 4, 1977.
Raymond, Rexie Brooks. Interview with Terry L. Birdwhistell, May 26, 1976.
Warth, Lillian Terry. Interview with Terry L. Birdwhistell, March 14, 1989.
White, Martin M. Interview with Terry L. Birdwhistell, February 5, 1979.

Archive Collections, University of Kentucky Libraries Special Collections Research Center

Chamberlain, Leo. Papers.
Clay, Laura. Photographic collection, pa46m4.
Creekmore, Maude. Journal and Scrapbook.
Didlake, Mary LeGrand. Miscellaneous Faculty Papers.
Donovan, Herman Lee. Papers.
Gillis, Ezra. Papers.
Harper, Ida Kenney Risque. Scrapbook, 1986ua001.
Ingels, Margaret. Papers.
Jewell Family. Papers.
Lafayette Studios. Photographs, 96pa101.
Lilly, Austin. Papers and photographs, 0000ua132.
Lyle Family Photographic Collection, pa62m49.
McClure, Virginia Clay. Diary.
McLaughlin, Marguerite. Papers and awards, 2005ua121.
McVey, Frances Jewell. Papers, 0000ua003.
McVey, Frank LeRond. Papers.
Nollau, Louis Edward. Photograph Print Collection, 1998ua002.
———. F Series Photographic Print Collection, 1998ua001.
Oversized Flat File Collection, 2001ua065.
Patterson, James K. Papers.
Postcard Collection, 2012ms276.
Stout, Florence Offutt. Papers.
Sweeney Family. Papers.
Tarpley, Cecil and Elizabeth Miller. Papers, 2000ua076.
Thompson, Abe. Photograph album, 1984ua004.
Tuttle, Margaret. Papers and photographs, 0000ua200.
Wilson, Alberta Server. Papers.
University of Kentucky. Annual Register.
———. Board of Trustees Minutes.
———. Faculty Senate Minutes.
———. General photographic prints, 1999ua081.
———. Glass plate negative collection, 2007ua014.

Bibliography

———. Matriculation ledgers, 2011ua026.
———. Portrait print collection, 1996ua005.

Books, Articles, and Theses

Alband, Jo Della. "A History of the Education of Women in Kentucky." Master's thesis, University of Kentucky, 1934.

Bailey, Beth. *From Front Porch to Back Seat: Courtship in Twentieth-Century America*. Baltimore: Johns Hopkins University Press, 1988.

Bashaw, Carolyn Terry. "'She Made a Tradition': Katherine S. Bowersox and Women at Berea College, 1907–1937." *Register of the Kentucky Historical Society* 89 (1991): 61–84.

———. *"Stalwart Women": A Historical Analysis of Deans of Women in the South*. New York: Teachers College Press, 1999.

———. "'We Who Live off the Edges': Deans of Women at Southern Coeducational Institutions and Access to the Community of Higher Education, 1907–1960." PhD diss., University of Georgia, 1992.

Birdwhistell, Terry L. "Divided We Fall: State College and the Normal School Movement in Kentucky, 1880–1910." *Register of the Kentucky Historical Society* 88 (October 1990): 431–456.

———. "An Educated Difference: Women at the University of Kentucky Through the Second World War." EdD diss., University of Kentucky, 1994.

———. "'Some Kind of Lawyer': Two Journeys from Classroom to Courtroom and Beyond." *University of Kentucky Law Journal* 84 (1996): 1075–1152.

Blair, Karen J. *The Clubwoman as Feminist: True Womanhood Redefined, 1868–1914*. New York: Holmes & Meier, 1980.

Blakey, George T. *Hard Times and New Deal in Kentucky:1929–1939*. Lexington: University Press of Kentucky, 1986.

Bordo, Susan. *Unbearable Weight: Feminism, Western Culture, and the Body*. Berkeley: University of California Press, 1993.

Breckinridge, Sophonisba P. *Madeline McDowell Breckinridge: A Leader in the New South*. Chicago: University of Chicago Press, 1921.

Brock, Loretta Gilliam. *A History of the Woman's Club of Central Kentucky, 1894–1994*. Lexington: Woman's Club of Central Kentucky, 1996.

Bush, Dana. "Plan Your Work and Work Your Plan: Home Economics and Efficient Living at Two State Funded Universities, 1900–1940." PhD diss., University of Kentucky, 2011.

Cahn, Susan K. *Coming on Strong: Gender and Sexuality in Women's Sport*. Urbana: University of Illinois Press, 2015.

Campbell, D'Ann. *Women at War with America: Private Lives in a Patriotic Era*. Cambridge, MA: Harvard University Press, 1984.

Bibliography

Carter, Susan B. "Academic Women Revisited: An Empirical Study of Changing Patterns of Women's Employment as College and University Faculty, 1890–1963." *Journal of Social History* 14 (Summer 1981): 675–699.

Cavanaugh, Virginia Frances. "Required Physical Education for Men and Women at the University of Kentucky, 1923–1933." Master's thesis, University of Kentucky, 1945.

Chafe, William H. T*he Paradox of Change: American Women in the Twentieth Century.* New York: Oxford University Press, 1991.

Clifford, Geraldine Joncich. *Lone Voyagers: Academic Women in Coeducational Universities, 1869–1937.* New York: Feminist Press, 1989.

Coleman, J. Winston, Jr. *A Centennial History of Sayre School.* Lexington, KY: Winburn Press, 1954.

Conable, Charlotte Williams. *Women at Cornell: The Myth of Equal Education.* Ithaca, NY: Cornell University Press, 1977.

Corley, Florence. "Higher Education for Southern Women: Four Church-Related Women's Colleges in Georgia, Agnes Scott, Shorter, Spelman, and Wesleyan, 1900–1920." PhD diss., Georgia State University, 1985.

Dahlgren, M., K. Dougherty, and A. Goodno. "The Role of Physical Space in Establishing Community." *Journal of the Student Personnel Association at Indiana University,* Special Issue, May 1, 2013: 62–86.

Delpar, Helen. "Coeds and the 'Lords of Creation': Women Students at the University of Alabama, 1893–1930." *Alabama Review* 42 (October 1989): 300–301.

Dorn, Charles. "'A Woman's World': The University of California, Berkeley, During the Second World War." *History of Education Quarterly* 48 (2008): 536–537.

Eisenmann, Linda. *Higher Education for Women in Postwar America, 1945–1965.* Baltimore: Johns Hopkins University Press, 2006.

———. "Reconsidering a Classic: Assessing the History of Women's Higher Education a Dozen Years after Barbara Solomon." *Harvard Educational Review* 67 (1997): 701.

Ellis, William E. "Frank LeRond McVey His Defense of Academic Freedom." *Register of the Kentucky Historical Society* 67 (January 1969): 37–54.

———. *A History of Eastern Kentucky University: The School of Opportunity.* Lexington: University Press of Kentucky, 2005.

———. *A History of Education in Kentucky.* Lexington: University Press of Kentucky, 2011.

Evans, Stephanie Y. *Black Women in the Ivory Tower, 1850–1954: An Intellectual History.* Gainesville: University Press of Florida, 2007.

Bibliography

Farnham, Christie Anne. *The Education of the Southern Belle: Higher Education and Student Socialization in the Antebellum South*. New York: New York University Press, 1994.

Farrell, David. "A Kentucky Collector: An Interview with W. Hugh Peal." *Kentucky Review*, 10 (1990): 48.

Fass, Paula S. *The Damned and the Beautiful: American Youth in the 1920s*. New York: Oxford University Press, 1977.

Fitzpatrick, Ellen. *Endless Crusade: Women Social Scientists and Progressive Reform*. New York: Oxford University Press, 1990.

Fuller, Paul E. *Laura Clay and the Women's Rights Movement*. Lexington: University Press of Kentucky, 1973.

Gavin, Lettie. *American Women in World War I: They also Served*. Niwot: University Press of Colorado, 1997.

Gillett, Margaret. *We Walked Very Warily: A History of Women at McGill*. Montreal: Eden Press, 1981.

Gillis, Ezra L. *The University of Kentucky, Its History and Development: A Series of Charts Depicting the More Important Data, 1862–1955*. Lexington: University of Kentucky, 1956.

Gordon, Lynn D. "Co-education on Two Campuses: Berkeley and Chicago, 1890–1912." In Mary Kelly, ed., *Woman's Being, Woman's Place: Female Identity and Vocation in American History*. Boston: G. K. Hall, 1979.

———. *Gender and Higher Education in the Progressive Era*. New Haven: Yale University Press, 1990.

Green, Judy, and Jeanne LaDuke. *Pioneering Women in American Mathematics: The Pre-1940 Ph.Ds*. Providence, RI: American Mathematical Society, 2009.

Hardin, John A. *Fifty Years of Segregation: Black Higher Education in Kentucky, 1904–1954*. Lexington: University Press of Kentucky, 1997.

Harris, Barbara. *Beyond Her Sphere: Women and the Professions in American History*. Westport, CT: Greenwood Press, 1978.

Harrison, Lowell H. *Western Kentucky University*. Lexington: University Press of Kentucky, 1987.

Harrison, Lowell H., and James C. Klotter. *A New History of Kentucky*. Lexington: University Press of Kentucky, 1997.

Hartford, Ellis Ford. "Highlights of Early Teacher Training in Kentucky." University of Kentucky, Bureau of School Service, 1974.

Hartmann, Susan B. *The Home Front and Beyond: American Women in the 1940s*. New York: Twayne Publishers, 1982.

Hay, Melba Porter. "The Lexington Civic League: Agent of Reform, 1900–1910." *Filson Club History Quarterly* 62 (July 1988): 336–355.

———. "Madeline McDowell Breckinridge: Kentucky Suffragist and Progressive Reformer." PhD diss., University of Kentucky, 1980.

———. *Madeline McDowell Breckinridge and the Battle for a New South.* Lexington: University Press of Kentucky, 2009.

Heilbrun, Carolyn G. *Writing a Woman's Life.* New York: W. W. Norton & Co., 1988.

Hoffecker, Carol D. *Beneath Thy Guiding Hand: A History of Women at the University of Delaware.* Newark: University of Delaware, 1994.

Hopkins, James F. *The University of Kentucky: Origins and Early Years.* Lexington: University of Kentucky Press, 1951.

Horowitz, Helen Lefkowitz. *Alma Mater: Design and Experience in the Women's Colleges from Their Nineteenth-Century Beginnings to the 1930s.* Boston: Beacon Press, 1984.

———. *Campus Life: Undergraduate Cultures from the End of the Eighteenth Century to the Present.* Chicago: University of Chicago Press, 1987.

Hronek, Pamela Claire. "Women and Normal Schools: Tempe Normal." PhD diss., Arizona State University, 1985.

Johnson, Joan Marie. *Southern Women at the Seven Sisters Colleges: Feminist Values and Social Activism, 1875–1915.* Athens: University of Georgia Press, 2008.

Kerr, Charles, ed. *History of Kentucky.* Chicago: American Historical Society, 1922.

Kiesel, Linda Raney. "Kentucky's Land-Grant Legacy: An Analysis of the Administrations of John Bryan Bowman and James Kennedy Patterson, 1865–1890." PhD diss., University of Kentucky, 2003.

Kilman, Gail. "Education at Wesleyan Female College and Randolph-Macon Woman's College, 1893–1907." PhD diss., University of Delaware, 1984.

Kinkead, Elizabeth Shelby. *History of Kentucky.* New York: American Book Co., 1896.

Klotter, James C. *The Breckinridges of Kentucky, 1760–1981.* Lexington: University Press of Kentucky, 1986.

———. *Kentucky: Portrait in Paradox, 1900–1950.* Lexington: University Press of Kentucky, 2006.

———. "Promise, Pessimism, and Perseverance: An Overview of Higher Education History in Kentucky." *Ohio Valley History* 6, no. 1 (Spring 2006): 45–60.

Layne, Margaret E., ed. *Women in Engineering: Pioneers and Trailblazers.* Reston, VA: American Society of Engineers, 2009.

Letters. University of Kentucky Literary Magazine.

Lopez, Elise, and Mary P. Koss. "History of Sexual Violence in Higher Education." *New Directions for Student Services* 161 (2018): 9–19.

Lucas, Marion B. "Berea College in the 1870s and 1880s: Student Life at a Racially Integrated Kentucky College." *Register of the Kentucky Historical Society* 98 (Winter 2000): 1–22.

Bibliography

Marshall, Anne E. *Creating a Confederate Kentucky: The Lost Cause and Civil War Memory in a Border State.* Chapel Hill: University of North Carolina Press, 2010.

McCandless, Amy Thompson. *Women's Higher Education in the Twentieth-Century American South.* Tuscaloosa: University of Alabama Press, 1999.

McGuigan, Dorothy Gies. *A Dangerous Experiment: 100 Years of Women at the University of Michigan.* Ann Arbor: Center for Continuing Education of Women, 1970.

McVey, Frances Jewell. "The Blossom Woman." *Mountain Life and Work* 1 (April 1934): 1–5.

———. "The Literature of Shakerism." Master's thesis, Columbia University, 1918.

———, ed. *A University Is a Place . . . A Spirit: Addresses and Articles by Frank LeRond McVey, President, UK, 1917–1940.* Lexington: University of Kentucky Press, 1944.

Miller-Bernal, Leslie. *Separate by Degree: Women Students' Experiences in Single-Sex and Coeducational Colleges.* New York: Peter Lang, 2000.

Morelock, Kolan Thomas. *Taking the Town: Collegiate and Community Culture in the Bluegrass, 1880–1917.* Lexington: University Press of Kentucky, 2008.

Moyen, Eric A. *Frank L. McVey and the University of Kentucky: A Progressive President and the Modernization of a Southern University.* Lexington: University Press of Kentucky, 2011.

Myers, Christine D. "Gendering the 'Wisconsin Idea': The Women's Self-Government Association and University Life, c. 1898–1948." In Joyce Goodman and Jane Martin, eds., *Gender, Colonialism, and Education.* London: Woburn Press, 2002.

Nickeson, Jennifer Anne. "Transforming Appalachia: Female Reformers in the Mountains, 1900–1941." PhD diss., State University of New York at Buffalo, 2016.

Ogren, Christine A. "Where Coeds Were Coeducated: Normal Schools in Wisconsin, 1870–1929." *Journal of the History of Education* 35 (Spring 1995): 1–26.

Payne, Mary Elizabeth. "Florence Offutt Stout: Teacher of Physical Education for Forty Years at the University of Kentucky." Master's thesis, University of Kentucky, 1941.

Pen, Ron. *I Wonder as I Wander: The Life of John Jacob Niles.* Lexington: University Press of Kentucky, 2010.

Powell, Sallie Lucille. "Constructing the Modern Girl, Kentucky Style : An Examination of Gender and Race through the Lens of Kentucky Girls' High School Basketball Prior to Title IX." PhD diss., University of Kentucky, 2012.

Bibliography

Pritchett, Rita J. "The Battle between Promise and Privilege: The History of Women's Basketball at the University of Kentucky, 1972–2002." PhD diss., University of Kentucky, 2007.

Radke-Moss, Andrea G. *Bright Epoch: Women and Coeducation in the American West.* Lincoln: University of Nebraska Press, 2008.

Richard, Deborah Eaton. "Women's Academies in Kentucky: Denominational/Non-denominational Differences in Character Formation." PhD diss., Southern Illinois University, 2000.

Rogers, Agnes. *Vassar Women: An Informal Study.* Poughkeepsie: Vassar College, 1940.

Rosenberg, Rosalind. *Beyond Separate Spheres: Intellectual Roots of Modern Feminism.* New Haven: Yale University Press, 1982.

———. "The Limits of Access: The History of Coeducation in America." In John Mack Faragher and Florence Howe, eds., *Women and Higher Education in American History: Essays from the Mount Holyoke College Sesquicentennial Symposia.* New York: Norton, 1988.

Rupp, Leila J. "'Imagine My Surprise': Women's Relationships in Historical Perspective." *Frontiers: A Journal of Women Studies* 5 (Autumn 1980): 61–70.

Rury, John L. *Education and Women's Work: Female Schooling and the Division of Labor in Urban America, 1878–1930.* Albany: SUNY Press, 1991.

Sartorius, Kelly C. "A Coeducational Pathway to Political and Economic Citizenship: Women's Student Government and a Philosophy and Practice of Women's US Higher Coeducation between 1890 and 1945." In Margaret A. Nash, ed., *Women's Higher Education in the United States: New Historical Perspectives.* New York: Palgrave Macmillan, 2018.

Sergio, Lisa. *A Measure Filled: The Life of Lena Madesin Phillips Drawn from her Autobiography.* New York: R. B. Luce, 1972.

Sicherman, Barbara. "College and Careers: Historical Perspectives on the Lives and Work Patterns of Women College Graduates." in John Mack Faragher and Florence Howe, eds., *Women and Higher Education in American History: Essays from the Mount Holyoke College Sesquicentennial Symposia.* New York: Norton, 1988.

Simmons, Christina. *Making Marriage Modern: Women's Sexuality from the Progressive Era to World War II.* New York: Oxford University Press, 2009.

Solomon, Barbara Miller. *In the Company of Educated Women: A History of Women and Higher Education in America.* New Haven: Yale University Press, 1985.

Sonenklar, Carol. *We Are a Strong and Articulate Voice: A History of Women at Penn State.* University Park: Pennsylvania State University Press, 2006.

Stanaland, Peggy. "The Early Years of Basketball in Kentucky." In Joan S. Hult and Marianna Trekell, eds., *A Century of Women's Basketball: From Frailty*

Bibliography

to Final Four. Reston, VA: American Alliance for Health, Physical Education, Recreation, and Dance, 1991.

Stanley, Gregory Kent. *Before Big Blue: Sports at the University of Kentucky, 1880–1940.* Lexington: University Press of Kentucky, 1996.

Starnes, Joe Daniel. "Required Physical Education for Men and Women at the University of Kentucky, 1913–1923." Master's thesis, University of Kentucky, 1948.

Stewart, Marjorie S., and Joyce Cotton Threlkeld. *Celebrating the Past, Building the Future: History of Home Economics at the University of Kentucky, 1906–1990.* Lexington: University of Kentucky College of Home Economics, 1990.

Stout, Florence Offutt. "Physical Education in Kentucky." *Mechanical Engineering and Electrical Engineering Record* 1 (May 1908): 24–42.

Swoboda, Marian J., and Audrey J. Roberts. "They Came to Learn, They Came to Teach, They Came to Stay." Madison, WI: Office of Women, 1980.

———. "'What if the Power Does Lie within Me?' Women Students at the University of Wisconsin, 1875–1900." *History of Higher Education Annual* 1984: 78–100.

Talbert, Charles Gano. *The University of Kentucky: The Maturing Years.* Lexington: University of Kentucky Press, 1965.

Taylor, Nancy D. "Rise of the Administrator in Higher Education: Focus on Professionalization of the Registrar at the University of Kentucky from 1910 to 1937." PhD diss., University of Kentucky, 2015.

Thelin, John R. *A History of American Higher Education.* Baltimore: Johns Hopkins University Press, 2004.

Thomas, James William. "Campus as Home: An Examination of the Impact of Student Housing at the University of Kentucky in the Progressive Era." PhD diss., University of Kentucky, 2017.

Tice, Karen W. *Queens of Academe: Beauty Pageantry, Student Bodies, and College Life.* New York: Oxford University Press, 2012.

———. "Queens of Academe: Campus Pageantry and Student Life." *Feminist Studies* 31 (Summer 2005): 250–283.

———. "School-Work and Mother-Work: The Interplay of Maternalism and Cultural Politics in the Educational Narratives of Kentucky Settlement Workers, 1910–1930." *Journal of Appalachian Studies* 4 (Fall 1998): 191–224.

Travis, Anthony R. "Sophonisba Breckinridge, Militant Feminist." *Mid-America: An Historical Review* 58 (April 1976): 111–118.

Verbrugge, Martha H. *Active Bodies: A History of Women's Physical Education in Twentieth-Century America.* New York: Oxford University Press, 2012.

Ware, Susan. *Beyond Suffrage: Women in the New Deal.* Cambridge, MA: Harvard University Press, 1981.

————. *Holding Their Own: American Women in the 1930s.* Boston: Twayne Publishers, 1982.

Westin, Jeane Eddy. *Making Do: How Women Survived the '30s.* Chicago: Follett, 1976.

Whisnant, David S. *All That Is Native and Fine.* Chapel Hill: University of North Carolina Press, 1983.

Wilson, Shannon H. *Berea College: An Illustrated History.* Lexington: University Press of Kentucky, 2006.

Wolfe, Margaret Ripley. *Daughters of Canaan: A Saga of Southern Women.* Lexington: University Press of Kentucky, 1995.

————. "Fallen Leaves and Missing Pages: Women in Kentucky History." *Register of the Kentucky Historical Society* 90 (Bicentennial Issue, 1992): 82.

Wood, Leila, Caitlin Sulley, Matt Kammer-Kerwick, Diane Follingstad, and Noël Busch-Armendariz. "Climate Surveys: An Inventory of Understanding Sexual Assault and Other Crimes of Interpersonal Violence at Institutions of Higher Education'" *Violence against Women* 23 (2017): 1249–1267.

Woody, Thomas. *A History of Women's Education in the United States.* 2 vols. New York: Science Press, 1929.

Wright, John D., Jr. *Transylvania: Tutor to the West.* Lexington: University Press of Kentucky, 2006.

Index

African Americans: Berea College, 4; Sarah Blanding, 158, 121–122; Kentucky State University, 10; Frances Jewell McVey, 192; University of Kentucky employees, 158–159
Agricultural and Mechanical College of Kentucky, 5–6
alcohol, 8, 54, 94, 118, 120–121, 157
Allen, J. Embry, 21, 35
alumnae luncheon, 31, 53
Alumni Association, 31, 47–48, 73
Alumni Gymnasium, 114, 123; dances, 45; women's basketball, 47; women's physical education, 35–37, 39–42
Alumni Hall, 34
American Association of Collegiate Alumni, 96
American Association of University Women, 84
Ammons, Bob, 173
Amos, Clifford, 153–154
Anderson, F. Paul, 109
Appalachian Settlement School movement, 60
Applegran, Clarence Oliver, 114
Ardery, William, 139
Army Specialized Training Program (ASTP), 171

Association of College Women, 53
Association of Land-Grant Colleges, 49
Association of Women Students (AWS), 160
Athletic Council (men's), 70, 113
Atkins, Mary, 27
Atkins, Roberta, 35
Auburn University, 4
automobiles, 118, 122–123, 133, 189, 190

Bailey, Beth, 102–103, 123
Baker Brothers Distillery, 104
Bakhaus, Betty, 127
Baldwin School, 57–58, 60–62, 65, 67, 84, 99–100, 107
Ball, Mira Snider, 1
band. *See* University of Kentucky marching band
Barber, Lannes Spurgem, 27
Barker, Henry Stites, 36, 43, 50–51, 53, 64, 83, 110
Barker, Kate, 37, 204n64
Barker Hall, 34
Barnard College, 147
Bartlett, Fred V., 19
Barton, Mary, 179
Bashaw, Carolyn Terry, 105, 167
basketball (men's), 114, 177, 182

237

basketball (women's), 64, 66, 69, 107, 113–114, 129, 164, 166, 168, 176; abolished, 110–112, 155; control over, 47–48, 50; organized, 46–47, 110; women's health, 145–146

Baxter, Annette, 58

Beall, Mary E., 87

beauty, 39, 125, 128–129, 134–135, 156, 164

Beckham, J. C. W., 38

Berea College, 4

Best, Katharine, 125

Bird, Philemon, 21

Blackburn, Lucy Berry, 36, 46, 73, 94, 126; matron for women, 17–19, 66; women's physical education, 42; women's study room, 25, 27, 102, 149

Blackburn, Luke B., 15

Blanding, Abraham Louis, 104, 215

Blanding, Ellen, 103–104

Blanding, Leonora, 103–104

Blanding, Sarah Anderson, 103–104

Blanding, Sarah Gibson, 101, 109–110, 117–120, 126, 128, 147, 151, 161, 166–167, 182, 191, 214; acting Dean of Women, 103; Columbia University, 115–116; Cornell, 222n7; family and early life, 103–105; London School of Economics, 132; meeting Frances Jewell McVey, 105–107; New Haven School of Gymnastics, 105; views on race, 158, 221–222n58; role in disbanding women's intercollegiate basketball, 111–112; senior portrait, 108; sex education, 152–153, 162; undergraduate experience, 105–108; woman's building, 148–149; women's rules, 155–157

Blanding, William de Saussure, 103–104

Blazer, Georgia Monroe, 1

Blessing, Martha White, 73

Bliss, Charlotte, 31

Board of Trustees, UK, 26–27, 41–42, 45, 50, 53, 82, 85–87, 149, 162, 165–166, 178; admission of women, 11–12; Domestic Science, 48–49; first woman member, 1; Elizabeth Shelby Kinkead, 43; matron for women, 17; Florence Offutt Stout, 37–38, 50; Woman's Building, 149, 162; women board members, 31–32; Women's Board of Control, 34–35, 82; women's housing, 21–22, 24, 33–34; World War II, 185

Boles, S. A. "Daddy," 70

Bordo, Susan, 201n19

Bower, Billy Frances Jackson, 178

Bowling Green, Kentucky, 5

Boyd, Paul, 105, 109, 139, 176–177

Boyd Hall, 160, 171–172

Bratt, Carolyn, 1

Bradley, Elizabeth B., 35

Bradley, E. U., 76

Bradley, Lee, 35

Breckinridge, Desha, 68

Breckinridge, Madeline McDowell, 64, 68, 104

Breckinridge, Sophonisba, 6, 11–12, 28, 53, 83, 95, 213n70

Breckinridge, W. C. P., 11–12

Brooks, Rexie, 55, 206–207n106

Broom Brigade, 13

Brown, Leigh, 158

Bryan, George G., 19

Bryan, John, 27

Bryn Mawr, 57, 167

Buckley, Leer, 124

Buell Armory, 40

Bull, Jacqueline P., 136
Bullock, "Miss," 17
Burchett, Woodrow, 135
Burkhart, Roy A., 162
Burnman, Anita, 151
Bush, Henry S., 27

Cadet Corps, 12–13, 15–16, 19, 26,
    41–42, 45, 125
Cambridge University, 149
Campbell-Hagerman College, 84
Canary Cottage, 157–158
Carleton College, 116–117
Carpenter, William Thomas, 29
Carr Boarding House, 22
Carrier-Lyle Corporation, 79
Carroll, Earl, 134–135
Catholic students, 128
Chafe, William, 118
Chautauqua School of Physical
    Education, 38
chemistry, 75–76, 84, 179
Chi Epsilon Chi, 31–33
Chi Omega, 78
Chorn, Sarah Marshall, 76
Civil War, 3, 9, 101, 107, 157
Civil Works Administration, 151
Clark, Thomas D., 136
Clay, Cassius M., Jr., 43
Clay, Henry, 60
Clay, Laura, 14, 31–34, 41, 48, 203n52
Clay, Miriam Gratz, 66
Clemson University, 4
Clifford, Geraldine Joncich, 3, 58
Coffman, Charlotte, 149
Colgate College, 146
College of Agriculture, UK, 30, 45,
    49, 85, 109, 165, 169–170, 178
College of Arts and Sciences, UK, 30,
    55, 105, 109, 137, 139, 174, 176
College of Commerce, UK, 30, 109,
    169

College of Engineering, UK, 29–30,
    43, 54–55, 70–71, 74, 81, 95, 109,
    169, 179, 186
College of Law, UK, 1, 30, 54–55,
    73–74, 78, 81, 109, 135, 169, 179,
    210n28
Collins, Mary C. Love, 78
Collins, Mary Lee, 153
Columbia University, 83–84,
    115–116, 132, 165, 167
commencement, 15, 19, 28–30, 48,
    147
Conable, Charlotte, 82
Conant, Caroline, 179
Conroy, Virginia Katherine,
    127–128
Cook, Lucille, 124
Cooper, Mary Hester, 117, 216n34
Cooper, Thomas Poe, 109, 165
Cornell, Laura Maybelle, 116
Cornell University, 3, 82, 116, 167
Cox, Lula May, 29
Crane, Adelaide E., 83, 85
Creekmore, Maude, 51
Cruikshank, Lucille, 78
Curtis, Henry E., 19
Cynthiana, Kentucky, 5

dancing, 39, 41–42, 45, 54, 60, 64,
    100, 102, 118, 123–124, 128,
    153–154, 162, 174, 183
Dantzler, Lehre L., 76, 87–88
dating, 120–121, 129
Davis, Mary Moore, 142
Dean of Men, UK, 109, 153
Dean of Women, UK, 14, 34, 48, 67,
    102, 114, 134, 142, 145; Sarah
    Blanding, 103, 105, 109–112,
    115–118, 120, 126, 128, 132, 147,
    149, 151–153, 155–156, 162,
    166–167; Virginia Franke,
    115–116, 124; Anna J. Hamilton,

51–53, 78, 80–82, 86–87; Jane
Haselden, 171; Sarah Holmes,
160, 167, 171, 174–178, 182–183,
185–187, 190; Frances Jewell,
90–91, 93–95, 97, 110; Josephine
Simrall, 90–91; Florence Offutt
Stout, 50–51, 53
DeMille, Cecil B., 128
Dent, Harry, 135
Depression, the (of the 1930s), 2,
109, 129, 130–131, 146–147,
153–154, 162–165, 220n30
Dicker, Joseph, 71
Didlake, George Ware, 28
Didlake, Mary LeGrand, 27–28, 35,
45, 203n41
Didlake, Nannie Bain, 28, 35
Ditto, Leola, 30
Domestic Science Department, UK,
14, 34, 48–50. *See also* Home
Economics Department, UK
Donovan, Herman Lee, 165–167,
169, 174, 176, 185
Donovan, Nell Stuart, 165–166
Downing, Harold H., 55
Downing, Joseph Milton, 27
Downing, Peter F., 24
Dudley School, 14
Dyer, Billy L., 180

Eastern Kentucky University, 5,
165–166
Eichelberger, Marietta, 116
Eisenmann, Linda, 185
Elkin, Fielding Clay, 25
English Department, UK, 30, 51–52,
65, 76–78, 87–88, 97, 107
enrollment, 5, 9–12, 16–17, 21–23,
26, 30, 53–54, 78, 80–82, 90, 102,
129, 131, 151–152, 169, 171, 179,
185–187
Erikson, Statie, 139, 140, 151

faculty, 13, 17, 19, 30, 37–38, 41,
42–43, 45–47, 52–56, 66–70,
76–78, 81, 116–117, 119, 129,
137, 160–162, 209
Faculty Senate, UK, 31–32, 37, 46,
86, 110, 112
Fass, Paula, 101–103
Faulkner, John Vick, 27
Fayette County Equal Rights
Association, 64, 73
Federal Emergency Relief Act, 151
Fee, John, 4
Fischer, Lydia Roberts, 176–177,
190
Fitzhugh, Lucy, 27
Florida State College for Women,
3–4
Florida State University, 3–4
Foster, Nettie Bell, 27–29, 203n42
Franke, Virginia, 115–116, 124
fraternities, 85–86, 95, 118, 120, 137,
154, 171, 181, 185
Frazee Hall, 123
Funkhouser, W. D., 109, 137

Garman, Harrison, 45
Georgetown College, 5, 116
Gildersleeve, Virginia G., 147
Gillespie, Elizabeth, 179
Gillis, Ezra, 45
Golden Jubilee celebration, 73–74.
See also parade(s)
Goman, Casey, 181–182
Gone with the Wind (Mitchell), 157
Good, Louise, 122, 217n46
Gordon, Gertrude Renz, 18
Gordon, Lynn, 9, 74, 121
Goucher College, 73, 119
Graduate School, UK, 109
Graham, Sallie A., 36
Green, Ella K. Porter, 73
Gregory, Mary Cottell, 73

Index

Grehan, Enoch, 70
Griffin, Gerald, 94
Gunn, Arabella "Belle" Clement, 19, 20, 25, 73, 202n27
gymnasium, Alumni, 114, 123; dances, 45; women's basketball, 47; women's physical education, 35–37, 39–42

Hailey, Mary Virginia, 145
Hamilton, Anna J., 51–53, 78, 80–82, 86–87
Hamilton College, 28, 124, 218n50
Harris, Barbara, 147
Haselden, Jane, 167–169, 171, 187, 223n9
Hay, Melba Porter, 55
Hayden, Bessie, 47–48
Heilbrun, Carolyn G., 213–214n81
Helm, Elizabeth, 113
Henderson, Olivia Elizabeth, 36
Henry Clay Society, 78
Hibler, Edna Parker, 42
Hickey, Margaret A., 175–176
Hill, Fred, 164
Hillenmeyer, Herb, 158
Hitchcock, Barbara, 120
Hodges, Harriet Claiborne, 45
Hodges, Mary, 45
Hoeing, Joseph, 15–16
Hoeing, Leonora, 15–16
Hoeing, Rebecca, 16
Holmes, Sarah Bennett, 132–133, 151, 160–161, 167, 169, 171, 174–178, 182, 185, 187, 190, 192, 223n9
Home Economics Department, UK, 55, 67, 74–75, 80–85, 116, 118, 139–141, 151, 167, 170. See also Domestic Science Department, UK
Hopkins, James, F., 201n13

Horowitz, Helen Lefkowitz, 10, 12, 14, 24, 86, 101, 118, 129
housing, 12–15, 21–22, 24, 26, 34–36, 42, 80–82, 86, 88, 90, 115, 123, 132, 139, 147–149, 151, 158, 160, 171–172, 185, 187, 190, 204, 211
Hunt, Irene I., 24

Idea, The, 56
Indiana University, 3
Ingels, Margaret, 70–72, 78, 79, 209–210n27
International Federation of Business and Professional Women, 73
intramural sports, 111–113, 140, 146

Jackson, Hugh R., 139
Jewell, Asa, 59
Jewell, Frances, 57–58, 61, 65, 70, 75, 76–77, 83, 85, 87, 93, 95–96; Baldwin School, 60, 62; Columbia University, 83–84; Dean of Women, 91; English faculty, 66–67; family, 59–60; marriage, 97–100; Shakers, 84, 211n48; Vassar College, 62–64; World War I service, 84. See also McVey, Frances Jewell
Jewell, John, 59
Jewell, Lizzie Berry, 59
Jewell, Robert "Bob," 59, 65
Johns Hopkins University, 90
Johnson, Anna Mayrell, 168
Johnson, Keen, 166
Johnson, Ralph E., 157
Jones, Bill, 188
Jones, J. Catron, 148
Jones, T. T., 153
Jones, Waller, 125
Journalism Department, UK, 67, 70, 76, 96, 178

Kappa Kappa Gamma, 107
Kastle, Joseph Hoening, 43,
    201–202n21
Kelly, Virginia, 113
Kentuckian, the, 86–87, 120–121,
    129; Anna J. Hamilton, 86;
    women's equality, 91–92; women
    students and World War II, 173,
    177, 184, 187
Kentucky Agricultural and
    Mechanical Society, 5
Kentucky Alumnus, 70, 78
Kentucky Association of Deans of
    Women, 183
Kentucky Club of Columbia Alumni,
    83
Kentucky Education Association, 38
Kentucky Equal Rights Association,
    14, 28, 31, 33, 48
Kentucky Federation of Women's
    Clubs, 51, 85
Kentucky House of Reform, 38
Kentucky Kernel: African American
    employees, 158; "Campus
    Courtesy Week," 180;
    coeducation, 92, 94, 124; Great
    Depression, 131; Frances Jewell as
    Dean of Women, 91; marriage
    and careers for women, 139, 142;
    student rules, 88, 123, 139, 142,
    145, 155–156; women engineering
    students, 179; women students'
    organizations, 145; women and
    World War II, 174–175, 177–178,
    181; women's academic success,
    124–125; women's band, 125;
    women's basketball, 112, 145–146;
    women's beauty contests, 128–
    129, 134–135
Kentucky state legislature, 5, 6, 12,
    32, 34–35, 101
Kentucky State University, 10

Kentucky University, 5, 6, 46–47
Kentucky Wesleyan College, 5
Kerth, Dorothy, 113
Kiler, William H., 35–36
King, Elizabeth W., 27
King, Margaret Isadora, 28–29, 45
Kinkead, George, 11, 21, 43
Kinkead, Elizabeth Shelby, 11,
    43–44, 67
Kinkead, Ellen Talbott, 11
Kinkead, William B., 11, 12, 43
Klair, William, 21
K-Men's Club, 92
Knott, J. Proctor, 15
Koppius, Martha, 179

Lafferty, W. T., 54
Lair, Ronald A. 146
League of Women Voters, 84, 88, 96
LeStourgeon, Elizabeth, 116, 117, 177
Letters campus publication, 119, 122,
    142
Lexington Alumnae Club, 147
Lexington Female Academy, 16
Lewis, Thomas Stone, 27
Library Science, UK, 74
Lilly, Anna D., 75
Lilly, Austin, 75, 76–78, 82
Lilly, Grant E., 75
Lincoln School (Lexington),
    104–105, 107
Lindenberger, Lillian, 149
Litsey, Sarah, 119, 217n38
London School of Economics, 132
Louisiana State University, 4
Louisville Girls' High School, 31, 51
Lowry, Catherine Bennett, 128
Luxon, Anne, 144
Lyons, Mary, 35

Main Building (UK administration
    offices), 15, 18, 23, 27, 30, 102, 148

marriage, 9, 24, 33, 49–50, 65, 70, 97,
99–100, 102, 116, 118–121,
142–144, 147, 160, 176
Marsh, John, 157
Maxwell Hall, 86
Maxwell Place, 18, 99, 154, 166
Maxwell Springs, 5, 15, 34
McCandless, Amy Thompson, 4
McCauliff, Mary, 27
McClure, Virginia Clay, 41
McConathy, James, 27
McCown, Anne Douglas "Doug,"
178
McDowell, Elizabeth, 178
McFarland, M. C., 13
McKenzie, Alexander St. Clair,
31–32
McLaughlin, Marguerite, 67–70, 76,
96, 209n24
McNamara, Irene, 94
McVey, Frances Jewell, 102, 105, 107,
115, 166–167, 171, 208;
appointment of Sarah Blanding as
Dean of Women, 103; death,
191–192; influence on Sarah
Blanding, 111; support of
students, 153–154; woman's
building, 148–149. *See also* Jewell,
Frances
McVey, Frank LeRond, 101, 103,
110–113, 115–116, 120–121,
130–132, 148–149, 153, 160,
165–167, 181, 191; Dean of
Women, 86, 87, 90–91; death of
Mabel Sawyer McVey, 96;
marriage to Frances Jewell,
97–100
McVey, Mabel Sawyer, 96, 213n73
McVey, Virginia, 116
McVey, William Pitt, 99
Meadowthorpe, 38
Melcher, Columbus, 109

Memorial Hall, 131
Miss Butler's School, 28
Mississippi State College for
Women, 3
Mississippi State University, 4
Mitchell, Margaret, 157
Moore, Barbara, 179
Moreland, Roy, 135
Morgan, Mildred, 152–153
Morrill Act (1862), 5
Mortar Board Leadership Society,
70, 107, 145, 149
Morton High School, 104–105
Morton Junior High School, 137,
176
Murray State University, 167–168
Murrill, Paul I. "Pi," 27
Mustaine, William W. H. "Musty,"
40
Myrick, Kathryn, 142, 143, 220n22

National American Woman Suffrage
Association, 75
National Federation of Business and
Professional Women's Clubs, 73
National Youth Administration, 151
Nelson, R. W., 43
Neville, John Henry, 42
Neville Literary Society, 203n37
New Deal, 150
New Haven Normal School of
Gymnastics, 37, 105
Newman, Roberta, 27
Niles, Rena, 119, 217n39
Normal Department, UK, 11–12, 21,
55; created, 6; entrance of women
students, 10–11; normal
certificate, 15–16; Philosophian
Society founded by, 25
Normal Department, University of
Wisconsin, 3
Northwestern University, 142

Oatridge, N.C., 139
Ochs, Pat, 182
O'Donnell, William Francis, 166
Offutt, Dan, 136
Offutt, Florence: assistant physical
 director, 36–37; marriage, 38. *See
 also* Stout, Florence Offutt
Offutt, Florence Graham, 36
O'Hara, Eugenia, 113
Omicron Delta Kappa, 181

Palmer, Mary Alice, 150
Panhellenic Association, 155
Panic of 1893, 21
parade(s): Golden Jubilee, 74; Home
 Economic students participating
 in, 82; May Day, 127; to new
 campus, 15; night shirt parade,
 41–42
Paretz, Rebecca, 78
Parker, Ethel Lee, 139, 141
Patterson, James K., 5–6, 14, 16–17,
 25, 27, 35, 37, 43, 45, 204; death
 of son, 28; and the first woman
 graduate from UK, 19; opposition
 to Domestic Science, 48–49;
 opposition to women board
 members, 32; retirement, 53; role
 in admission of women students,
 11–12; women's physical
 education, 40–41
Patterson, Walter K., 34, 148, 204n56
Patterson, William Andrew "Billy,"
 28
Patterson Hall, 34, 35, 42, 45, 51, 78,
 81–83, 85–86, 88, 95, 115, 132,
 134, 139, 156, 159–160, 162, 172,
 211
Patterson House, 148, 150, 211n44
Payne, Robert T., 19
Peabody College, 165
Peal, W. Hugh, 77

Pence, Merry Lewis, 117
Pence, Sally, 117
Pennsylvania State University, 3
Pepper, Ella Offutt, 37–38
Pepper, James E., 37–38
Peters, Iva L., 119
Pettit, Katherine, 60
Phi Beta Kappa, 124, 159, 178
Phillips, Lena Madesin, 73
Philosophian Society, 25, 26
physical education, 36–39, 42, 47, 50,
 67, 80, 105, 107, 111–112, 116,
 118, 129
Piggot, Clare, 159
Pleasant View, 60, 64, 99
Plummer, Neil, 178
Pollitt, Mabel Hardy, 76
Prewitt, Burton, 94
Progressive Era, 7, 9, 33, 110
Public Relations, UK, 164, 177, 182
Pugh, Betty Jane, 177

Radke-Moss, Andrea, 3, 7, 55–56
Reedy, Daniel, 137
Reynolds, Nellie, 27
Richardson, Clarence H., 54
Robards, Mildred O., 135, 219n11
Roberts, Augusta, 148, 219
rules, 7–8, 13–14, 16, 18–19, 26–28,
 41–42, 53–54, 47, 81, 83, 114,
 122–124, 126–127, 130, 132–133,
 139, 142, 145, 153, 155, 160, 171,
 176, 190

Saffarrans, Ada, 14, 201n15
Saffarrans, Ada Meade, 14
Saffarrans, Daniel, 14
Sartorius, Kelly C., 91
Satterwhite, Ella Graham, 36–37
Satterwhite, Mrs. Maurice, 36
Sayre School, 19, 28, 60, 62, 64–65,
 67, 72–73

Science Hill Academy, 19
Scribbler's Club, UK, 122
Semple, Ellen Churchill, 206n97
Semple, Patty Blackburn, 206n97
Semple Collegiate School, 51
Server, Alberta Wilson, 136–138,
219n12
Server, James Milton "Big Jim," 137,
219n12
sex education, 152–153, 162
Shakers, 84, 211n48
Shaw, Bess, 46
Shelby House, 151–152
Simmons, Christina, 144
Simrall, Josephine, 90–91, 212n67
Smith, Elizabeth King, 73, 88
Smith, Frances, 156
Smith, Rebecca, 71
Smith Hall, 149
smoking, 19, 31, 94, 118, 120, 124,
127–128, 150
Snider, Patricia, 177–178
Solomon, Barbara Miller, 9, 65,
102
sororities, 78, 86, 97, 107, 115, 118,
121, 124, 128, 149, 155, 190
Southern Association of College
Women, 84
Stanaland, Peggy, 110
Stanford University, 31
State College. See University of
Kentucky
State Normal School for Colored
Persons, 10
Stebbins, Dorothy, 125, 218n52
Stephenson, Helen, 179
Stoll, Richard C., 27
Stoll Field, 165, 168
Stout, Florence Offutt, 38–41, 43,
45–46, 67, 78, 105, 116, 139,
206n95, 209n20; first woman
dean, 50–51; opposition to

women's basketball, 47–48,
110–112. See also Offutt, Florence
Stout, Robert Lee, 38, 43
student government, 88, 90–91,
106–107, 123, 126, 132, 149, 153,
155, 180, 188
Student Union, UK, 154, 160, 181,
187
suffrage, women's, 2, 33, 65, 71, 73,
75, 83–84, 88, 95, 101, 109
SUKY, 70
Sulzer, Elmer, 125, 132
State College Cadet, The, 26
Sweeney, Mary, 84–85, 116
Sweeney, Sunshine, 85, 212n52
Sweet Briar College, 90

tennis team (women's), 113
Terry, Lila Beatrice, 28, 203n43
Terry, Lillian, 172
Tevis, Betty, 172, 177–178, 224n35
Thelin, John, 9, 74, 181
Theta Sigma Phi, 70, 128
Tice, Karen, 129
Tompson, Lunette, 22
Transylvania University, 5, 84, 124,
167
Tucker, Nannie Susan, 48
Tupper, Sarah, 116
Turk, C. J., 109
Tuttle, Franklin E., 76
Tuttle, Margaret, 76

Underwood, John C., 5
University Athletic Committee, UK,
47–48
University of Alabama, 4
University of California, Berkeley, 3,
74
University of Chicago, 28, 31, 37, 45,
53, 83, 95, 116
University of Cincinnati, 90

University of Florida, 4
University of Georgia, 4
University of Illinois, 117
University of Iowa, 3
University of Kansas, 3
University of Kentucky, 10. *See also*
    specific colleges and departments
University of Kentucky marching
    band: all-male band, 188; hazing,
    182; May Day Parade, 127;
    women allowed as members, 181;
    women's band, 125–126, 132–133
University of Louisville, 5
University of Maryland, 4
University of Michigan, 3, 181
University of Minnesota, 3
University of Mississippi, 3
University of Missouri, 3
University of North Carolina, 3–4
University of North Carolina,
    Greensboro, 3
University of South Carolina, 4
University of Tennessee, 4
University of Wisconsin, 3, 9

Vassar College, 62–64, 65, 67, 83, 87,
    107, 115, 191, 206n97
violence on campus, 8, 13
Virginia Tech, 4

Wallace, Caroline Embry Allen, 35
Ware, Susan, 131
Warner, Callie, 19, 21, 202n29
Wayne, Margaret Jane, 179
Weaver, Rufus Lee, 27
Wellesley College, 12, 53, 90, 119
Western Kentucky University, 5, 165
Western State Normal School, 5, 165
White, James, 17
White, Martha, 73
White, Martin M., 130, 174
White Hall, 26, 42

Whiting, Pierre, 158
Wiedeman, Mary, 179
Wiest, Edward, 109
Wilmott, John Webb, 27
Williams College, 65
Willmott, Jennie, 29
Wilson, Alberta, 136–138, 219n12
Wilson, Shannon H., 4
Wolfe, Margaret Ripley, 33
Woman's Building, UK, 80, 147–149,
    160–162, 220n38
Woman's Club, UK, 84, 96
Woman's College of Baltimore. *See*
    Goucher College
Woman's College of the University
    of North Carolina. *See* University
    of North Carolina, Greensboro
Woman's League, UK, 88, 89, 107
Women's Administrative Council,
    UK, 106, 107, 124
Women's Advisory Committee of the
    National War Manpower
    Commission, 175
Women's Athletic Association, UK,
    92, 112, 114
Women's Athletic Council, UK, 112
Women's Board of Control, UK,
    34–36, 82–83, 86, 88, 90, 95
women's health, 16, 38, 45, 50, 73, 87,
    94, 99, 110–112, 145–146, 157
Woodlands (Woodland Park) 6, 12,
    105
Woods, John Joseph, 27
Woolridge, Jim, 180
World War I, 24, 73–74, 78, 88, 101,
    118, 130, 137, 164–165;
    enrollment decrease, 83; women
    faculty and the war effort, 84–85
World War II, 164, 169, 190, 191,
    192; expanded opportunities for
    women, 165; impact on women
    faculty, 176–177; impact on

women's housing, 171; male soldiers on campus, 171–173; postwar concern for women students, 182–188; women student leaders, 177–179; women students' and war effort, 174–175

Yale Summer School of Physical Education, 38
Young Women's Democratic Club, 150
YWCA (Young Women's Christian Association), 73, 78, 84, 88, 116, 148, 152

Topics in Kentucky History

James C. Klotter, Series Editor

Books in the Series

The Family Legacy of Henry Clay: In the Shadow of a Kentucky Patriarch
Lindsey Apple

Kentucky and the Great War: World War I on the Home Front
David J. Bettez

Our Rightful Place: A History of Women at the University of Kentucky, 1880–1945
Terry L. Birdwhistell and Deirdre A. Scaggs

George Keats of Kentucky: A Life
Lawrence M. Crutcher

Enid Yandell: Kentucky's Pioneer Sculptor
Juilee Decker

A History of Education in Kentucky
William E. Ellis

Madeline McDowell Breckinridge and the Battle for a New South
Melba Porter Hay

Committed to Victory: The Kentucky Home Front During World War II
Richard E. Holl

Alben Barkley: A Life in Politics
James K. Libbey

Henry Watterson and the New South: The Politics of Empire, Free Trade, and Globalization
Daniel S. Margolies

Murder and Madness: The Myth of the Kentucky Tragedy
Matthew G. Schoenbachler

How Kentucky Became Southern: A Tale of Outlaws, Horse Thieves, Gamblers, and Breeders
Maryjean Wall

Madam Belle: Sex, Money, and Influence in a Southern Brothel
Maryjean Wall